Central Banking

Central Banking

Fourth Edition

M. H. DE KOCK, PH.D. (HARVARD)
Former Governor of South African Reserve Bank

St. Martin's Press New York

First published 1939 by Staples Press
Reprinted 1942
Second edition 1946
Reprinted 1949, 1950, 1952
Third edition 1954
Reprinted 1956, 1958, 1960, 1961, 1965, 1967, 1969

Fourth edition first published in the United States of America in 1974
 For information, write:
St. Martin's Press, Inc., 175 Fifth Avenue, New York, N.Y. 10010

Printed in Great Britain

Library of Congress Catalog Card Number: 74-78896

AFFILIATED PUBLISHERS: Macmillan Limited, London
—also at Bombay, Calcutta, Madras and Melbourne

Preface to Fourth Edition

In this edition, the book has not only been brought up to date but completely revised, in view of the significant changes and developments which have taken place in the fields of central banking and monetary policy during the nineteen years since the publication of the previous edition. A great deal of obsolete or less essential material has been deleted and new material introduced into all chapters. In fact, a considerable proportion of most chapters has been virtually rewritten, with the object also of improving the presentation of facts and analyses.

While the general form and sequence of the previous edition have been largely retained, the subject of Variable Reserve Requirements has been treated more extensively in a separate chapter, owing to its increased importance, instead of including it again in the chapter on Other Methods of Credit Control, some of which have also become more prominent. On the other hand, two chapters have been omitted, namely, those on the International Monetary Fund and the Recent Revival of Monetary Policy, not only because in the present context these chapters contained a lot of obsolete or irrelevant detail, but also because the principal features of the subjects concerned had inevitably to be referred to in several other chapters.

Cape Town
September, 1973

M. H. de Kock

Contents

CHAPTER ONE

The Rise of Central Banking

Evolution of Central Banks

Prior to the commencement of the twentieth century there had been no clearly defined concept of central banking. A gradual evolution had been taking place in various countries over a long period of years, but the process had not always been a conscious one, and a systematic and consistent technique had not yet been developed and formulated. The temperament and discretion of individual managements had played the principal part in the decisions and operations of the bank which had, as it were, become the centre of the monetary and banking system in each of several countries.

In many of the older countries, one bank gradually came to assume more and more the position of a central bank, due mainly to its enjoying the sole or the principal right of note issue and acting as the Government's banker and agent. They were not originally called central banks, but were generally known as banks of issue or as national banks. The regulation of the note issue subject to safeguards imposed by the State, and the maintenance of the convertibility of their notes into gold or silver or both where such was in force, were the principal functions of these banks. In due course, such banks of issue acquired other functions, duties and powers until the term 'central bank' came to be generally used and to have a more or less standardized meaning.

Of the existing central banks, the Riksbank of Sweden is the oldest in the sense that it was the first to be established, but the Bank of England was the first bank of issue to assume the position of a central bank and to develop what are now generally recognized as the fundamentals of the art of central banking. The history of the Bank of England is thus universally accepted as illustrating the evolution of central banking principles and technique.

Bank of England

The Bank of England was brought into being by public subscription in 1694 for the express purpose of advancing money to the Government, in return for the privilege of note issue conferred under a charter granted to it in an Act of Parliament. This privilege was subject to limitations, but with every renewal of its charter the right to issue notes was renewed and extended in exchange for further loans to the Government or for other considerations. The Bank came to acquire at least a partial monopoly of note issue in England in the sense that only banking firms or partnerships of not more than six persons were also permitted to issue notes. It was not until 1826 that other joint-stock banks were granted the right of issue, and then only if they were established outside a 65-mile radius from London. The Bank, however, retained its privileged position in that legislation passed in 1833 declared only its notes to be legal tender. Moreover, under the Bank Act of 1844 the issues of all the other banks were limited to the amounts in circulation at that time, and provision was made for their lapsing in certain circumstances, e.g. in the case of amalgamation with or absorption by another bank. In 1826 the Bank was also authorized to open branches in other parts of England.

Its partial monopoly of note issue, in addition to the gradual expansion of its function as the banker and agent of the Government, placed the Bank of England at an early stage of its career in a special position vis-à-vis the other banks. The private banks of the eighteenth century had discovered that there was an advantage in keeping an account with the Bank of England, as it was the bank whose notes commanded the greatest confidence and the widest circulation and as it was becoming more and more the Government's banker and agent. The tendency to keep larger balances with the Bank grew as time went on, and when the widespread establishment of joint-stock banks in England began in 1826, the Bank of England had already come to be regarded as the custodian of the cash reserves of the private banks, and thus of the country's gold reserves. This tradition of maintaining balances with the Bank was also taken up by the joint-stock banks, and its position as the centre of the English banking structure was further strengthened in 1854, when the plan was adopted of settling the differences between the various banks at the end of each clearing by transfers between their respective accounts at the Bank.

The next development was that the Bank came to accept the position of being the 'lender of last resort', as Bagehot called it, and to assume responsibility for endeavouring to maintain not only the currency but also the credit system of the country on a sound basis. The close relationship between currency and credit was forcibly brought to the Bank's attention by the crises of 1847, 1857 and 1866. It had under the Bank Act to maintain a minimum gold reserve against its note issue and to redeem its notes on demand in gold coin; and those crises clearly demonstrated the extent to which the position of the Bank could be affected by speculation and undue expansion of credit, and, accordingly, the need for taking steps in good time to protect its gold reserve. On the other hand, it was brought home to the Bank that in certain circumstances financial panic could easily be brought about by the fear that the requisite banking facilities could not be obtained, and that it could be promptly allayed by the assurance that all legitimate requirements would be met by the Bank, although at temporarily higher rates with the object of limiting the demand for accommodation to the most urgent and essential needs and securing the contraction of credit as a whole.

The use of Bank Rate as an important instrument of credit policy was now firmly established, and the Bank's regulatory function received greater prominence. The crisis of 1873 was promptly and successfully handled by the Bank; and similarly, in 1890, when a serious emergency was created by widespread and excessive speculation in foreign securities culminating in the failure of Baring Brothers, the Bank succeeded by prompt action in allaying public alarm and averting a general panic. In neither case was it necessary for the Government to suspend the gold-cover requirements of the Bank Act, which had to be resorted to in the crises of 1847, 1857 and 1866.

The successful application of its paternal influence in these emergency situations not only gave the Bank of England great prestige and established it finally as the central bank of Great Britain, but also stimulated the development of central banking in other parts of the world.

Development of Other Central Banks

In various countries, during the course of the nineteenth century, the State either endowed an existing bank with the sole or principal right of note issue, or caused a new bank of issue to be established with special powers and privileges, accompanied by varying degrees of State control and supervision.

The Riksbank of Sweden, which had sprung from a privately owned bank founded in 1656 and reorganized as a State bank in 1668, followed in the footsteps of the Bank of England and gradually developed into a central bank. During a large part of its earlier career it enjoyed a monopoly of note issue which was reaffirmed by legislation in 1809, but the 'enskilda' banks which were established from 1830 onwards took the liberty of issuing their own notes and later obtained legal authority for their issues. It was not until 1897 that the sole right of issue was finally restored to the Riksbank.

The Bank of France, which was founded in 1800 partly with the aid of State funds but mainly with private capital, was closely connected with the State from the beginning. It became the Government's banker and received the exclusive right of note issue in Paris. The Government claimed a participation in the control of the Bank through the appointment of the Governor and two Sub-Governors, while the shareholders were represented by a board of fifteen Regents elected by the two hundred largest shareholders. In 1848 its scope and capital were enlarged as a result of the transformation of nine provincial banks with note-issuing powers into branches of the Bank of France. In due course more branches were established and the Bank obtained a monopoly of note issue in the whole of France.

The Bank of the Netherlands was established in 1814 after the old Bank of Amsterdam had for various reasons become discredited. The need was felt for a bank of the new type which was developing in England, Sweden and France, as referred to above. It was accordingly granted the sole right of note issue and made the Government's banker. It was founded with private capital, but the President and Secretary of the Managing Board were appointed by the Government, while the other members of the Managing Board and the Board of Directors were elected by the shareholders.

The National Bank of Austria was instituted in 1817 in order to restore order in the monetary position of Austria, which had seriously deteriorated as a result of the excessive issue and depreciation of Government paper money. The Bank received the exclusive privilege of note issue and proceeded to convert the Government money into its own notes as far as circumstances would permit. This process was almost completed by the end of 1847, but owing to the wars and uprisings in which Austria was involved between 1847 and 1866 the Government again resorted to the issue of paper currency, and several loans had also to be made to the Government by the Bank. The Bank was reorganized as the Bank of Austria-Hungary in 1878, and subsequently steps were taken to retire the Government paper money and to place the monetary system on a sound basis.

The Bank of Norway, which was opened in 1817, was brought into being by private capital, but its Governor and Vice-Governor were appointed by the King and the directors were elected by the Legislature. It was accorded the sole right of issue and made the Government's banker, and its further development followed on much the same lines as the Riksbank of Sweden.

The National Bank of Copenhagen, now known as the National Bank of Denmark, was founded with private capital in 1818 to take over the business of the Rigsbank, a State bank which had been created in 1813 to withdraw the depreciated Government paper money from circulation and to issue bank notes in their place. The National Bank became the sole bank of issue and was called upon to reorganize the monetary system. The only State control was in the form of the appointment by the Government of two out of the four or five managers, while the Board of Directors was elected by the shareholders.

The National Bank of Belgium was created in 1850 as the sole bank of issue and the financial agent of the Government. Prior to that date there were four banks of issue, and the notes of none of these banks had a national circulation, nor did they operate successfully as agents of the Treasury. The National Bank was a privately owned institution, but the Governor of the Bank was to be appointed by the Government.

The Bank of Spain, which had sprung from a State bank founded in 1829, was established under that name in 1856. At first it had to share the right of issue with the provincial banks, and was not granted a monopoly of note issue till 1873. Although the capital was raised by private subscription, the appointment of the Governor of the Bank rested with the Government.

The Bank of Russia was founded in 1860 as a State bank with the declared object of consolidating the monetary circulation and the floating debt of the Russian Empire. The country had suffered greatly from the evils of depreciated Government paper money and from the lack of proper banking facilities. The Bank was granted the sole right to issue bank notes and was called upon to stabilize the currency and promote the development of commerce, industry and agriculture by means of short-term credits. The Governor and Deputy Governor were appointed by the Government, while a Council consisting of Treasury officials was instituted to supervise the operations of the Bank.

The Reichsbank of Germany was founded in 1875 on the Bank of Prussia, whose ownership rested partly with the State but mainly with private shareholders. At the time of the formation of the German Empire there were in the several German States thirty-three banks of issue, of which the Bank of Prussia was the most important. It was agreed that these banks should retain their right of issue subject to certain limitations and to a uniform set of regulations, but that there should be a central bank of issue which was also to act as banker to the Imperial Government and to pursue, like the Bank of England, a bank-rate policy for the protection of the gold reserve and the credit structure of Germany. The Bank of Prussia was taken as the nucleus of such a bank which was called the Reichsbank. The Prussian Government was paid out its share of the capital and surplus, and the whole of the capital of the Reichsbank was obtained by private subscription. The Imperial Government, however, reserved to itself the power of appointing the Management Board, while the shareholders were to be represented by a council elected by themselves.

The Bank of Japan was set up in 1882 to restore order out of the chaos caused by the excessive issues of notes by the several national banks. These banks were ordered to withdraw their notes within a certain period, and the Bank of Japan obtained the sole right of issue. It was a joint-stock company, but the whole directorate of the Bank consisting of the Governor, Deputy Governor and four directors were to be appointed by the Government.

In such countries as Portugal, Roumania, Bulgaria, Serbia, Turkey, Java, Egypt and Algeria, banks with a monopoly of note issue were also brought into being during the nineteenth century.*

Thus, by the end of the nineteenth century almost every country in Europe,† along with Japan, Java and Persia in the East, and Egypt and Algeria in Africa, had established a bank of issue with special privileges and powers. All these banks became the bankers and financial agents of the Governments of their respective countries; and in different ways or in varying degrees they also assumed the other functions which were developed by the Bank of England and which have come to be regarded as essential functions of 'central banks'.

* In connection with this historical survey of the development of central banks, the author wishes to acknowledge his indebtedness, in particular, to the following works: Andréadès: *History of Bank of England*; Conant: *History of Modern Banks of Issue*; Dunbar: *Theory and History of Banking*; Mackenzie: *Banking Systems of Great Britain, France, Germany, and the United States of America*; Willis and Beckhart: *Foreign Banking Systems*.

† The Bank of Italy was established in 1893 but did not receive the sole right of note issue until 1926, while the Swiss National Bank did not start operations until 1907.

Establishment of New Central Banks

At the beginning of the twentieth century all the countries of the New World, and such countries of the Old World as China and India, were still without central banks, and, in most cases, even without partial centralization of the note issue. In the United States of America,* every bank established under the National Banking Act had the right to issue notes against deposit with the Federal Treasury of an equivalent amount of certain Government securities, and none of these banks acted exclusively as the banker or fiscal agent of the United States Government or as a lender of last resort. A more or less similar state of affairs prevailed in South and Central America and in Canada, Australia, South Africa, New Zealand, etc.

The financial panic of 1907 drew so much attention to the glaring weakness of the decentralized banking system of the United States that a special commission was appointed and an exhaustive inquiry ordered into the monetary and banking systems of the older countries. The outcome of this was the establishment, in 1914, of a central banking system for the United States in the form of twelve Federal Reserve Banks, each having authority over a defined area, with a co-ordinating Federal Reserve Board at Washington. These banks were granted a partial monopoly of the note issue and became the fiscal agents of the Government, the custodians of banking reserves, the banks of rediscount, and the lenders of last resort in their respective territories. While the constitution of these banks was different in several respects from that of the central banks of Europe and their powers more closely circumscribed by legislation, they performed practically the same functions and adopted the same practices.

Provision was made for State participation in the administration of the Federal Reserve System through the appointment of the members of the Federal Reserve Board by the President of

* It deserves to be mentioned that the First Bank of the United States (1792–1812) and the Second Bank of the United States (1816–30) had been institutions resembling the central banking type in some ways, and that the failure to secure a renewal of the charter of the Second Bank had deferred central banking development in the United States for nearly eighty years.

the United States, and then through the appointment by the Federal Reserve Board of three out of the nine directors of each Federal Reserve Bank, including the chairman. The other six directors were to be elected by those commercial banks which became members of the System in their respective districts, and while three of these could be bankers, the other three were to be representative of the commercial, industrial and agricultural interests of the community. Moreover, the member banks subscribed the whole capital of the Federal Reserve Banks and had to keep with the latter the minimum reserves against their deposit liabilities as laid down by law.

Although the Federal Reserve Banks of the United States were virtually superimposed upon an extensively developed banking structure, in contrast to the gradual development of central banks alongside commercial banks in the older countries, and were for that reason opposed and obstructed by certain sections of the community, they soon succeeded in working their way into the financial system of the United States and proved to be of great benefit and assistance to the Government and the banks during the war and post-war period (1917–20). The comparative success of the Federal Reserve System, under the unfavourable conditions emanating from unit banking as opposed to branch banking and from the existence of banking laws in each of the forty-eight States in addition to the Federal banking laws, played an important part in focusing attention on the desirability of having a central banking system in any country.

Moreover, the International Financial Conference, which was held at Brussels in 1920, passed a resolution to the effect that all countries which had not yet established a Central Bank should proceed to do so as soon as possible, not only with a view to facilitating the restoration and maintenance of stability in their monetary and banking systems but also in the interest of world co-operation.

Since that time, commencing with the South African Reserve Bank in 1921, central banks have been established not only in the existing independent or self-governing countries which did not yet have a central bank, but also in the many new independent states which have been created during the past fifty years, as shown in the following table:

1921 South African Reserve Bank
1922 Reserve Bank of Peru (reconstituted as Central Reserve Bank of Peru in 1931)
Bank of Latvia
Bank of Lithuania
1923 Bank of the Republic of Colombia
1924 National Bank of Hungary
Bank of Poland
Commonwealth Bank of Australia and Bank of the Republic of Uruguay converted into central banks
1925 National Bank of Albania
1926 National Bank of Czechoslovakia
Central Bank of Chile
Central Bank of Guatemala (reconstituted as Bank of Guatemala in 1946)
1927 Central Bank of Ecuador
Bank of Estonia converted into a central bank
1928 Central Bank of China
National Bank of Iran
Central Bank of Bolivia
Bank of Greece (in place of National Bank of Greece)
National Bank of Iceland converted into a central bank
1929 National Bank of Yugoslavia (in place of former National Bank of Serbia)
1931 Central Bank of the Republic of Turkey
1932 Bank of Mexico converted into a central bank
1934 Reserve Bank of New Zealand
Central Reserve Bank of El Salvador
1935 Bank of Canada
Reserve Bank of India
Central Bank of the Argentine Republic
1936 Bank of the Republic of Paraguay (reconstituted as Bank of Paraguay in 1944)
1937 National Bank of Costa Rica
1939 Bank of Afghanistan
1940 Central Bank of Venezuela
1941 National Bank of Nicaragua converted into a central bank
1942 Central Bank of Ireland
Bank of Thailand
State Bank of Ethiopia
1945 National Bank of Poland (in place of Bank of Poland)
1947 Central Bank of the Dominican Republic
1948 State Bank of Pakistan

Bank of the German States – Bank Deutscher Länder (in place of Reichsbank in West Germany)
Central Bank of the Philippines
1949 National Bank of Iraq
1950 Central Bank of Ceylon
National Bank of Cuba
Bank of Korea
Central Bank of Honduras
Central Bank of Costa Rica (in place of National Bank of Costa Rica)
German Bank of Issue – Deutsche Notenbank (in place of Reichsbank in East Germany)
1952 Central Bank of Belgian Congo (replaced by Monetary Council in 1960 and by National Bank of Congo in 1964)
Union Bank of Burma converted into central bank
Central Bank of Paraguay (in place of Bank of Paraguay)
Bank of Issue of Associated States of Indo-China (split into the National Banks of Cambodia, Laos and Vietnam in 1955)
1953 Bank of Indonesia (in place of Bank of Java)
1954 Bank of Israel
1955 National Bank of Libya (renamed Bank of Libya in 1963)
1956 Central Bank of Syria
Central Bank of Iraq (in place of National Bank of Iraq)
Bank of Rhodesia and Nyasaland (split into Reserve Bank of Rhodesia, Bank of Zambia and Reserve Bank of Malawi in 1964)
Central Bank of Nepal
1957 German Federal Bank – Deutsche Bundesbank (in place of Bank Deutscher Länder)
Bank of Ghana
Central Bank of Surinam
1958 Central Bank of Nigeria
Central Bank of Malaya (renamed Central Bank of Malaysia in 1963)
Central Bank of Tunisia
1959 Bank of Morocco
Reserve Bank of Australia (Commonwealth Bank split into Reserve Bank and Commonwealth Banking Corporation)
Central Bank of West African States
Central Bank of Equatorial Africa and Cameroon
1960 Bank of Republic of Guinea
Bank of Sudan
Bank of Jamaica

National Bank of Somalia converted into a central bank
1961 Central Bank of Egypt (in place of National Bank of Egypt)
Central Bank of Nicaragua (in place of National Bank of Nicaragua)
Central Bank of Iran (in place of National Bank of Iran)
Central Bank of Iceland (in place of National Bank of Iceland)
1962 Central Bank of Algeria (in place of Bank of Algeria)
Bank of Republic of Mali
Bank of the Netherlands Antilles
1963 Central Bank of Cyprus
National Bank of Ethiopia (in place of State Bank of Ethiopia)
Central Bank of Jordan
Bank of Sierra Leone
1964 Bank of Lebanon
Central Bank of Trinidad and Tobago
Bank of Burundi
National Bank of Rwanda
1965 Central Bank of Brazil
Bank of Guyana
1966 Central Bank of Kenya
Bank of Tanzania
Bank of Uganda
1967 Central Bank of Uruguay (in place of Bank of Republic of Uruguay)
1968 Central Bank of Malta
Central Bank of Mali (in place of Bank of Republic of Mali)
1969 Central Bank of Kuwait
Central Bank of Republic of Equatorial Guinea
1971 Central Bank of The Gambia

Present Position of Central Banking

At present, therefore, there is virtually no country which has not set up a central bank of its own.* This world-wide establishment

* Brazil was the last of the earlier independent countries to establish a special central bank, namely, the Central Bank of Brazil in 1965. Previously the Bank of Brazil, in addition to its commercial banking business, did perform some central banking functions, such as holding deposits of the other banks and rediscounting for them, and acting as the Government's banker and agent, but it did not have the right of note issue which was vested in the Treasury, and the control of the money and exchange markets

of central banks can be attributed to the growing realization that under modern conditions of banking and business it was a great advantage to any country irrespective of the stage of economic development, to have centralized monetary reserves and the control of currency and credit vested in one bank which had the support of the State and was subject to some form of State supervision and participation. Another factor was the realization that a central bank offered the best means of communication and co-operation between the banking system of one country and that of another.

While there are substantial differences in the constitutional structure and in the statutory powers of the various central banks, most of them show a tendency in practice to conform to, or work up to, a similar pattern in respect of their functions and methods. In the absence of uniform conditions, local improvisations and adjustments are, of course, resorted to in many cases. Thus, the methods vary in degree and sometimes in kind as between one central bank and another, depending upon the particular stage of economic development of a country; the volume and variety of its material resources; the make-up of its banking and credit structure generally; the nature of its international financial relationship (whether a creditor or a debtor country); the state of development of its capital market; and the degree of organization and activity of its money market. The point is, however, that underneath all these variations there lies a large measure of agreement in practice, and central bankers are to be found all over the world with more or less the same outlook on monetary and banking matters.

The methods of central banks also vary in kind and in degree as between one period and another, in accordance with the need for adjustment to fundamental changes in economic conditions and in the trend of political thought and action; and where some central banks are compelled by such circumstances to adjust their methods or adopt new ones, others faced with somewhat similar circumstances tend sooner or later to follow suit wholly or partly and directly or indirectly.

---

and bank reserve requirements was also exercised by the Treasury through its Superintendency of Money and Credit. These functions have been entrusted to the new Central Bank.

Central banking has become an entirely separate branch of banking, as distinct from the functions and operations of commercial banks, merchant banks, industrial banks, agricultural banks, savings banks, hire-purchase banks, investment banks, etc. Central banks have developed their own code of rules and practices, which can be described as 'the art of central banking' but which, in a changing world, is still in the process of evolution and subject to periodical readjustment. It is now also legitimate to speak of 'the science of central banking'.

A clearly defined concept has been evolved, a central bank being generally recognized as the bank which constitutes the apex of the monetary and banking structure of its country and which performs, as best it can in the national economic interest, the following functions:

1. The regulation of currency in accordance with the requirements of business and the general public, for which purpose it is granted either the sole right of note issue or at least a partial monopoly thereof.
2. The performance of general banking and agency services for the Government.
3. The custody of the cash reserves of the commercial banks.
4. The custody and management of the nation's reserves of international currency.
5. The provision of credit facilities in the form of rediscounts or collateral advances, to commercial banks, discount houses, bill brokers and dealers, or other banking institutions, in its capacity as the bankers' bank, and the general acceptance of the responsibility of lender of last resort.
6. The settlement of clearance balances between the banks, and the provision of facilities for the transfer of funds between all important centres.
7. The control of credit in accordance with the needs of business and the economy generally and for the purpose of carrying out the broad monetary policy adopted by the Government.

While the older central banks performed the functions enumerated above mostly as the result of tradition, the newer central banks had some of those functions specifically entrusted to them by statute. Preambles stipulating particular objectives of monetary policy were also introduced in the thirties. For example, in the preamble to the Bank of Canada Act that bank was directed 'to regulate credit and currency, to control and protect the external value of the national monetary unit and to mitigate by its influence fluctuations in the general level of production, trade, prices and employment so far as may be possible within the scope of monetary action'; and the preamble to the Reserve Bank of India Act referred to that bank as being constituted 'to regulate the issue of bank-notes and the keeping of reserves with a view to securing monetary stability in India, and generally to operate the currency and credit system of the country to its advantage'.

Moreover, the statutes of many of the newer central banks circumscribe their powers and functions to such an extent that those statutes amount almost to a definition of what a central bank should or should not do. The noticeable trend in central banking legislation towards a more or less standard type, after allowing for the political constitution and the stage of economic development of different countries, affords a practical illustration of the existence of a clearly defined concept of central banking.

Characteristics of a Central Bank

The question as to which function more particularly characterized a bank as a central bank had exercised the minds of several economists during the inter-war period when the surge of new central banks began to manifest itself. For example, Hawtrey[1] regarded its function as the lender of last resort as the essential characteristic of a central bank and pointed out that, while the right of note issue gave a bank a great advantage in facing the responsibilities of the lender of last resort, it could nevertheless perform that function without the right of issue. Vera Smith,[2] on the other hand, said that 'the primary definition of central banking is a banking system in which a single bank has either a complete or a residuary monopoly in the note issue', and that 'it was out of monopolies in the note issue that were derived the secondary functions and characteristics of our modern central banks', whereas Shaw[3] held that 'the one true, but at the same time all-sufficing function of a central bank is control of credit'.

Kisch and Elkin[4] considered that 'the essential function of a central bank is the maintenance of the stability of the monetary standard', which 'involves the control of the monetary circulation', while Jauncey[5] said that 'clearing is the main operation of central banking'. In the Statutes of the Bank for International Settlements, on the other hand, a central bank was defined as 'the bank in any country to which has been entrusted the duty of regulating the volume of currency and credit in that country'.

Moreover, the fact that several central banks were named reserve banks, such as the Federal Reserve Banks of the United States, the South African Reserve Bank, the Central Reserve Bank of Peru, the Reserve Bank of Australia, the Reserve Bank of New Zealand, and the Reserve Bank of India, would appear to show that in the opinion of some authorities the custody of bank reserves was the characteristic function of a central bank.

In practice, however, it is difficult to single out any particular function as the characteristic one or name all the functions in the order of their importance, since they are interrelated and complementary. For example, a specific loan operation of a central bank (i.e. in its capacity as a bank of rediscount) might have been caused by a commercial bank requiring more note currency (involving the central bank as the bank of issue) or foreign exchange or gold (involving the central bank as the custodian of the nation's reserves), or having to replenish its cash reserves and clearing balances (involving the central bank as the custodian of the cash reserves of the commercial banks and the bank of central clearance) which it could not obtain from any other source owing to general monetary stringency (involving the central bank as lender of last resort); and before effecting the rediscount, the central bank might have raised its discount rate or imposed certain conditions in its capacity as the controller of credit.

A true central bank should always be ready to perform any of the functions enumerated above if the conditions and circumstances in its area of operation render it necessary or desirable for it to do so. The guiding principle for a central bank, whatever function or group of functions it performs at any particular moment, is that it should act only in the public interest and without regard to profit as a primary consideration.

The following seven chapters deal separately with the seven main functions of central banks, as there is a considerable advantage in also tracing the separate development of the various functions and as this is the only satisfactory way of setting out in detail the operations connected therewith. The essential unity and the interdependence of these functions under modern conditions must, however, be constantly borne in mind; and to facilitate this, the inter-connections between one function and another will off and on be brought out in each of those chapters. In the chapter on the Control of Credit attention will be drawn to the fact that it is through the function of credit control, in particular, that the other functions are united and made to serve a common purpose.

The same considerations apply to the four chapters devoted to a separate analysis of the development of the various methods of credit control.

References

1 Hawtrey, R. G. *Art of Central Banking*. Cass, 1932. p. 131.
2 Smith, Vera. *Rationale of Central Banking*. P. S. King & Son, 1936. p. 148.
3 Shaw, W. A. *Theory and Principles of Central Banking*. Pitman, 1930. pp. v and 78–80.
4 Kisch, C. H. & Elkin, W. A. *Central Banks*, 4 ed. Macmillan, 1930. p. 74.
5 Jauncey, L. C. *Australia's Government Bank*. Cranley & Day, 1933. p. 166.

CHAPTER TWO

The Bank of Issue

Evolution of Issue Function

The privilege of note issue was almost everywhere associated with the origin and development of central banks. In fact, until the beginning of the twentieth century they were generally known as banks of issue.

The issue of notes as of other currency was always claimed to be a prerogative of the State, but whereas in the case of metallic currency the State retained its prerogative, it decided, with few exceptions, to hand the issue of notes over to banks when they, like note currency itself, arose and developed out of the need for further means of facilitating the exchange of goods. Banks were given the right to issue notes, or, where banks had already put into circulation notes of their own in one form or another, they were legally authorized to continue issuing notes, subject to certain safeguards imposed by law. In some countries the note issue was entrusted to banks owing to the heavy depreciation of, and the consequent loss of public confidence in, notes issued by the State, while in others it was done in return for loans to the State or because the issue of notes was considered more appropriate in the hands of banks than those of the State.

In due course, as more banks came to be established in each country and note currency came into greater use with the rapid expansion of trade, the need for uniformity in the note circulation and for better regulation of the note issue caused almost every country to introduce specific legislation granting one bank either a complete monopoly of the note issue or a residuary monopoly, as Vera Smith[1] called it. This stage was reached, for example, in the Netherlands in 1814, England in 1844, France in 1848, Germany in 1875, Sweden in 1897, United States in 1914, South Africa in 1921, Colombia in 1923, Australia in 1924, Chile in 1925, Italy in 1926, New Zealand in 1934, Canada in 1935, Venezuela in 1940, Ireland in 1942, etc. In some cases, as in England and Sweden, the bank which was ultimately granted the monopoly of the note issue was also the first joint-stock bank to be established in those countries, but in many countries it was given to a new bank which was created under a special law or charter for the purpose, *inter alia*, of securing uniformity in the note issue. In all cases, however, the banks entrusted with the sole or residuary monopoly of note issue became the recognized central banks of their respective countries; and this monopoly privilege was a primary factor in their development into central banks with special duties and responsibilities of a semi-public character.

In the case of most of the central banks which today enjoy a complete monopoly of the note issue, the other banks were required by law to redeem their notes as they were paid in or to withdraw their notes from circulation within a stated period, as in Sweden, Switzerland, South Africa, Colombia, Chile and New Zealand; or the central bank was required to take over the issues of the other banks subject to certain conditions and provisions for their redemption, as in France, Spain, Japan and Italy. In England the other banks were allowed under the Act of 1844 to retain their note issues, but they were limited to the individual amounts outstanding at that time and provision was made for their lapsing in certain circumstances, the final extinction taking place in 1920; in Germany, where thirty-three note-issuing banks were in existence on the establishment of the Reichsbank in 1875, all but four had, owing to the restrictions imposed on their issues, surrendered their right of issue to the Reichsbank long before 1935 when the privilege of the remaining four was withdrawn; and in Canada, where the chartered banks were permitted to continue issuing notes after the establishment of the Bank of

Canada in 1935, subject to their note issues being gradually reduced in accordance with a prescribed schedule to 25 per cent of their unimpaired paid-up capital, the Bank of Canada was subsequently given the sole right to issue notes as from 1st January, 1945.

There are, at present, only a few central banks which do not yet enjoy a complete monopoly of the note issue. Those of the United States have, at least, a residuary monopoly. In the United States, the issues of the national banks were limited to the outstanding amounts of the special Government bonds carrying the privilege of cover for such notes, and these were to be gradually redeemed. There are, however, still limited amounts of Government notes in circulation as relics of the past. The Federal Reserve notes now represent the great bulk and the elastic element of the note circulation,* and for practical purposes the Federal Reserve System may be said to have a monopoly of the note issue.

Concentration of Note Issues in Central Banks

The main reasons for the concentration of the note issue of almost every country in a central bank were the following:

(1) Every country found it necessary or desirable not only to bring about uniformity in its note circulation according as notes became more and more the principal form of hand-to-hand currency, but also to attain effective State supervision over a credit instrument which had, for the sake of convenience, to be declared by law to be legal-tender money. Although this uniformity and State supervision could also have been achieved by means of a direct State issue, the many examples of depreciation of Government notes in the past and the consequent public distrust of Government issues caused the State to concentrate the note issue in one bank, even if it was in many cases a State bank. In other words, Governments considered it advisable in

* At the end of 1970 Federal Reserve notes amounted to $50·2 billion out of a total of $50·8 billion notes in circulation outside the Treasury and the Federal Reserve Banks.

the circumstances to exercise their supervision over the note circulation indirectly through a central bank governed by special legislation, rather than directly through a Government Department.

(2) With the increasing use of deposit money created by the commercial banks and the growing need for some form of credit control by a central bank, it came to be more generally realized that a monopoly of the note issue in itself tended to give a central bank some measure of control over undue credit expansion by the commercial banks, since the expansion of credit obviously led to an increased demand for note currency. Except in special circumstances, such as when net favourable balances of payments over a period of years or other factors provided the commercial banks with large credit balances at the central bank, the commercial banks must sooner or later borrow from the central bank in order to obtain the additional supply of notes required for the larger payments of wages and salaries arising out of their credit expansion and the consequent increased economic activity, since they could not issue notes themselves. In the absence of special circumstances, therefore, the sole right of note issue tended at least to give the central bank a better opportunity of exercising such influence over credit expansion by commercial banks as it considered to be appropriate under the prevailing conditions.

(3) It also came to be recognized that the concentration of the note issue in one bank which, moreover, enjoyed the support of the State, gave such notes a distinctive prestige not attaching to notes issued by several banks – a prestige which proved to be of great value in a crisis or other emergency.[2]

(4) Since the issue of notes could in certain circumstances be a valuable source of profit and since Governments preferred for various reasons not to issue notes themselves, it appeared to be more advantageous to concentrate the note issue in one bank and provide for participation in its profits than to leave the right of issue in the hands of several banks, even if they were subject to tax on the amount of their notes in circulation.

Regulation of Note Issues

Apart from uniformity, it was important to have elasticity in the note issue with a view to meeting the legitimate currency requirements of business and the general public. The note circulation should operate automatically and be capable of expanding according as the demand for currency increased (whether as the result of expanding business activity and larger pay-rolls or seasonal factors such as during harvesting and holiday periods), and of contracting according as the demand for currency declined because of contraction of business and smaller pay-rolls or seasonal dullness. Willis,[3] for example, referred to the 'recognized principle of bank-note circulation' as 'dictating that the issue of notes shall take place when and as demanded by those who have business transactions to perform, or wages to pay'.

The question as to how far elasticity in the note circulation could be carried without unduly weakening the security of the notes and shaking public confidence, or facilitating the creation of unsound economic conditions, was the subject of controversy for over a hundred years. During that period there were, roughly speaking, three different methods evolved by legislators in connection with the regulation of note issues.

The first was the system of a partial fiduciary issue, which was introduced in England in 1844 and subsequently adopted by several countries. The primary feature of this system was that of a fixed amount laid down by law, which could be covered only by Government securities, while all notes issued in excess of this amount had to be fully covered by gold. This method of note regulation was frequently criticized in England as being too inelastic, on the ground that an internal or external drain of gold caused an undue contraction of currency and credit, and also that it was not sufficiently adaptable to heavy demands for currency in financial panics and other emergencies. On the other hand, the view was held that it served at least a useful purpose as a brake on undue expansion of currency and credit in times of prosperity. In spite of frequent attacks on the relatively inelastic English system of note issue, even by Governmental Commissions of inquiry, it continued to remain in force, mainly as a matter of tradition.

It was not until 1928 that elasticity in the note issue of England was specially provided for in the form of legal authority to the Treasury to permit the Bank of England to increase its fiduciary issue above £260 million (the amount fixed at that time), to a specified amount for not more than two years altogether from the date on which the authority was originally given. The fiduciary issue was increased, for the first time, by £15 million to £275 million in August, 1931, in order to protect the credit base from the drain of gold which was then taking place. This increase was interpreted in a very unfavourable light on the Continent, since it was regarded as the beginning of inflationary tendencies, and it helped to increase the outflow of gold. The disadvantage of this expedient was, as the *Statist* pointed out at the time, that 'elasticity can only be obtained at the cost of a definite loss of confidence', inasmuch as it 'attracts unnecessary attention when that attention is least desirable'. The Macmillan Committee on Finance and Industry had also in the same year stated that 'an approach by the Bank of England to the Treasury for permission to increase the fiduciary issue would be interpreted as a sign of weakness, and be the occasion of nervousness at a time when the opposite effect on sentiment was to be desired' (page 140 of Report).

Subsequently, however, greater use was made of this expedient. In March, 1933, the fiduciary issue was reduced to the original figure of £260 million, owing to the inflow of gold at that time; and in December, 1936, it was further reduced to £200 million to compensate for the sale of gold to the Bank of England by the Exchange Equalization Account. In November, 1937, it was raised to £220 million in order to protect the reserve against heavy seasonal expansion in the note circulation due to Christmas demands, and reduced again to £200 million in January, 1938, when the note circulation declined. In December, 1938, it was increased to £230 million for the same reason as in the preceding year; and early in January, 1939, it was further increased to £400 million in order to facilitate the transfer of £200 million gold (at the statutory price of about eighty-five shillings per fine ounce) from the Bank of England to the Exchange Equalization Account. In the following month, however, it was reduced to £300 million as a result of revaluation of the remainder of the Bank's gold holdings at current market price. It was then raised to £580 million in September, 1939, when all the gold held in the issue department of the Bank, and valued at about £280 million at the market price, was transferred to the Exchange Account with the object of 'concentrating the country's resources in one reserve'.

Thus, the position since September, 1939, has been that the note issue of the Bank of England has been directly covered* only by Government securities and a small amount of other securities and coin.

The former English system of a partial fiduciary issue was, with some variations, also followed by Italy prior to 1926, and by Japan, Sweden, Norway and Finland.

The second method was that followed by France between 1870 and 1928, and by England and Japan since 1939 and 1941 respectively, namely, that of a maximum limit for the note circulation in the form of an amount fixed from time to time and without any gold cover being prescribed by law. The essential difference between the system previously followed by France and that in force in England and Japan during the war and post-war periods, was that in the latter countries the Legislature delegated to the Treasury the power to raise the maximum limit at any time and to any amount during the period covered by specific authority or general emergency powers, whereas in the former the Legislature retained that prerogative. France abandoned its method of a maximum issue fixed by the Legislature because, according to Lemoine,[4] it 'was altogether too rigid and incapable of sufficient adjustment to the requirements of the present-day money markets', and also because it 'provides no guaranty against inflation' owing to the possibility of 'raising the limit by Parliamentary action whether such action is warranted or not'. In this connection it is interesting to note that in England the ultimate control by Parliament over the maximum limit for the note issue was restored in February, 1954, when the limit was fixed at £1,575 million, as compared with £580 million in September, 1939. By the end of 1970 the limit had been raised to £3,700 million.

* It should be borne in mind, however, that the gold and foreign exchange reserves were concentrated in the Exchange Equalization Account, and that such reserves were available for external purposes.

The third method was that of prescribing a minimum percentage gold reserve* against the note issue, the remainder of the notes to be covered by certain specified assets such as trade bills and Government securities, and, in most cases, also a minimum reserve against the deposits of the central bank. This method of note regulation, which also provided formally for temporary suspension of the full reserve requirements subject to certain conditions, had by 1928 spread over a large part of the world and was further adopted by many of the new central banks which were established after that date. In some countries, however, the central banks were allowed to include foreign exchange along with gold in the legal minimum reserve. The evolution of this system of note regulation represented a deliberate attempt to attain the highest degree of elasticity compatible with adequate security in the note circulation.

The principle of a minimum percentage metallic cover for note issues had already been adopted, before the middle of the nineteenth century, in the Netherlands and Java (40 per cent) and Belgium (one-third). At first a maximum limit for the uncovered notes was also laid down, but in the Netherlands, for example, the limit was removed in 1863 when instead the minimum percentage reserve was made applicable to the current account liabilities as well as the note liabilities of the Netherlands Bank.

In Germany, on the other hand, with the establishment of the Reichsbank in 1875, an additional limit apart from a minimum reserve of one-third was imposed on the note issue in that beyond a certain fixed amount the notes were to be fully covered by cash in hand (i.e. gold bullion, German or foreign gold coin and other German coin). The additional limit showed the influence of the former English system, but a novel feature was added to it, namely, that the Reichsbank could issue notes in excess of this limit subject to the payment of a tax at the rate of 5 per cent per annum on any such excess of notes. The idea behind this method was to impart elasticity to the note circulation, while at the same

* Prior to the general adoption of the gold standard during the latter part of the nineteenth century, the countries which still maintained the silver or bi-metallic standard used to prescribe a minimum reserve comprising both gold and silver coin and bullion.

time it discouraged the central bank from following a policy of undue expansion by imposing a tax on the uncovered excess. Another novel feature was the provision that, apart from the minimum reserve requirements, the remainder of the notes were to be covered by discounted paper having a maturity of not more than three months. No provision, however, was made for a minimum reserve against the deposits of the Reichsbank, as was done in the case of the Netherlands Bank.

When the United States finally decided in 1913 to establish a central banking system, these new principles were incorporated in the provisions for the regulation of the note issues of the Federal Reserve Banks, but with various modifications. It was provided that the Federal Reserve Banks should maintain a minimum gold reserve of 40 per cent against all their notes in circulation, and that they should also hold a reserve of 35 per cent against their deposits. At first, in addition to the minimum gold reserve of 40 per cent the notes were to be fully covered by trade or agricultural bills discounted for the member banks by the Federal Reserve Banks. This was prompted by the desire for a so-called 'pure asset currency', which would not only be a very safe and sound currency but would also expand or contract in accordance with the volume of business, as it was expected that the volume of discounted bills in the hands of the Federal Reserve Banks would reflect fairly accurately the volume of business activity in the United States. This was, however, found not to be the case, and the Federal Reserve Banks experienced difficulty at times in providing adequate note currency.

The next step was taken in 1916, when the base of the note issue was broadened by admitting as cover the short-term collateral notes of the member banks which represented another means of member-bank borrowing from the Federal Reserve Banks, and also the bills and acceptances bought by the latter in the open market, while in 1917 gold was admitted as direct cover and only for the remainder were notes to be covered by bills and collateral notes. Finally, in 1932 direct obligations of the United States were temporarily* admitted as additional backing for

* The provision declaring the Federal Reserve Banks' own holdings of Government securities (in contrast to those held under collateral notes) to

Federal Reserve notes, owing to the heavy demand for currency for domestic hoarding and the demand for gold from abroad at that time.

Further elasticity was provided in the form of permitting, in an emergency, a temporary shortfall in the gold reserve against notes rather than a temporary excess of notes above the amount covered in accordance with the reserve requirements, as in the case of the Reichsbank. Provision was made for authority to suspend the full reserve requirements for thirty days and to renew the suspension for periods of fifteen days each, subject to the payment by the Federal Reserve Banks of a graduated percentage tax on the amount of the shortfall in the gold reserves and to the raising of their discount and interest rates at least by the percentage of the tax to be so paid.

The basic provisions of the Federal Reserve Act of the United States (as amended up to 1917), relating to the regulation of the note issue and to the reserve against deposits as well as notes, were incorporated in the statutes of many of the new central banks which were established thereafter, beginning with the South African Reserve Bank in 1921, and were also adopted by Italy in 1926 and France in 1928 when they reorganized their currency systems. Even Germany decided, on the occasion of the reorganization of the Reichsbank in 1924, to adopt the modifications previously introduced by the United States, with the exception of the reserve against deposits; and in 1933, after the Reichsbank had lost most of its gold and exchange reserves owing to the flight of capital, it was also empowered, as was done in the case of the Federal Reserve Banks in 1932, to use its own holdings of Government bonds in addition to commercial bills discounted, as cover for notes.

A further development in the direction of elasticity was that of prescribing merely a minimum percentage gold reserve against notes and deposits and making the notes a first charge on all the assets of the central bank, as has been done in the Netherlands since 1863 and in South Africa since 1930. Thus, by discarding the principle of specifying the particular kinds of assets which

---

be eligible collateral for Federal Reserve notes, was extended from time to time until the question of a time limit was finally eliminated in 1945.

may be used as cover for that part of the note issue not covered by gold, the central bank was given greater freedom of action. The widespread adoption of the principle of a minimum reserve against the deposits as well as the notes of the central bank was already a belated legal recognition of the fact that the deposits represented no less a liability of the central bank than its notes did, since the former were convertible into the latter on demand; and thus it was only logical not to prescribe any specific security for the note issue other than a minimum cover of gold or of gold and foreign exchange, as was done in the case of deposits.

Finally, despite the foregoing historical record of legislative measures designed to ensure both the maintenance of substantial direct restraint and the provision of adequate elasticity for note issues by central banks, many countries were compelled, some already under the stress of the world depression of 1930–3 and others subsequently under war or post-war conditions, to suspend or abolish the reserve requirements, or to repeal the penal conditions attached to temporary suspension, or at least to reduce the minimum reserve. It is obvious, therefore, that for various reasons elasticity has become the predominant factor in the issue of note currency.

State Notes versus Bank Notes

While the State practically everywhere entrusted the note issue to a central bank, and while this was generally accepted as proof in itself that the central bank was found by experience to be the most suitable and appropriate medium for the issue of note currency, there were some adherents of the view that in the interest of the community the State alone should issue notes. Shaw[5] even expounded the view that a State note issue based on full value was the only means of securing an 'uncontrolled, automatic, self-regulating note currency', and that the State should use the central bank, if at all, only for the distribution of notes as in the case of metallic currency.

The following quotations will suffice to illustrate Shaw's reasoning:

'The principles of the true or ideal paper money, viz. a State-issued paper money of full face value, guaranteed by a full cover redemption fund composed of securities, issued automatically, retired automatically, self-regulating, never redundant, never deficient, neutral in its effect on prices, but rising equal to any strain upon it, guaranteed against debasement by the State which issues it, and incapable of debasement by the community which purchases and uses it'; 'so long as a State sells paper money at a full face value the public will only buy so much as it absolutely needs, and so much as it actually can afford to pay for'; and 'every known case of deliberate depreciation of currency has been the act of a needy Government which has imposed its will upon a Central Bank.'

It is difficult to understand why a needy Government should not hesitate to bring pressure to bear on the central bank to debase the note currency, but would refrain from debasing notes when it was the issuer itself, just because it had originally undertaken to issue full value currency and only in response to actual demand from the public. 'Necessity knows no law', and, moreover, history reveals many illustrations of currency depreciation owing to the over-issue of notes by the State.

It is true that there are also many examples of currency depreciation due to needy Governments imposing their will upon central banks, but if the latter had resisted indefinitely the former would have resorted to other means of achieving their object. In this as in other matters, central banks are frequently confronted with the necessity of choosing the lesser of two evils. The resistance which is usually offered by a central bank against unsound monetary and financial policies on the part of the State is at least one advantage in favour of the central bank being the issuer of notes.

It is also difficult to understand why a State issue should be the only, or the best, medium of securing an automatic, self-regulating note currency. At least in every country where bank deposits constitute a more important means of payment than note currency, the issue of notes by the central bank is not a controlled factor in the sense that conscious and deliberate policy is imparted to it. Conscious policy, if any, is directed towards the control of credit, and the issue of notes proceeds automatically, contracting and expanding, as Shaw demands of an ideal paper currency, in accordance with the needs of business and the general public. In other words, the central bank does not take the initiative in the issue of notes. In the modern economy the creation of bank credit, either central bank or commercial bank credit, reveals itself in the first instance in the form of deposit money, while the secondary effect is an expansion of the automatic demand for notes.

Furthermore, since it is generally recognized, even by Shaw, that the control of credit belongs essentially to the central bank, and since the concentration of the note issue in the central bank has proved to be of great advantage in the carrying out of its function of controlling credit, it follows that the two functions should continue to be co-ordinated and to be exercised by the central bank subject to the general supervision of the State, rather than directly by the State.

Economic opinion in general is definitely against a State note issue, on account of the temptation in which Governments are placed and the comparative ease with which Governments as big disbursers of money can in the long run force their notes into circulation. As Lewinski[6] pointed out, 'bank-notes are, with rare exceptions, issued but on the demand of the recipient parties', whereas Government paper money can be 'put into the channels of circulation in exchange for services and goods' and need not be 'preceded by any demand for them'.

There are, moreover, no central bank notes which do not comply with Shaw's requirement of 'paper money of full face value, guaranteed by a full cover redemption fund composed of securities'. Whether specific collateral against notes issued by the central bank is prescribed by law or not, all central bank notes are fully backed by such assets as gold, foreign exchange, coin, trade bills, Treasury bills, Government bonds or other securities. In short, central banks only issue notes in exchange for value, although it must be admitted that the different kinds of assets which may be, or in certain circumstances have to be, accepted by a central bank in exchange for its notes are not all of equal value in the long run as a backing for the currency. This aspect of the matter will be further discussed in Chapter 5.

Phenomenal World-Wide Increase in Note Issues

Note issues showed a considerable expansion between 1914 and 1929, due not only to the abnormal increase in the total money supply consequent upon the net inflationary repercussions of World War I but also to the general displacement of gold coin with notes on account of the abandonment of the gold-specie standard. Between 1929 and 1938 there was again a large increase in some countries, but during and after World War II a phenomenal increase took place in the note issues of all kinds of countries, as illustrated by the following table:*

Note Issues at End of Year

(Base: 1929 = 100)

Country	1938	1944	1952	1960	1970
United States	179	885	1,048	1,080	1,810
United Kingdom	135	314	387	540	938
France	160	845	3,133	5,970	11,200
Canada	144	572	835	1,000	1,900
Australia	117	486	814	1,010	1,580
South Africa	211	667	1,022	1,230	2,830
Sweden	186	438	804	1,160	2,040
Switzerland	175	355	513	735	1,440
Argentina	90	189	1,524	8,490	61,100
Chile	226	738	3,633	45,170	1,245,000

The large increase in the note circulation of some countries between 1929 and 1938 was associated with the expansion of bank credit in response to an official policy of cheap money to stimulate the economy, or with currency depreciation and re-

* To maintain the indices for 1960 and 1970 on a comparable basis with the earlier indices, due allowance was made for the conversion of French francs and Argentine pesos into new francs and pesos at the rate of 100 old units for 1 new unit, in 1960 and 1970 respectively, and of Chilean pesos into escudos at the rate of 1,000 for 1 in 1960, as well as for the change-over from South African and Australian pounds to rands and dollars respectively, at the rate of 2 new units per pound, which accompanied the decimalization of these currencies in 1961 and 1966 respectively.

valuation of gold reserves or a net favourable balance of payments. There was also a tendency in certain countries towards an increased use of note currency relative to the use of bank deposits. In the United States, as Whittlesey pointed out in 1943, the increased use of currency had been going on for a quarter of a century, and this 'is less a symptom of reversion to more primitive financial methods than an indication of certain shifts in the distribution of income and in methods of conducting trade'.[7] Thus, bank deposits (including savings deposits) as a multiple of the note circulation[8] declined in the United States from 11·1 in 1929 to 7·6 in 1938 and continued to decline to 5·5 in 1952; in Switzerland from 13·0 to 8·0 and 4·6 respectively; in Sweden from 11·8 to 8·2 and 4·5 respectively; and in Germany from 5·9 to 4·3 and 3·4 respectively. On the other hand, the multiple remained almost constant in the United Kingdom and France between 1929 and 1952.

As far as the sharp increase in note issues between 1938 and 1944 was concerned, the basic factor in the belligerent countries was, of course, the enormous war expenditure, a large part of which had to be financed directly or indirectly by the creation of bank credit. The total money supply was thus considerably increased from time to time, not only to meet the actual requirements of a war economy and a rising price level, but also to keep interest rates on war loans as low as possible. In addition, a relative increase in the use of notes was induced by war conditions, e.g. larger holdings of currency by the banks, the business community and the public for emergency purposes; heavy cash payments to the armed forces and their dependants; the growth in wage payments relative to the increase in other income shares,[9] etc.

With regard to the neutral countries, the abnormal increase in note issues between 1938 and 1944 was due mainly to a marked rise in the price level, expansion of economic activity and favourable balances of payments which resulted from war conditions over a large part of the world.

Since the end of the war in 1945, the rapid increase in the note issues of all countries has continued to manifest itself in varying degrees, as shown in the foregoing table. This is to be attributed not only to the notable expansion of the volume of world production and trade, but also to the persistent universal, and in some countries astronomical, inflation of credit, wages and prices which will be discussed later.

References

1 Smith, Vera. *Rationale of Central Banking*. Cass, 1936. p. 148: 'A residuary monopoly denotes a case where there are a number of note issuers, but all of these except one are working under narrow limitations, and this one authority is responsible for the bulk of the circulation.'
2 Dunbar, C. F. *Theory and History of Banking*, 3 ed. Putnam, 1918. pp. 79–80.
3 Willis, H. P. *Theory and Practice of Central Banking*. Harper, 1936. p. 264.
4 Lemoine, R. J., in *Foreign Banking Systems*, Ed. Willis & Beckhart. Henry Holt, 1929. p. 533.
5 Shaw, W. A. *Theory and Principles of Central Banking*. Pitman, 1930. pp. 30–80.
6 Lewinski, J. S. *Money, Credit and Prices*. King, 1929. p. 55.
7 Whittlesey, C. R. *The Effect of War on Currency and Deposits*. National Bureau of Economic Research, 1943. p. 4.
8 *Annual Report of the Bank for International Settlements for 1952–53*. p. 165.
9 Whittlesey, *op. cit.* p. 24.

CHAPTER THREE

The Government's Banker, Agent and Adviser

Introduction

Central banks everywhere fulfil the functions of banker, agent and adviser of the Government. In fact, the older institutions performed these functions even before they developed into real central banks; and it was as banks with the sole or principal right of note issue that they came to be the bankers of their respective Governments. This association of the function of note issue with that of banker to the Government was thus automatically accepted in the case of the new central banks.

As the Government's banker the central bank conducts the banking accounts of Government departments, boards and enterprises; it makes temporary advances to the Government in anticipation of the collection of taxes or the raising of loans from the public, and extraordinary advances during a depression, war or other emergency; and it carries out the Government's transactions involving purchases or sales of foreign currencies. The central bank is also called upon to perform various services as the Government's financial agent, and it acts generally as a financial adviser of the Government.

Government Banking Accounts

In keeping the banking accounts of Government* departments and institutions, the central bank performs the same functions as the commercial bank ordinarily performs for its customers. It accepts their deposits† of cash, cheques or drafts, and undertakes the collection of the cheques and drafts drawn on other banks; it supplies them with the cash required for salaries and wages and other cash disbursements and also debits their accounts with the amounts of cheques or vouchers drawn by them on it and presented for payment by other customers; it transfers funds for the Government from one account to another or from one centre to another, etc.

The control over the Government accounts is usually centralized in the Treasury, except in the case of State enterprises or boards which are managed independently of the Treasury and which, therefore, make their own arrangements with the central bank.

Owing to the magnitude of the Government's financial operations, the keeping of the Government banking accounts obviously entails an enormous amount of clerical work and expense. In the case of many central banks, the State has provided for remuneration either directly in the form of a specific payment to the central bank based on the turnover of the accounts or an agreed annual amount, or indirectly through an arrangement whereby the Government has to maintain a minimum credit balance in its accounts with the central bank, even if it has to borrow from the latter at times in order to maintain the requisite balance. In other cases, however, the central bank has under its charter or statute, or under a private agreement with the Government, to conduct the Government accounts free of charge; and as with permanent loans to the State in the case of the older central banks, this obligation on the part of the central

* In many countries the central bank keeps the accounts not only of the Central or Federal Government, but also of the Provinces or States.

† In the United States the Federal Treasury has continued to hold a substantial amount of actual cash and also to keep some of its deposits with commercial banks, whether arising out of the proceeds of issues of Government securities or out of deposits of current receipts in places distant from Reserve Bank cities.

bank is usually associated with its enjoyment of the privilege of note issue and any other privileges which may have been conferred by legislation.

The central bank operates as the Government's banker, not only because it is more convenient and economical to the Government, but also because of the intimate connection between public finance and monetary affairs. The State is in every country the largest receiver of revenue and has in most countries also become the biggest borrower; and its expenditures have come to play an increasingly important part in the economic life of the nation. The central bank, on the other hand, is charged with the duty and responsibility of controlling or adjusting credit in the national economic interest and carrying out the monetary policy adopted by the Government. As the manifold financial activities of the State can in certain circumstances exercise a disturbing influence on money-market conditions* and exchange rates and counteract the credit policy of the central bank, the centralization of Government banking operations in the central bank at least gives the latter a better opportunity of judging the general financial situation at any time, giving the appropriate advice to the Government and taking the necessary remedial measures.

Another banking service rendered by the central bank is that of providing the Government with the foreign exchange required to meet its external debt service or its purchases of goods and other disbursements abroad, or buying any surplus foreign exchange which may accrue to the Government from foreign loans or from other sources. In many debtor countries the Government requires relatively large amounts of foreign exchange to meet interest and other charges abroad; and the central bank has to acquire the requisite foreign exchange by purchase

* In this connection the view is held in some circles that, to prevent immobilization of banking funds resulting from large Government balances with the central bank at certain times, Government deposits should be kept with the commercial banks rather than the central bank. Such immobilization, however, can best be prevented, to the extent that the central bank considers it necessary or desirable to do so, through the carrying out of suitable open-market operations, which will be discussed in Chapter 10.

in the open market or by agreement with the commercial banks or the principal export industries, or by a combination of these methods.

Government's Agent and Adviser

In general, it may be said that the older central banks are required to perform a greater number and variety of services as agents of the Government than in the case of the newer central banks. The main reason for this is that, owing to the late appearance of the latter, the Treasuries of the countries concerned were already well developed and organized for the carrying out of such duties. The trend has, however, been in the direction of passing some of these duties to the central bank from time to time. The Reserve Bank of New Zealand and the Bank of Canada, for example, were entrusted with the management of the national debt in 1936.

With the older central banks, the process of undertaking financial services for the Government developed more or less in accordance with the growing needs of the State. The Bank of England, for example, first took over from the Exchequer the duty of receiving subscriptions for Government loans in 1718. Then it undertook in 1751 the service of paying interest on the national debt. In due course it assumed all the other duties connected with the administration and management of the national debt, such as the keeping of transfer registers in respect of Government stocks; the receipt of subscriptions for Government loans and the making of all other arrangements in connection with the flotation, conversion or redemption of Government loans; the issue and redemption of Treasury bills; and the giving of advice and information regarding the state and trend of the money and capital markets, the terms and other conditions on which new Government loans can be issued or old loans converted, etc.

Like the Bank of England, the Federal Reserve Banks of the United States perform numerous services as agents and advisers to the Treasury and Government institutions generally. They have, for example, taken over from the Treasury all the work connected with the distribution of its securities, whether bonds, Treasury notes or Treasury bills; they receive subscriptions for new issues and deliver the securities to subscribers; they cash interest coupons and pay off maturing obligations; they act as agents for the Reconstruction Finance Corporation, Home Owners' Loan Corporation, and other similar Government agencies. In one way or another, such general services are also rendered by many other central banks.

Central banks, moreover, perform special agency services for the State. In all the countries which have introduced exchange stabilization or equalization funds, or payments or clearing agreements with other countries, the central banks have been entrusted with the administration of these funds and agreements, keeping separate banking accounts for these purposes and carrying out all the transactions in gold and foreign exchange connected therewith. The central bank likewise acts as the Government's agent where exchange control, whether as a war or other measure, is in force.

Advances by Central Bank to Government (prior to 1914)

The obligation on the part of the central bank to grant advances to the Government was closely associated with its right of note issue, and in due course also with its function as the lender of last resort.

In the case of the Bank of England and several other central banks, the privilege of note issue was originally granted or extended in return for loans to the Government. The original capital of the Bank of England was £1,200,000, and the whole of this amount was advanced to the Government. In 1697 and in 1709, when the Government was again in need of funds, the Bank was authorized to increase its capital and its note issue in return for further loans to the Government. By 1721 the permanent debt of the Government to the Bank had risen in this manner to £9,375,000, and to £14,686,000 in 1800. This amount was reduced in 1833 to £11,015,000, at which figure the permanent debt of the Government to the Bank has remained ever since. This debt to the Bank has throughout its career been closely associated with its enjoyment of certain privileges conferred by legislation.

With regard to temporary advances, the Bank began in 1718 to make advances to the Government 'in anticipation of the land and malt taxes, and upon exchequer bills and other securities'.[1] During the eighteenth century and until the forties of the nineteenth century, the Government financed most of its short-term requirements by means of Exchequer bills. The Bank of England itself usually held some Exchequer bills in its portfolio which it either purchased as an investment or rediscounted for third parties, and granted temporary advances to the Government to make up the deficiency between the issues of Exchequer bills and the needs of the Government. For various reasons, however, the Exchequer bill declined in popularity after 1840, and the Bank was called upon to make larger advances. These advances came to be known as ways and means advances. Owing to the increasing needs of the Government, the Treasury bill was introduced in 1877 and made an attractive investment for the surplus funds of banks and the public by giving it a fixed currency (usually three months) and issuing it by tender under discount.[2] As a result of the extensive use of Treasury bills, the Bank was no longer required to make ways and means advances to any great extent.

Prior to 1914 the Bank of France had on several occasions to make substantial advances to the Government, for example, at the time of the Revolution in 1848 and the Franco-Prussian War in 1870, and in connection with the payment of the indemnity by France to Germany in 1871. These advances were intended to be of a temporary nature, and the greater part of these loans was repaid over a period of years, but beginning in 1857 each renewal of its charter and of its privilege of note issue was accompanied by an agreement on the part of the Bank of France to grant the Government a permanent loan. In 1897, when the permanent loan had increased to 180,000,000 francs, the Bank agreed to make it a non-interest bearing debt. According to Conant,[3] however, these renunciations of interest were offset by the fact that the Government carried in its current account at the Bank a sum which was usually equal to the amount of these loans. In 1911 the permanent debt of the Government to the Bank was increased by a further 20,000,000 francs to a total of 200,000,000 francs.

The Netherlands Bank was obliged by law in 1888 to grant accommodation to the Government in the form of advances on current account, subject to such advances not exceeding Fl. 5,000,000 at any time and to interest being paid at the rate for ordinary advances. In 1903 the maximum for the Bank's advances to the Government was raised to Fl. 15,000,000, and it was enacted that no interest should be charged thereon by the Bank.[4]

The Reichsbank of Germany was authorized to discount Treasury bills or Treasury certificates directly for the Treasury or for third parties, but prior to 1914 it was seldom called upon to hold much Treasury paper in its portfolio.

In general, therefore, it could be said that up to the time of World War I (1914–18) the financial relations between the State and the central bank were governed by a tradition that, in the interest of sound finance, the central bank should only be required, apart from a permanent or special loan in return for the monopoly of note issue, to grant advances to the Government which would be repaid within a relatively short period out of the proceeds of taxes or loans raised from the public.

The fundamental principle underlying this tradition was the recognition of the fact that, other things being equal, the granting of advances by the central bank to the Government brings about not only a direct increase in the quantity of money in circulation, but also an increase in the cash resources of the commercial banks* and, therefore, in their capacity to expand credit through increased advances, discounts and investments. The granting of advances to the Government by the central bank is thus a potential source of inflation.

When, however, in anticipation of receipts from taxation or

* Where, however, the Government borrows from the central bank for the purpose of buying foreign exchange to meet commitments abroad, the effect will be a reduction in the gold and exchange reserves of the central bank, i.e. a change in the composition of its assets and not in the total of its assets or in the quantity of money in circulation or in the cash resources of the commercial banks. This will also be the case when the receiving banks are indebted to the central bank and take the opportunity to reduce or discharge such debts.

from public loans, the Government needs funds which cannot conveniently or economically be obtained from the money market, either because of temporary stringency or because the issues and maturities of Treasury bills or other short-term securities could not be properly adjusted to the requirements of the Government, the central bank can perform a useful function by granting temporary advances to the Government. In the first place, if such an advance is liquidated within a short period, it does not serve as a source of inflation *per se*. Secondly, there are occasions during the year when, owing to a desire for liquidity by those liable for heavy dividend or tax payments, a temporary stringency arises, and when central bank accommodation to the Government not only provides the latter with its needs for the time being but also helps to counteract the stringency by placing more funds at the disposal of the market. In other words, the quantity of money is increased at a time when the velocity of circulation has declined.

The tradition regarding the necessity of limiting advances to the Government in the interest of sound currency applied, of course, also to other direct or indirect forms of central bank accommodation to the Government, such as discounting Treasury bills for the Government, subscribing to Government loans, buying Government securities in the open market or making advances on relatively favourable terms to banks and the public against Government securities. Thus, during the period under review the central banks usually held in their portfolios relatively small amounts of Government bonds and Treasury bills, which they obtained in the course of their rediscount and open-market operations as a matter of credit policy, or which they acquired as investments to defray part of their expenses or as cover for the fiduciary portion of their note issues where, as in England, such was the practice.

It was in this atmosphere that the Federal Reserve Act of the United States was passed in 1913, and accordingly the spirit as well as the letter of the law aimed at limiting the powers of the Federal Reserve Banks to grant accommodation to the Government, and thus also the capacity of the Government to demand accommodation from them. With regard to temporary accommodation, the Federal Reserve Act did not grant the Federal

Reserve Banks the power to make advances on current account to the Government or to discount Treasury certificates or bills for the Government, but it was arranged that Treasury overdrafts for a few days could be liquidated by means of a one-day certificate of indebtedness, issued by the Treasury to a Federal Reserve Bank to cover the amount of the overdraft on any particular day and replaced by another on the following day and so on until the proceeds of taxes, bonds or notes balanced the Government's accounts.

The Federal Reserve Banks were also not given the power to rediscount Treasury certificates or bills for third parties, but they were authorized to rediscount for member banks their customers' paper issued or drawn for the purpose of carrying or trading in bonds and notes of the United States Government and endorsed by the member banks themselves, subject to a maximum maturity of ninety days for such paper. Furthermore, they were empowered to buy and sell Government bonds and notes, but only in the open market; and this power was intended to give the Federal Reserve Banks some control over money-market conditions by enabling them to conduct open-market operations like the Bank of England and the Reichsbank did at the time. In other words, it was not contemplated that the power to buy Government securities in the market should be used for the purpose of granting indirect accommodation to the Government.

Central Bank Accommodation to the State since 1914

The huge cost of the war of 1914–18 and the enormous loan requirements of the State placed a heavy burden on the credit structure of every country which was involved in that war. Under the stress of this burden, central banking traditions had to be set aside and the central banks of all the belligerent countries had to assist in the process of adaptation to war economy. They were obliged to contribute, directly and indirectly, towards the financing of the war and of the extraordinary post-war expenditures. In other words, their actions were governed mainly by the requirements of war finance and post-war readjustment.

Towards the end of 1919 the central banks of Great Britain and the United States were released from the domination of State finance, and a policy of deflation was adopted which was continued until April, 1921. In such countries, however, as France, Germany, Italy and Belgium, the creation of central bank credit under pressure from the Government was continued for several years after the war; and as a result of this inflationary method of finance their currencies suffered varying degrees of depreciation, from one-fifth of the pre-war gold parity in France to 1/1,000,000,000,000th in Germany.

During the great depression of 1930–3 many central banks, old and new, were again called upon to make special advances to their Governments or to support Government credit in one way or another; and some of them continued to do so in the course of carrying out an official cheap-money and expansionist policy. This creation of central bank credit was rendered possible by the general suspension of the gold standard.

With the outbreak of another war in Europe in September, 1939, and its subsequent world-wide extension, central banks were once more required to come to the aid of their respective Governments in war finance and the maintenance of cheap money.

Great Britain

In Great Britain substantial use was made of ways and means advances by the Bank of England to the Government during the period 1914–19, while the Bank also increased its holdings of Government and other securities. This creation of central bank credit caused an increase in the cash of the commercial banks, which in turn enabled them to buy more Government securities and increase their advances. Moreover, the issue of currency notes* by the Treasury had the same expansionist effect as central bank credit. In general, however, less use was made in Great Britain of central bank credit (including the Treasury notes) and greater use of taxation and of the capital resources of

* The amount of Treasury currency notes at the time of their amalgamation with the Bank of England note issue in 1928 was £285,000,000.

the community than in the other belligerent countries of Europe.

With regard to the financial crisis of 1931 and its aftermath, the Bank of England was not called upon to do much in the way of advances to the Government, but it increased its holdings of Government securities on various occasions between 1932 and 1939 as a means of supporting Government credit and as a matter of monetary policy.*

During World War II the Bank's contribution to war finance and to the maintenance of cheap money was reflected in the increase in its total holdings of Government debt from £700 million on 6th September, 1939, to £1,710 million in December, 1945. After the war the Bank's holdings of Government debt continued to show a net increase at varying rates, depending upon the prevailing economic conditions and monetary policies, and amounted to £2,270 million at the end of 1956 and £4,100 million at the end of 1970.

United States

In 1917–19 the Federal Reserve Banks increased their holdings of Government securities and made large advances to member banks against their promissory notes covered by Government securities, and indirectly to non-member banks as well. The expansion of central bank credit was even facilitated by making the advances against Government securities at interest rates equal to or lower than those carried by the securities themselves, and also at preferential rates as compared with commercial paper. No great use was, however, made of certificates of indebtedness as a means of direct accommodation to the Government.

As in the case of the Bank of England, the Federal Reserve Banks increased their open-market purchases of Government securities during the years 1931–3, but on a much larger scale. For example, they increased their holdings of Government securities from about $300 million in 1929 to $2,430 million by the end of 1933. These operations formed part of a monetary

* See the section on 'Open-Market Operations in Great Britain' in Chapter 10.

policy designed to promote reflation and counteract deflation and depression.*

When the United States entered the war in December, 1941, the Federal Reserve Banks' holdings of Government securities stood at $2,184 million. As in 1917–19, the Federal Reserve System was called upon to assist in financing the Government's war effort by increasing its holdings of Government securities either through open-market operations† or through advances to member banks against Government securities. In October, 1942, all the Federal Reserve Banks reduced the rate for advances to member banks secured by Government obligations maturing or callable in one year or less from 1 to ½ per cent; and the Federal Reserve System also undertook to buy Treasury bills from member banks at ⅜ per cent, with the latter retaining an option to repurchase the bills at any time before maturity. In November, 1942, the Federal Reserve Bulletin reported that 'in recent months the Federal Reserve System has made large purchases of Government securities principally for the purpose of providing to the banks an adequate amount of reserves to form the basis for such purchases of United States Government securities as are offered to the banks'.

The System's holdings of Government securities bought in the open market or acquired directly from member banks increased from $2,184 million on 3rd December, 1941, to $24,300 million in December, 1945. After the war the System's holdings of Government debt showed a net decrease to $20,300 million at the end of 1950, but thereafter the trend was strongly upward to $24,900 million at the end of 1956 and $40,800 million and $62,100 million at the end of 1965 and 1970 respectively.

* See the section on 'Open-Market Operations in the United States' in Chapter 10.

† In March, 1942, the Federal Reserve System was also authorized to buy or sell Government securities (and certain Government-guaranteed securities having a maturity not exceeding six months) directly from or to the United States Government, provided that the aggregate amount of such securities acquired directly from the Government which were held at any one time by the twelve Federal Reserve Banks did not exceed $5,000 million.

France

In France it was the general practice for the Government in an emergency to resort to direct borrowing from the central bank, rather than to the indirect method of requiring the central bank to increase its holdings of Government securities by purchase or subscription. During the war of 1914–18 the Bank of France was obliged to make enormous advances to the Government, since for various reasons increased taxation was not adopted as an important means of war finance. This inflationary method was continued by France after 1918, when a series of budget deficits caused the Government to resort to further borrowing from the Bank until the advances reached the huge total of 38,000 million francs in July, 1926.

These advances were finally repaid in 1928 partly out of a new long-term loan floated by the Government, and partly out of the profit resulting from the revaluation of the Bank's gold and exchange holdings when the franc was finally stabilized at one-fifth of its former gold parity. Under a convention concluded in the same year, however, the Bank agreed to grant the Government a loan of 3,000 million francs without interest, in addition to the old permanent loan of 200 million francs referred to previously.

During the period 1931–5, a further series of budget deficits caused heavy borrowing by the Government in the form of Treasury notes with currencies ranging from three to twenty-four months, owing to the difficulty of floating long-term loans on favourable terms. By the beginning of 1935, the banks and other institutions had so many Treasury notes in their portfolios that they were unwilling to buy more, since under prevailing practice the Bank of France rediscounted these notes only when they had a maturity of less than three months. In this emergency the Treasury approached the Bank with a view to its rediscounting, or accepting as collateral for advances, Treasury notes and National Defence notes with maturities exceeding three months. The Bank at first declined to do so on the grounds, firstly, that Government borrowing from the Bank over and above the permanent loan of 3,200 million francs was forbidden under the convention of 1928, and secondly, that the rediscounting of

Treasury paper under such conditions would be tantamount to an indirect loan to the Treasury and would be strongly conducive to inflation. The Bank ultimately submitted, but on the condition that advances on the security of such Treasury obligations be published as a separate item in the weekly report of the Bank, 'so that the public might be informed if the amount rose too rapidly and became a threat of inflation'.[5]

The accentuation of the financial emergency in France by the continued flight of capital caused the Government to exert further pressure on the Bank, which then discounted Treasury bills on a considerable scale and grouped them together with commercial bills for more than a year. Under a convention of June, 1936, these indirect borrowings from the Bank, amounting at the time to 13·8 billion francs, were consolidated and regularized as provisional non-interest bearing advances to the State, and provision was made for additional borrowing facilities of 10 billion francs. During 1937–8 other conventions were concluded between the Bank and the State, providing for further facilities up to 30 billion francs.

These provisional advances had reached a total of over 50 billion francs in November, 1938, when a further convention was concluded between the Bank and the State, under which the profit resulting from the revaluation of the Bank's gold holdings at 170 francs to the £ was allocated towards part repayment of the provisional advances and the permanent State debt to the Bank was raised from 3·2 to 10 billion francs. The provisional advances which were reduced by these means to 20·6 billion francs on 17th November, 1938, remained at that level till the outbreak of war in September, 1939, and were finally repaid in March, 1940, out of the profit on the further revaluation of the Bank's gold holdings. In the meantime, however, new advances had to be granted to the Government, amounting to 32·6 billion francs by the end of May, 1940, shortly before the collapse of France.

During the German occupation, the Bank's advances to the Government grew by leaps and bounds and amounted to 442 billion francs by the end of 1944, due primarily to the costs of the army of occupation. After the war the Bank's claims on the Government continued their rapid increase, amounting to 802 billion francs at the end of 1952 and 1,224 billion at the end of September, 1959. In the following month a new agreement was concluded by the Government with the Bank, providing for the consolidation of the interest-free loans which had in the meantime been increased to 50 billion francs, and the existing 'provisional' advances, under the heading of 'Loans to the State', amounting to a total of 650 billion francs, and for the consolidation of the remaining advances under the heading of 'Advances to the State', with an initial maximum limit of 500 billion francs, i.e. 1,150 billion francs altogether. At the end of 1963, i.e. after the conversion of old francs into new francs at the rate of 100 to 1, the Bank's total credit to the Government amounted to 11·48 billion francs, and to 11·68 billion at the end of 1970.

Margaret Myers[6] said of the Bank of France, as early as 1936, that 'the history of the relationship between Bank and Government resolves itself into a series of struggles in which the Bank has striven to maintain its independence and the Government has tried to bend the Bank to its own interests'. The subsequent experience of the Bank with permanent, provisional and temporary credits to the Government, which proved to have been far worse than up to 1936, and the series of depreciations which the franc had to undergo until by the end of 1969 it represented only about 1 per cent* of its pre-1914 parity with the US dollar, have shown clearly the dangers and disadvantages to a country emanating from undue Government pressure on the central bank in times of financial strain. It must be added, however, that the agreement of 1959 would appear to have succeeded in restraining the creation of additional central bank credit for the Government.

Germany

In Germany the central bank was also called upon to take a leading part in the financing of the war of 1914–18 and of the Government's post-war requirements. The procedure adopted

* The parity of the new franc in 1972, namely 5·116 francs per US dollar, was almost the same as the pre-1914 parity of the old franc, but the new franc is the equivalent of 100 old francs. Moreover, it must be borne in mind that the dollar itself was devalued in terms of gold by almost 41 per cent in 1934, and about 8 per cent at the end of 1971.

was that of discounting by the Reichsbank of three-months' Treasury bills or Treasury certificates, in anticipation of public loans to be floated every six months. During the first two years of the war the proceeds of such loans were sufficient to repay the Treasury bills discounted by the Reichsbank, but thereafter there was a progressive increase in the excess of Treasury bills outstanding over loans issued. At the end of 1918 the floating debt of the German Government amounted to 55·2 billion marks, a large part of which consisted of bills discounted directly by the Reichsbank. Under the difficult conditions with which the Government and the Reichsbank were faced during the post-war period, the process of inflation through the discounting of Treasury bills and other methods of credit creation by the Reichsbank was accelerated until it reached astronomical proportions towards the end of 1923.* The resultant depreciation and collapse of the mark was followed by the establishment of the Rentenbank and the stabilization of the mark on the basis of 1 rentenmark (or goldmark) for 1,000,000,000,000 paper marks. The Rentenbank was ordered to grant the Government a credit of 1,200 million rentenmarks, of which 300 million were to be used for the repayment of the Treasury bills held by the Reichsbank, and no further Treasury bills were to be discounted with the Reichsbank.

The Reichsbank was reconstituted in 1924 with the aid of the Dawes loan and made independent of the Government. Under the new law its powers of granting accommodation to the Government were narrowly defined. It was authorized to make advances to the Government to a maximum of 100 million reichsmarks, but at the end of each year (altered in 1930 to 15th July) the Government was to be free of direct debt to the Reichsbank. To the Post Office and the Railways the Reichsbank could also grant short-term credits up to a maximum of 200 million reichsmarks. Finally, the Reichsbank was empowered to discount Treasury bills for third parties up to a maximum of 400 million reichsmarks.

* Treasury bills outstanding amounted to 191,580,465,422 billion marks in the middle of November, 1923, and Reichsbank notes in circulation to 496,507,425,000 billion marks in December, 1923. (Parchmann, *Die Reichsbank*, pp. 27–39.)

With the financial stringency in Germany resulting from the large withdrawal of foreign balances in 1931 and the difficulty of obtaining and renewing foreign credits, and with an intensive Government programme of relief and reconstruction after 1933, the Reichsbank was again called upon to place its credit at the disposal of the German economy, but rather in the form of rediscounts to the commercial banks and other financial institutions than direct accommodation to the Government. This was reflected in the increase in the discounts and advances of the Reichsbank from 2,537 million reichsmarks at the end of 1930 to 8,200 million reichsmarks at the end of June, 1939. Under the law of 1939, however, the Reichsbank was empowered to grant credits to the Government up to a maximum amount determined by the Führer, and to hold Treasury bills with a maturity of not more than three months, to a total specified by the Führer.

These powers were freely used after June, 1939, first in connection with preparation and mobilization and then with actual war,* as was reflected in two items of the Reichsbank statement: (1) 'bills and cheques', which included Treasury bills and which increased from 8 billion reichsmarks in June, 1939, to 15 billion in December, 1940, and 63 billion in December, 1944; and (2) 'notes in circulation', which increased from 8 billion reichsmarks in December, 1938, to 14 billion in December, 1940, and 50 billion in December, 1944.

In 1948, under the currency reform, the existing Government debts were cancelled completely, while all holdings of currency and bank deposits above 60 Reichsmarks per person were converted into the new Deutsche marks at the effective rate of 100 to 6·5. But the banks, whose assets consisted mainly of Government debt in one form or another, had to be given claims on the Government sufficient to equate their assets and liabilities in their balance sheets after the conversion.† These claims, which were called 'Equalization Claims', represented a new form of

* 'The Reichsbank recognized the manifest duty at the outbreak of the war of placing itself at the disposal of the Reich for the financing of the Reich's projects, not only indirectly through utilizing the latent possibilities of the German money market, but also directly through contributing its own credit resources.' *Annual Report of Reichsbank for 1939*.

† This procedure was also applicable to the insurance companies.

Government debt, albeit on a much smaller scale. The central bank at the time, the Bank Deutscher Länder (reconstituted as the Deutsche Bundesbank in 1957), thus received Equalization Claims of about 8 billion Deutsche marks, but after 1955 a substantial proportion of these claims was converted into Treasury bills and Treasury bonds for the purpose of its open-market operations as an instrument of monetary policy. Moreover, the Bundesbank was authorized to grant short-term credits to the Federal Government and State Governments as well as certain Government organizations for which it acts as banker, but in all cases prescribed limits were laid down by law.* The Bank was also empowered to grant credits to the Federal Government for the fulfilment of its commitments as a member of the International Monetary Fund, the International Bank, and the European Fund. At the end of 1970 the Bank's total claims on the Government sector amounted to 14·6 billion marks, compared with 7·8 billion at the end of 1960.

Relations between State and New Central Banks

As a result of the unfortunate experiences which central banks had with the financing of Governments during the 1914–18 war and post-war period, the large number of central banks which were newly established or reorganized after that war had their powers of making advances to the State or buying Government securities severely restricted.

The central banks of Chile and Colombia, for example, were prohibited from buying, or making advances against, Government and Municipal obligations to a total amount in excess of 30 per cent of their paid-up capital and surplus, and also from granting floating credits or allowing overdrafts to their Govern-

* The following explanation of these restrictions by Schmidt is deserving of mention: 'As the credit-granting of the central bank to the public authorities could form a dangerous source of inflation, the Bundesbank Law contains particularly stringent and restrictive provisions regarding this part of its business.' See *Eight European Central Banks* published under the auspices of the Bank for International Settlements by George Allen and Unwin, Ltd. in 1963, p. 80.

ments. The South African Reserve Bank was allowed only to buy, or make advances against, Government securities and Treasury bills of not more than six months' currency, and to invest sums not exceeding capital and reserve in Government securities of not more than two years' currency. The Reserve Bank of Peru was authorized to acquire Government securities only if offered by banks as collateral for their promissory notes to be discounted by the Bank, subject to a maximum currency of ninety days for the promissory notes and subject also to a maximum advance of 90 per cent of the market value of Government securities; and it was prohibited from granting loans on current account to the Government.

The National Bank of Czechoslovakia was not allowed to grant directly or indirectly any credit to the State, or to acquire State bonds for its own account, except that one-half of the reserve fund was to be invested in State bonds of the Republic, but it was authorized to make advances against Government securities for a period not exceeding three months. The National Banks of Austria and Hungary were prohibited from entering into business relations with the State which involved the granting of loans or credits to the State, but they were allowed to make advances against Government securities for not more than three months and to discount three months' bills drawn by State commercial undertakings provided they were managed as independent enterprises with separate accounts. The powers of the reorganized Reichsbank were, as stated previously, also narrowly defined.

Under the stress, however, of the world-wide depression of 1930–3, many of these central banks became the victims of Government pressure. Not only were their powers of granting accommodation to the State increased or the restrictions thereon suspended, but they were virtually obliged to provide the financial facilities demanded by their Governments.

With regard to the new central banks which were established after 1933, those of Argentina and El Salvador, for example, were subject at first to severe restrictions in their relations with the State. The Central Bank of Argentina could make advances to the Government subject to a maximum of 10 per cent of the estimated revenue for the fiscal year, and that of El Salvador up to 10 per cent of the estimated customs revenue. With regard to Government securities, the Central Bank of Argentina could buy Government securities only within strict limits, while that of El Salvador was prohibited from holding Government securities as investments. Subsequently, however, these restrictions were substantially lessened or suspended.

The central banks of India, New Zealand and Canada, on the other hand, had fewer restrictions imposed on them from the outset; but these restrictions were also subsequently relaxed. For example, under the amendments of its Act in 1936 and 1937 the Reserve Bank of New Zealand was authorized to grant advances to the Government up to the full amount of the estimated revenue for the fiscal year, and to buy or advance against Government and Government-guaranteed bonds of any amount and any maturity, as well as to buy or rediscount Treasury bills maturing within three months. Moreover, it was empowered to grant accommodation to the Government, by way of overdraft, for the purpose of financing the purchase and marketing of any New Zealand produce under the Primary Products Marketing Act; and it was also given the power to underwrite Government loans.

The process of minimizing or relaxing restrictions on the granting of central bank credit to the Government sector also manifested itself in many of the countries which created central banks during and after World War II. As examples of new central banks subject to substantial restrictions, however, mention can be made of the Central Bank of Kenya and the Bank of Zambia, which were established in 1966 and 1964 respectively. With regard to the former, it was provided that the aggregate of the Bank's direct advances to the Government and the value of Government and Government guaranteed securities owned by the Bank or held as collateral for loans to banks, was not at any time to exceed 240 million shillings. As far as the Bank of Zambia is concerned, the outstanding amount of the Bank's loans and advances to the Government was not at any time to exceed 20 per cent of the estimated recurrent revenue for the fiscal year, while the total amount of Government securities held by the Bank as collateral for advances or otherwise was not at any time to exceed 25 per cent of its demand liabilities.

Present Position of Government Debt in Central Bank Assets

The phenomenal creation of central bank credit through advances to the Government or holdings of Government securities (whether as a matter of general monetary and financial policy or as a means of financing war or defence or other special expenditures) brought about a considerable change in the composition, as well as a manifold increase in the total, of the assets of central banks in many countries.

The following table gives the total amount of claims on the Government sector held by various central banks at the end of 1970, as compared with their foreign assets (including gold) and also those of other monetary authorities in certain countries where the Treasury and/or an Exchange Fund holds the principal or a substantial amount of foreign assets.

The table shows that the central bank's claims on Government far exceed the foreign assets of the monetary authorities in the United States, United Kingdom, Sweden, Japan, India, Indonesia, Argentina, Chile, Mexico, Egypt and Zaïre, whereas the opposite was the case in West Germany, France, Netherlands, Switzerland, Canada, Australia, South Africa, Zambia, Kenya and Venezuela.

In connection with this table, however, certain other factors must also be taken into account. In the first place, in some countries the central bank's claims on Government include Government securities received in exchange for the foreign assets which are held in an Exchange Account or Fund under the control of the Treasury. In the United Kingdom and Canada, for example, virtually all the gold and foreign exchange reserves have been concentrated in such an official entity. Secondly, the central banks of some countries, particularly the United States and the United Kingdom, conduct open-market operations in Government securities on a large scale and must, therefore, always have an adequate supply of such securities for trading purposes, but do not normally have substantial claims, if any, on the banking and private sectors, whereas in France, for example, the central bank's claims on the latter sectors usually far exceed its claims on the Government.

Central Bank Claims on Government and Foreign Assets of Monetary Authorities at End of 1970*
(in millions of national currency)

Country		Claims on Government	Foreign Assets
United States	$	62,100	14,500
United Kingdom	£	4,000	1,366
Sweden	Kr.	9,860	3,940
Japan	Yen	2,992,000	1,583,000
India	Ru.	43,000	6,410
Indonesia	Ru.	111,650	83,180
Argentina	Pe.	6,450	2,550
Mexico	Pe.	13,680 (Sep.)	9,300
Chile	Es.	9,575	4,832
United Arab Republic	£	517	101
Zaïre	Za.	169	93
West Germany	Dm.	14,600	51,700
France	Fr.	11,680	28,540
Netherlands	Gu.	210	11,690
Switzerland	Fr.	1,670	22,140
Canada	$	4,240	4,820
Australia	$	1,095	1,542
South Africa	Ra.	379	760
Kenya	Sh.	164	1,585
Zambia	Kw.	9	367
Venezuela	Bo.	1,031	4,004

* *Source: International Financial Statistics* (IMF), except for the central banks' claims on Government in the United Kingdom, United States and Canada, which it was considered necessary to extract from the publications of the banks concerned.

All that the table purports to show is the extent to which Government debt has, for one reason or another, come to occupy a major position in the assets of central banks in various parts of the world, as compared with other central banks whose foreign assets still constitute a significant proportion of their total assets or at least exceed their holdings of Government debt.

Conclusion

Monetary history contains many examples of inflation and currency depreciation resulting mainly from excessive credit creation on behalf of the State. While the gold standard had automatically imposed a large measure of discipline on the monetary authorities and the economy as a whole, 'managed money' permitted the State to resort to the central bank as a ready and convenient means of obtaining credit, which would enable it to take the line of least resistance. In fact, experience has shown that heavy Government borrowing, either directly from the central bank or indirectly through the latter's open-market operations and rediscounts of Treasury bills or loans against Government securities which also increased the credit-creating capacity of the commercial banks, has been a principal source of inflation* in many countries. In this respect, therefore, it is not just a coincidence that the degree of expansion of central bank credit for Government purposes (the so-called monetization of Government debt) has had some relationship with the extent of currency depreciation, not only in terms of gold but more particularly in terms of goods and services.

References

1 Gilbart, J. W., in *History, Principles and Practice of Banking*, Vol. I, Ed. Sykes. Longmans, 1922. p. 36.
2 King, W. T. C. *History of the London Discount Market*. Routledge, 1936. pp. 9, 13 and 275–7.
3 Conant, C. A. *History of Modern Banks of Issue*, 5 ed. Putnam, 1927. p. 67.
4 *Foreign Banking Systems*, Ed. Willis & Beckhart. Henry Holt, 1929. p. 738.
5 Myers, M. *Paris as a Financial Centre*. King, 1936. pp. 16–17.
6 *Ibid.* p. 45.

* It is admitted that a large and prolonged increase in foreign assets, particularly through the inflow of capital, has also at times been an important source of inflation in various countries. But whereas an increase in foreign assets serves directly to increase a country's capacity to pay for foreign goods and services, as well as its internal money supply, an increase of central bank credit for the Government tends to increase only the latter.

CHAPTER FOUR

The Custodian of the Cash Reserves of the Commercial Banks

Evolution of Reserve Function

The central bank became the custodian of the commercial banks' cash reserves by a process of evolution which was closely associated with its functions as the bank of issue and the Government's banker.

In England, for example, the private banks of the eighteenth century had discovered that there was an advantage in keeping an account with the Bank of England, for the reasons that it was the bank whose notes commanded the greatest confidence and the widest circulation in the country and that it was developing more and more as the Government's banker and agent. The tendency to keep larger balances with the Bank of England grew as time went on, until it became the traditional practice of the private banks to entrust their surplus cash to the Bank. When the widespread establishment of joint-stock banks in England began in 1826, the custom of maintaining balances with the Bank was also adopted by these banks. The Scottish and Irish banks similarly found it convenient and advantageous to keep balances with the Bank of England. The practice was further developed when the Bank opened branches in various parts of England and when, in 1854, it assumed the function of a settlement bank, i.e. settlement of the clearance differences between banks.

This process of evolution also took place in other countries according as one bank became the sole or principal bank of issue and the Government's banker. Thus, like the Bank of England and for the same reasons the special bank of issue in every other country came to be accepted as the custodian of the commercial banks' cash reserves (i.e. apart from their normal till-money requirements); and, as will be explained in the following chapter, it was the custody of the banks' cash reserves plus the sole or principal right of note issue which automatically made the special bank of issue also the custodian of its country's metallic reserves. In fact, the custody of reserves was part and parcel of the development of such banks into central banks.

With the establishment of the Federal Reserve Banks in the United States in 1914, a new principle regarding bank reserves was introduced, namely, a statutory provision that member banks had to maintain with their respective Reserve Banks minimum credit balances depending upon the amount of their demand and time deposits; and this feature was incorporated, in one form or another, in the statutes of many of the central banks which were subsequently established all over the world, as well as some of the older central banks. On the whole, it can be said that, for reasons of convenience and mutual advantage if not because of legal provisions, commercial banks everywhere have come to entrust their cash reserves to the central bank.

Significance of Centralized Cash Reserves

The centralization of cash reserves in the central bank is a source of great strength to the banking system of any country. Centralized cash reserves can at least serve as the basis of a larger and more elastic credit structure than if the same amount were scattered among the individual banks. It is obvious that, when bank reserves are pooled in one institution which is, moreover, charged with the responsibility of safeguarding the national economic interest, such reserves can be employed to the fullest extent possible and in the most effective manner during periods of seasonal strain and in financial crises or general emergencies.

Referring to 'the shift of required reserves from the vaults of member banks to the vaults of the Federal Reserve Banks', Burgess[1] pointed out that it 'was not simply a change in physical location', but that it 'made a change in the character and effectiveness of the reserves and enabled them to serve more adequately their original purposes'. He also emphasized that there are two kinds of emergencies to be met. In the one case, when only a few banks need additional funds, the reserves 'can be shifted to the point where the need is greatest at any time', while in the other, when the need for funds is general, the centralized reserves can be used to increase the total amount of funds available.

The centralization of cash reserves is conducive to economy in their use and to increased elasticity and liquidity of the banking system and of the credit structure as a whole, but only in an indirect manner. It is, in fact, the central bank's function of rediscount and lender of last resort which directly serves to promote such economy, elasticity and liquidity. In the absence of a central bank and centralized reserves, each of the commercial banks would, for example, have to carry more cash in order to cope with seasonal strains and possible emergencies than if there were a central bank from which the banks could, directly or indirectly and individually or collectively, obtain the necessary accommodation at such times. In short, with a central bank to fall back upon in case of need the commercial banks can with safety conduct either a larger volume of business with the same cash reserve or the same amount of business with a smaller reserve than if they have to depend only on their own individual resources and on such money-market facilities as are available. The important point about centralized cash reserves is, however, that they serve to increase the capacity of the central bank to rediscount or otherwise create credit for the purpose of meeting the cash requirements of the commercial banks or of the money market generally.

The statutory provision for the holding by commercial banks of minimum credit balances with the central bank, which was first introduced in the United States, was designed to secure at least a minimum of the advantages of centralized cash reserves and to strengthen the general financial position of the central bank and its capacity to control credit in the common interest. It was, in other words, the urgency of a strong central banking structure and the absence of banking tradition in regard to the holding of cash reserves in a central bank which were mainly responsible for the imposition of such statutory requirements in many countries.

Statutory Minimum Cash Reserves

Under the original Federal Reserve Act of the United States, the member banks* were required to hold minimum cash reserves amounting to 5 per cent of their time deposits and 12, 15 or 18 per cent of demand deposits† depending upon whether they were country banks, reserve city banks or central reserve city banks respectively. Of these reserves, they had to hold certain minimum proportions in the Federal Reserve Bank of their particular district and in their own vaults, and the balance either in the former or the latter or both. In 1917, however, an important alteration was made. Instead of distinguishing between the minimum reserves to be kept with the Reserve Bank and those in their own vaults, the law laid down merely the minimum reserves which the member banks should keep with their Reserve Bank and which were fixed at 3 per cent of their time deposits and 7, 10 or 13 per cent of their demand deposits depending upon whether they were country, reserve city or central reserve city banks.‡ As to the remainder of their cash reserves, member

* All the national banks (operating under the National Bank Act) had to become member banks, while the State Banks (operating under laws or charters of the individual States) which conformed to certain requirements and conditions could become members on application. Of 13,687 commercial banks in operation at the end of 1970, there were 5,766 member banks. These member banks, however, hold over 80 per cent of the total deposits at commercial banks in the United States.

† The distinction made between time and demand deposits was to the effect that the former were deposits subject to notice of withdrawal within not less than thirty days, and the latter in less than thirty days.

‡ Under the original Act provision was made for three central reserve cities, but these were subsequently reduced to two (New York and Chicago) and finally removed from the classification of member banks in 1962, leaving only reserve city banks and country banks.

banks were left entirely to their own discretion as to what amount they should keep on hand as till money or as reserves in their own vaults or as working balances with correspondent banks or as excess balances with their Federal Reserve Banks.*

When the establishment of the South African Reserve Bank was under consideration in 1920, it was decided to incorporate this feature of the Federal Reserve Act and to require 'every bank transacting business in the Union of South Africa' to maintain with the Reserve Bank minimum reserve balances amounting to 3 per cent of their time liabilities in South Africa and 13 per cent of their demand liabilities (reduced to 10 per cent in 1923).

This provision for minimum credit balances with the central bank was also adopted in the case of the new central banks which were created in South America during the twenties. In Chile, for example, the commercial banks were required to hold with the central bank at least 20 per cent and 8 per cent of their demand and time liabilities respectively; and in Colombia commercial banks had to keep with the central bank at least one-half of the total minimum cash reserves prescribed in respect of their demand and time deposits.

Mexico followed suit in 1932 under the new law of the Bank of Mexico, which required all banks accepting deposits for less than thirty days to keep with the Bank minimum credit balances equivalent to 5 per cent of their deposit liabilities. In New Zealand, on the establishment of the Reserve Bank in 1934, it was laid down that 'all banks carrying on business in New Zealand' were to maintain balances in the Bank amounting to not less than 3 per cent of their time liabilities and 7 per cent of their demand liabilities in New Zealand. In India, minimum balances were also to be kept with the Reserve Bank by the 'scheduled' banks on the basis of 2 per cent of time liabilities and 5 per cent of demand liabilities, but contrary to the practice in the United States, South Africa, Chile and New Zealand, demand liabilities in India were interpreted as liabilities to be met on demand, i.e. within twenty-four hours, instead of within

* In 1960 member banks were allowed to count all their holdings of note currency and coin as reserves for the purpose of the legal minimum reserve requirement.

thirty days. In Argentina, the banks had to maintain total cash reserves equal to not less than 8 per cent of their time deposits and 16 per cent of their demand deposits, and of these minimum reserves two-thirds had to be held with the Central Bank. In Brazil, the other banks had to keep 4 per cent of their time deposits and 8 per cent of their demand deposits with the Bank of Brazil; and in Paraguay, the banks had to maintain 20 per cent of their sight deposits, 15 per cent of their fixed deposits and 10 per cent of their savings-account deposits with the Bank of Paraguay.

With regard to the Bank of Canada which was set up in 1935, it was decided to make no distinction between demand and time liabilities in respect of legal reserve requirements. The 'chartered' banks were required to hold cash reserves equal to not less than 5 per cent of all their deposit liabilities within Canada, but they were allowed to include in the minimum reserves not only their balances with the Bank of Canada, but also Bank of Canada notes held in their tills or vaults. This method of prescribing minimum cash reserves for commercial banks, without providing specifically for minimum credit balances with the central bank, was also followed by several other countries.

New Methods Investigated and Introduced in United States

In the meantime, a Committee of officers of the Federal Reserve System had been appointed at the end of 1929, to inquire into ways and means of establishing bank reserves 'on a more logical or effective basis than now appears to be possible under present laws'. According to their report, the existing system of legal requirements for member bank reserves had 'not operated to relate the expansion of member bank credit to the needs of trade and industry, nor has it adequately reflected changes in the volume and activity of member bank credit'. They held that, although the law 'in requiring lower reserves against time deposits than against demand deposits, and lower reserves against the demand deposits of country banks than against the demand deposits of reserve and central reserve city banks may have been expected to impose higher reserves on more active deposits than on less active deposits', in practice it did not sufficiently take into account the velocity of the turnover of deposits. Moreover, whenever there was a shift from demand to time deposits, the existing system permitted a large expansion in the total volume of bank credit without a corresponding increase in the cash reserves which member banks had to maintain with the Reserve Banks.[2]

To remedy these defects, the Committee considered that an entirely new approach to the reserve problem was necessary. They proposed that 'the formula used in calculating reserve requirements take into account directly, instead of indirectly as in the existing law, the activity as well as the volume of the deposits held by each individual member bank, without regard to the location of the bank or the terms of withdrawal on which the deposits are technically held', and, therefore, that 'each member bank be required to hold a reserve equivalent to (*a*) 5 per cent of its total net deposits, plus (*b*) 50 per cent of the average daily withdrawals actually made from all of its deposit accounts'.[3] Their proposals thus provided for the removal of the distinction between time and demand deposits and between country, reserve city and central reserve city banks, and for the inclusion in the legal reserves of member banks of their vault cash, with certain limitations.

It was considered by the Committee that their proposed formula would increase the Reserve Banks' powers of control over credit conditions, particularly since in a period of rapidly expanding activity and growing speculation the velocity or rate of turnover of deposits would also tend to increase considerably, and this would automatically increase the reserve balances which the member banks would be required to keep with the Reserve Banks under section (*b*) of the formula. Moreover, under this formula a shift from demand to time deposits would not increase the credit-creating capacity of the member banks to nearly the same extent as under the old system.

In 1932 the Federal Reserve Board[4] expressed the opinion 'that the adoption of a system of reserves based on velocity of accounts as well as on their volume, as recommended by the System's Committee on reserves, would be an important step in strengthening the influence that the Federal Reserve System could exert in the direction of sound credit conditions'.

The Committee's proposals were not, however, translated into law.* Instead, while the old formula as amended in 1917 was retained, legislation was formally passed in 1933 and 1935 authorizing the Board of Governors of the Federal Reserve System (formerly Federal Reserve Board) to change the member banks' reserve requirements by regulation 'in order to prevent injurious credit expansion or contraction', the minimum reserve percentages not to be less than those laid down in 1917 nor more than twice such percentages. The power to change the minimum reserves to be kept with the Reserve Banks by the member banks was intended as an additional means of enabling the Reserve Banks to contract or expand the credit-creating capacity of the member banks.

This power to prescribe variable minimum cash reserves to be maintained with the central bank by the commercial banks, and in some cases also certain other credit institutions, was likewise granted to many of the central banks which were created after 1935, either from their inception or subsequent thereto, as well as to many of the new central banks which had been established prior to that date on the basis of fixed minimum reserves. Moreover, in the meantime, even many of the older central banks, which previously relied merely on custom or tradition, have acquired the authority to prescribe minimum cash-reserve requirements for commercial banks, whether by law or formal voluntary agreement, but in general the purpose has been to use it only as an instrument of monetary policy in special circumstances, and without any legal provision for a normal minimum reserve ratio to be maintained as a credit balance with the central banks, as in the case of most of the new central banks. Thus, in Sweden it was introduced in 1937, followed by Italy in 1947, West Germany in 1948, Netherlands in 1954, Switzerland in 1955, Japan in 1957, Great Britain in 1958, Belgium in 1961 and France in 1967. It must, however, be added that in almost all cases a maximum reserve ratio, with or without a minimum ratio, has been laid down.

* The new formula proposed by the committee was tried out by Mexico for a period (1936–41). See Chapter 11.

The use of this additional instrument of monetary policy in various countries will be discussed in detail in Chapter 11.

General Observations

It was shown that the older central banks were gradually and voluntarily entrusted by the commercial banks with the custody of their cash reserves, because of the convenience and other advantages which accrued therefrom to banks individually and to the banking system as a whole; that the custody of bank reserves was part and parcel of the development of central banks as such; and that the statutory provision for the holding by commercial banks of minimum credit balances with the central bank, which was first adopted by the United States and followed by many other countries, was designed to secure at least a minimum of the advantages of centralized cash reserves.

With regard to the introduction of minimum cash-reserve requirements, there was at first a tendency to stress the advantages not only of increased safety and solvency but also of increased liquidity of the commercial banks as a direct result of their having to maintain minimum balances with the central bank. In due course, it came to be generally realized that the increased liquidity of the commercial banks was derived from the rediscount and lending facilities afforded by the central bank, and not from the holding of minimum reserve balances which as such were practically immobilized from the point of view of current operations. There was, however, a close connection between the two in the sense that the centralization of cash reserves increased the scope and extent of the facilities which could be afforded by the central bank. The increase in liquidity was thus an indirect rather than a direct result of centralized cash reserves.

More emphasis was also placed during the thirties on the fact that the obligation imposed on commercial banks to keep minimum cash reserves in the central bank gave the latter a minimum amount of funds with which it could operate, and not only strengthened its financial position but also gave it some means of control over the banking and credit situation.

In the United States, the Committee on Bank Reserves[5] reported in 1931 that 'it is no longer the primary function of legal reserve requirements to assure or preserve the liquidity of the individual member bank', and that 'the two main functions of legal requirements for member bank reserves under our present banking structure are, first, to operate in the direction of sound credit conditions by exerting an influence on changes in the volume of bank credit, and, secondly, to provide the Federal Reserve Banks with sufficient resources to enable them to pursue an effective banking and credit policy'; and in England, where there were no statutory cash-reserve requirements, the Macmillan Committee[6] stated in the same year that 'the main reason for expecting the banks to keep reserves above the minimum needed for daily convenience is no longer primarily the safety and solvency of the banks themselves, as it was in former times, but the necessity for providing the Central Institution with adequate resources wherewith to manage the monetary system and safely furnish the member institutions with precisely those conveniences, for rapidly liquidating earning assets, upon which the latter depend when determining the amount of their cash reserves'.

Moreover, Gregory[7] drew attention to the fact that 'the ease with which the central bank can affect the money market situation at any given moment will vary (in addition to other environmental conditions) . . . with the reserve requirements which are imposed by law or by custom upon the other banks'; and in discussing the disparity between the imposition of legal cash-reserve minima in countries where central banking was relatively new and the absence of such minima in countries where central banking had already reached an advanced stage, the Midland Bank *Monthly Review*[8] commented that 'this disparity is partly to be explained by the desire to place new central banks in possession of sufficient funds to pay their way and perform their controlling functions'.

In conclusion, the greater measure of control which was associated with the centralization of bank reserves, and particularly with the initial statutory provisions for minimum reserves, induced several countries to explore ways and means of improving and facilitating that control. This led to the central banks of many countries being empowered to vary the requirements for minimum credit balances to be maintained with the central bank by the other banks, depending upon the prevailing monetary and economic conditions, and in recent times an extensive use of this power as an instrument of credit control has been made in various countries, as will be shown later.

References

1 Burgess, W. R. *Reserve Banks and the Money Market*, Rev. ed. Harper, 1936. pp. 26–7.
2 *Report of the Committee on Bank Reserves of the Federal Reserve System*. 1931. p. 5.
3 *Ibid.* p. 6.
4 *Annual Report of the Federal Reserve Board for 1932*. p. 26.
5 *Report of the Committee on Bank Reserves of the Federal Reserve System*. 1931. p. 5.
6 *Report of the Macmillan Committee on Finance and Industry*. 1931. p. 158.
7 Gregory, T. E. *Gold, Unemployment and Capitalism*. King, 1933. p. 168.
8 Midland Bank *Monthly Review*. May–June, 1937.

CHAPTER FIVE

The Custodian of the Nation's Reserves of International Currency

Centralization of Metallic Reserves

The central bank's function of holding the nation's metallic reserves was automatically derived from its functions as the bank of issue and the custodian of the commercial banks' cash reserves.

According as one bank obtained a complete or residuary monopoly of the note issue, and according as the use and circulation of note currency increased, the other banks had to hand over sufficient of their metallic reserves* to that bank in order to meet the growing demand for notes which they could not issue themselves. The metallic reserves of the commercial banks were also concentrated more and more in the bank of issue according as the latter came to be increasingly entrusted with the custody of their surplus cash and to develop into a central bank. In short, the central bank acquired its holding of metallic reserves and, in many cases, also of foreign exchange as a counterpart of its issue of notes and its custody of the commercial banks' cash reserves.

As the bank of issue, it had under the gold specie standard, which prevailed over a large part of the world until 1914, to redeem its notes in gold coin on demand, and it had, therefore, in any case to hold sufficient gold for the purpose of redeeming such

* Gold or silver or gold and silver, depending upon the monetary standard and the legal requirements in force at the time.

notes as might be presented for payment from time to time. In due course, however, it was realized that currency and credit were closely related, and that the commercial banks relied upon their deposits with the bank of issue being also convertible into gold if and when required. The metallic reserves of the bank of issue thus came to be recognized as the basis of the entire banking system; and the formal acceptance by it of the responsibility of maintaining the monetary standard laid down by law or otherwise safeguarding the value of the national currency, was another essential link in the process of its evolution as a central bank.

Reserve Requirements

With a view to regulating note issues and safeguarding the convertibility of notes, minimum reserve requirements or other limitations were imposed by law on banks of issue. In Chapter 2 details were given of the different methods evolved by legislators in connection with the regulation of note issues.

As regards legal reserve requirements, there were two principal methods. The first was that of a partial fiduciary issue introduced in England in 1844, namely, a fixed amount laid down by law from time to time which need be covered only by Government securities, while all notes issued in excess of this amount must be fully covered by gold. This method was followed by England until the outbreak of war in September, 1939, when all the gold held in the issue department of the Bank of England was transferred to the Exchange Equalization Account and the note issue as such became a total fiduciary issue, subject to a maximum limit prescribed by the Treasury and Parliament from time to time. The system of a partial fiduciary issue was, in one way or another, adopted by such countries as Sweden, Norway and Finland; and it was also followed by Italy prior to 1926, and by Japan prior to 1941. Like England, Japan then switched over to a flexible maximum issue without any statutory requirement of a minimum reserve.

The second method was that of prescribing a minimum percentage gold reserve against the note issue, as well as a minimum reserve against the deposits of the central bank.* The principle of a proportional metallic reserve (gold and/or silver) against note issues had been introduced in the Netherlands, Java and Belgium before the middle of the nineteenth century, but it was not until 1863 that the minimum reserve of 40 per cent was also made applicable to the current deposits of the Netherlands Bank. In Germany, with the establishment of the Reichsbank in 1875, a minimum gold reserve of one-third was laid down only in respect of the note issue, but beyond a certain fixed amount the notes were to be fully covered by gold coin and bullion, although the Reichsbank was permitted to exceed this limit subject to the payment of a tax on any such excess of notes. When the Federal Reserve System of the United States was created in 1913, the principle of a minimum proportional gold reserve was adopted in respect of both the notes and deposits of the Federal Reserve Banks, as in the Netherlands and Belgium, and provision was made for the temporary suspension of the reserve requirements subject to certain conditions, as in Germany, but with important modifications.

Thus, in the United States the latter provision took the form of permitting, in an emergency, a temporary shortfall in the gold reserve† against the note issue rather than a temporary excess of notes above the amount covered in accordance with the reserve requirements. The Federal Reserve Banks were authorized, with the consent of the Federal Reserve Board, to suspend the full reserve requirements for thirty days and to renew the suspension for periods of fifteen days each, subject to the payment of a graduated percentage tax on the amount of the shortfall in the gold reserves and to the raising of their discount and interest rates at least by the percentage of the tax to be so paid. The motive underlying this formal provision for temporary suspension of reserve requirements was to introduce additional elasticity into the monetary system and to increase the central bank's

* By applying the principle of the minimum reserve also to the deposits of the central bank, legal recognition was given to the fact that its deposits represented no less a liability than its notes, the former being convertible into the latter on demand.

† After deducting the minimum reserve to be maintained against the deposits.

capacity to cope with such emergencies as might arise, for example, from the loss of gold due to an unfavourable turn in the balance of payments or from an inadequate domestic supply of money; and the conditions attached thereto were designed, firstly, to deprive the central bank, by a special tax, of any incentive to follow a policy of undue expansion, and, secondly, to compel the central bank, through increases in its discount and interest rates, to aim at credit contraction and economic readjustment where necessary for the purpose of remedying the deficiency in its reserves.

The basic provisions for reserve requirements in respect of the notes and deposits of the Federal Reserve Banks, and for their temporary suspension, were incorporated in one form or another in the statutes of most of the new central banks which were established during the twenties, and were also adopted by France, Italy, Austria, Bulgaria and Greece when they reorganized their currency systems during that period. There were, however, some modifications and deviations from the particular provisions of the Federal Reserve Act. For example, the reserve against current deposits as well as notes of the Bank of France was to consist only of gold, whereas in the case of the Federal Reserve Banks the reserve against deposits could consist not only of gold bullion and coin but also of other 'lawful money' (i.e. silver coin, silver certificates, 'Greenback' notes and national bank notes).* In South Africa silver coin† was also admitted but restricted to one-fifth of the minimum reserve against deposits, and in Peru and Mexico to one-tenth and one-fifth respectively of the minimum reserve against notes and deposits combined. In some countries, moreover, the central bank was allowed to include foreign exchange along with gold in the minimum reserve against notes and deposits, which will be discussed later in this chapter.

Furthermore, there were differences in respect of the reserve percentages. The Federal Reserve Banks had to maintain mini-

* The provision for the inclusion of 'lawful money' in the reserve against deposits was repealed in 1945. Such reserve was henceforth to consist only of gold, i.e. gold certificates as in the case of the reserve against notes.

† The provision for the inclusion of silver coin was eliminated from the new South African Reserve Bank Act of 1944.

mum reserves of 40 per cent against their note issues and 35 per cent against their deposits, while most countries adopted the same percentage for deposits as for notes, e.g. 33⅓ per cent in Belgium and Bulgaria, 35 per cent in France, Roumania and Yugoslavia, 40 per cent in the Netherlands, Italy, Greece and South Africa, 50 per cent in Chile and Peru, and 60 per cent in Colombia.

During the severe depression of 1930–3, however, those countries which suffered a heavy loss of gold and foreign exchange found themselves seriously embarrassed by the penal conditions attached to the temporary suspension of reserve requirements. In particular, the provision for the raising of discount and interest rates on a graduated scale was found to be unduly rigid in its application, since it necessitated the central bank raising its rates to a level fraught with great danger to the national economic interest. Some of these countries tried to avoid the issue by lowering the reserve requirements and/or revaluing the reserves according as their currencies depreciated and/or by admitting the inclusion of certain other assets in the legal reserves, while others formally abolished the penal conditions (e.g. South Africa in 1932 and New Zealand and Bulgaria in 1936) or allowed them to be disregarded. Thus, when the Bank of Canada Act was passed in 1934, it was provided that the Bank could suspend the reserve requirements with the consent of the Government, and without any liability in respect of special taxation or any obligation to raise its rates; and this was also adopted by other new central banks. With regard to the United States, although the penal conditions were retained in the Federal Reserve Act, it was provided under special legislation in 1933 that those conditions were not to apply when the suspension was necessitated by reason of open-market operations or direct purchases of Treasury bills or other Government obligations undertaken by the Federal Reserve Banks, at the request of the Treasury, for the expansion of credit in an economic emergency or in other specified circumstances.

Between 1930 and 1939 the minimum reserve ratios for central banks were reduced in many countries, not only due to the impact of the world depression of 1930–3 but also because it was in line with the continuing trend towards greater elasticity in monetary policy and the recommendation made by the International Economic Conference of 1933 in favour of a 25 per cent reserve ratio. Thus, such countries as Czechoslovakia, Hungary, Bulgaria, Yugoslavia, Denmark, Mexico and Chile reduced their minimum reserve ratios to 25 per cent, while some of the central banks which were established after 1933, for example, those of Canada, Argentina, New Zealand and El Salvador, commenced operations under statutes requiring only a 25 per cent ratio. Certain countries, however, lowered their reserve ratios merely to 30 per cent, e.g. South Africa, Latvia and Ecuador. On the other hand, Germany,* Italy, Greece, Peru and Bolivia, instead of reducing the reserve requirements, suspended such provisions indefinitely during the thirties.

After the outbreak of war in 1939, France, and subsequently Canada, Denmark, Norway, Holland and Belgium also formally suspended their reserve requirements. The suspension of the reserve provisions in England and Japan has already been referred to. These indefinite suspensions were resorted to for the purpose of meeting the actual or anticipated increases in the note circulation under wartime conditions, and/or with a view to transferring the gold reserves of the central bank to a State exchange organization (as in Great Britain and Canada) or otherwise rendering gold and exchange reserves available for meeting adverse balances of payments.

The next important changes in reserve requirements were the reduction, for the first time, in the minimum reserves to be maintained by the Federal Reserve Banks of the United States, namely, from 40 and 35 per cent of their notes and deposits respectively to 25 per cent of both their notes and deposits; and the abolition of the former minimum reserve of 25 per cent against the note issue of the Commonwealth Bank of Australia. In the United States, the lowering of the original reserve requirements in June, 1945, 'was occasioned by the rapid fall in the ratio of reserves to note and deposit liabilities in all Federal

* Under the Reichsbank law of 1939, the question of reserve requirements was avoided by merely providing that 'gold and foreign exchange holdings, which are at the disposal of the Reichsbank, shall be admitted as note cover in addition to the cover specified' under another subsection, namely, fixed-interest securities, Treasury bills, commercial bills and collateral loans.

Reserve Banks during the past three years, which has resulted mainly from the financing of the war' and, to a smaller extent, from the decrease in their total reserves, 'reflecting cash payments to foreign countries for materials needed in the war and for the maintenance of United States troops abroad'.[1] In Australia, on the other hand, the reserve requirement was abolished in 1945 on the ground that there was no longer any need for an internal reserve, and that the whole of the Commonwealth Bank's reserve 'should be available for use as required to meet external commitments'.[2]

In Guatemala, the new law of December, 1945, also refrained from imposing a specific minimum reserve of gold and exchange to be held by the central bank, and stipulated that the Bank of Guatemala was to utilize its international reserves 'for the protection of the stability of the currency against temporary disequilibria in the balance of payments'. However, while no reserve requirement was specifically laid down, certain levels of international reserves were prescribed as criteria for particular purposes, e.g. for determining when emergency measures were to be adopted, or how the Bank's exchange reserves may be invested from the point of view of liquidity, or whether the Bank may acquire Government or other first-class bonds in the domestic market. The main novel feature was that these levels of reserves, expressed in percentages, were related to the annual average of total sales of exchange during the three preceding years, rather than to the Bank's current note and deposit liabilities. This was done on the ground that, for a country like Guatemala, the level or trend of sales of foreign exchange afforded a better guide for monetary and exchange policy than the level or trend of the central bank's domestic liabilities.

Since 1946 the trend towards liberalization has continued in one form or another. In the first place, most of the countries which had suspended reserve requirements before or during the war, did not subsequently re-introduce them. Secondly, certain other countries which had not previously done so, also decided to abolish or suspend their reserve provisions, e.g. Sweden, Czechoslovakia, Argentina, New Zealand and Chile. In New Zealand, for example, it was merely laid down that 'it shall be the duty of the Reserve Bank to maintain reserves which, in the opinion of the Board of Directors, will provide a reasonable margin for contingencies, after taking into account prospective receipts and disbursements of overseas funds, and having regard to the economic position within New Zealand'; while in Czechoslovakia the reserves were to be dependent upon the requirements of the balance of payments position. Likewise, the new Central Bank of Ceylon (1950) was only required to maintain international reserves adequate to meet any foreseeable deficits in the balance of payments; but various criteria were laid down to which the Bank must have regard in judging the adequacy of the reserves, including estimates of the prospective receipts and payments of foreign exchange, the volume and maturity of the central bank's own liabilities in foreign exchange, and the volume and maturity of the foreign exchange assets and liabilities of the Government, banking institutions and other persons in Ceylon.

This pattern of stipulating general objectives, directives or criteria instead of laying down specific reserve requirements in relation to the note issue or the note and deposit liabilities of the central bank, was followed in the case of various other new central banks. In some of these the reference to reserves was of a very general nature. For example, it was mentioned only as one of the three objectives prescribed for the Bank of Korea (1950), namely, 'to administer the nation's international monetary reserves in the interests of achieving and maintaining an orderly pattern of international trade and exchange relationships'; and in the case of the Bundesbank of West Germany (1957) there was merely a general directive to the effect that the Bank 'shall regulate the money circulation and the supply of credit to the economy with the aim of safeguarding the currency and shall ensure the due execution by banks of payments within the country as well as to and from foreign countries'. In Kenya, however, a particular as well as a general directive was laid down, namely, that the Central Bank (1966) 'shall at all times use its best endeavours to maintain a reserve of external assets at an aggregate amount of not less than the value of four months' imports as recorded and averaged for the last three preceding years'.

Furthermore, the United States which had originally given the principle of minimum reserve ratios a tremendous impetus over a large part of the world, and which had maintained it continuously, although the ratio was reduced to 25 per cent in 1945, decided in March, 1965, to 'eliminate' the reserve requirement against the deposit liabilities of the Federal Reserve Banks. This step was taken because the reserve ratio in respect of their combined note and deposit liabilities had already dropped to 27½ per cent and was expected to continue its downward trend, due to the constant increase in these liabilities and the persistent decline in the gold reserve, and because it was considered advisable to 'assure the world of the availability of United States monetary gold for legitimate monetary uses in international commerce'.[3] Then in March, 1968, in view of the increase in currency 'in response to the demands of a growing economy', the reserve requirement against the note issues of the Federal Reserve Banks was also 'eliminated', because 'its repeal would help to make absolutely clear that the United States gold stock is fully available to serve its primary purpose as an international monetary reserve'.[4]

However, some of the new central banks created after the war were required to hold minimum reserves of gold and foreign exchange, e.g. 20 per cent of notes and demand deposits in Indonesia, 25 per cent in Burma, Cuba, Nigeria and Rhodesia, and 50 per cent in the Dominican Republic, Surinam and Zambia.* Moreover, a few countries which had suspended reserve requirements during the war, re-introduced them, e.g. the Netherlands in 1956 and Belgium in 1957, the new ratios being 50 per cent gold and foreign exchange in the former and 33⅓ per cent gold in the latter, against notes and deposits in both cases. There were also some central banks which maintained their reserve ratios unchanged during and after the war, e.g. 40 per cent gold against notes in Switzerland and 25 per cent gold and foreign exchange against notes and deposits in Mexico.

In South Africa, on the other hand, while the principle of a minimum gold-reserve ratio against the note and deposit liabilities of the central bank was retained throughout, the reserve

* In Zambia the reserve ratio was reduced to 25 per cent in respect of any increase in the central bank's notes and demand deposits after 25th June, 1965.

requirements were liberalized in two respects in 1948. In the first place, the ratio which had been reduced from 40 to 30 per cent in 1933, was lowered further to 25 per cent; and secondly, the Reserve Bank was permitted to deduct its holding of foreign exchange from its liabilities to the public before calculating the reserve ratio. The latter measure was regarded as a logical one in the prevailing circumstances, because the Bank had relatively large holdings of sterling and other currencies which represented the counterpart of an equivalent amount of its liabilities, and because the deduction of foreign exchange from the liabilities was preferred, on principle, to its inclusion with gold in the reserves.

Thus, while most of the central banks of the world are no longer required by law to maintain minimum reserves of international currency against their note issues or both their note and deposit liabilities, there is still a substantial number of countries which have adhered to the principle of specific reserve requirements, although most of them have come to include in their reserves not only their actual holdings of foreign exchange but also their automatic and/or special drawing rights on the International Monetary Fund, which will be discussed later.

Use of Foreign Exchange as a Legal or a Technical Reserve

Prior to World War I, little use had been made of foreign exchange as a direct and specific reserve against note issues. Up to that time it was only colonial territories such as Java, India, the Philippines and the Malay States, and countries like Mexico, Egypt and Panama, which had officially followed the one or other form of exchange standard. India, for example, abandoned the silver standard in 1893 in favour of a system under which its currency was redeemable either in gold or in drafts on London; and in the Philippines, under legislation introduced in 1903, reserves of United States currency had to be held in the form of balances or investments in New York as Philippine currency was redeemable in drafts on New York. In an informal manner Russia and Austria-Hungary also followed an exchange standard. Apart from these examples of exchange standards, the central banks of Sweden, Norway and Denmark were allowed, within limits, to include in the reserve against their note issues their net balances with each other, although their notes were legally redeemable only in gold.

During the twenties and thirties, however, modified forms of the gold exchange standard came to be extensively adopted as a means of stabilizing currencies and economizing in the use of gold, and foreign exchange was admitted by law as part of the minimum reserve to be held by central banks in a large number and variety of other countries, such as Germany, Italy, Belgium, Austria, Hungary, Roumania, Poland, Bulgaria, Greece, Finland, Chile, Colombia, Mexico, Argentina, Peru, Australia, India, Bolivia, Ecuador and El Salvador. In some of these countries the amount of foreign exchange which could be included in the legal reserve was limited to a certain proportion of such reserve, varying from one-tenth to one-half, whereas in others the relative proportions of gold and foreign exchange were left to the discretion of the central bank.

At first it was laid down by law or regulation that the admissible foreign exchange was to consist only of balances, bills and other specified assets payable in a gold currency, although in some cases New York and London were prescribed as the only eligible centres. On the suspension of gold payments by Great Britain in 1931 and the depreciation of sterling in terms of gold, sterling was rendered ineligible as a reserve for central banks which had to continue maintaining a gold exchange standard, but a 'sterling area' came into being, comprising those countries which kept their currencies linked with sterling or subsequently decided to re-link with sterling at the old or a new parity and which, in many cases, formally adopted a 'sterling exchange standard', with sterling as the whole or part of the legal reserve. A 'dollar group' with a 'dollar exchange standard' also emerged from the confusion of fluctuating currencies. As regards the remaining countries which had previously followed a gold exchange standard, the foreign assets eligible for inclusion in the legal reserve were defined, after the general suspension of gold payments, as those payable in the principal banking centres of Europe and America, or in the leading world markets, or in currencies not subject to extraordinary fluctuations or not subject to restrictions in the countries concerned.

Apart from the central banks which, under the one or other form of exchange standard, held increasing amounts of foreign exchange as legal reserves, there was also a growing tendency on the part of other central banks to participate in foreign exchange transactions and to hold foreign exchange, although not permitted to include it in their legal reserves. Even prior to World War I the central banks of such countries as Germany, Austria-Hungary, Holland and Belgium had regularly followed the practice of holding substantial amounts of foreign bills in their portfolios as a first line of defence for their currencies. Since that time, however, whatever monetary standards were in force, the central banks of most countries came, either as a natural development in credit and exchange control or as an emergency measure, to play an increasingly important part in foreign exchange operations and to aim at maintaining balances and liquid investments in the centre or centres with which their countries had important commercial and financial relations. Their foreign assets, in addition to being a source of revenue, performed the functions of a 'buffer' or 'shock-absorber' and served as an instrument for the regulation of exchange rates, while their dealings in foreign exchange were also used as one of the means of regulating money-market conditions.

In many countries the central bank virtually became a central exchange bank, acquiring the surplus exchange which accrued from a favourable balance of payments and making up the shortfall which had to be met in the event of an unfavourable balance. These central banks continued to perform this function after the abandonment of the gold standard, but usually for the profit or loss of the Government.

In Great Britain, on the other hand, the old principle of the Bank of England that direct participation in exchange transactions for its own account was not a proper sphere of activity for a central bank, and that it should exert its influence on exchange rates through its control of money-market and credit conditions and also, under the gold standard, through its redeeming its notes in gold, tended to persist. This was, no doubt, due mainly to the existence in London of a broad and active international money market and to sterling having been for so long the predominant international currency. After the abandonment of the gold standard in September, 1931, however, the Bank of England operated in the exchange market to some extent as a stabilizing factor until the Exchange Equalization Account was established in July, 1932. It was then called upon to take a more active and controlling part in exchange operations in its capacity as agent of the Account, in addition to carrying out transactions for account of the many central banks which deal with the London exchange market through the Bank.

In the United States and parts of Continental Europe, the central banks were generally inclined to follow a middle course. The Federal Reserve Bank of New York, for example, in spite of the development of the New York money market and the increasing use of the dollar as an international currency, operated in the exchange market for its own account (as well as for central bank customers) and held foreign bills as a secondary reserve and as an aid to regulating exchange rates, until the gold standard was suspended in the United States in the beginning of 1933. Thereafter the Treasury, as in Great Britain and some other countries, assumed the responsibility of regulating foreign exchange, while using the machinery of the Federal Reserve Bank of New York for this purpose.

In recent times most central banks have, in one way or another, been called upon to undertake more intensive exchange regulation and control. In Central and Eastern Europe, Latin America and Asia, the repercussions of the great depression of 1930–3 caused the central banks to be granted wide powers for the purpose of controlling the exchange markets of their countries in accordance with instructions laid down by legislation or regulation; and for obvious reasons the outbreak of World War II rendered rigid exchange control necessary in belligerent countries generally, while the disruptions brought about by the war also necessitated control in neutral countries. Since the war some form or degree of exchange control has been maintained in many countries, but normally within the limits permitted or sanctioned by the International Monetary Fund depending particularly upon the balance of payments position of the member countries concerned.

The question of exchange regulation and control will again be referred to in later chapters. The point to be established here is merely that most central banks will, directly or indirectly and as a matter of general policy and financial control or because of necessity, continue to play an important part in foreign exchange operations and to aim at maintaining a substantial amount of foreign exchange as a first line of defence for their currencies, whether such foreign exchange is admissible as part of a legal reserve or not.

Purposes of Gold and Exchange Reserves

The obvious purpose of a central bank holding gold and foreign exchange would appear to be that of having at its disposal a reserve of international currency, with a view to meeting at any time an adverse balance of payments and maintaining the external value of its currency. To the extent, however, that a central bank was required by law to maintain a minimum reserve against its note issue or against both its note and deposit liabilities, as was the case in most countries prior to World War II, its holding of gold and foreign exchange was immobilized and not available for the purpose of balancing international accounts. The existence of a reserve requirement, therefore, virtually meant that a central bank had to hold two different kinds of reserves, the one an internal or impounded reserve (i.e. against the domestic monetary circulation) and the other an external or free reserve (i.e. freely available for active use as international currency).

The immobilization of the internal reserve, however, was lessened by the provision, in many countries, for temporary suspension of the reserve requirement in abnormal circumstances. Apart from the release of reserves during such a suspension, there was an automatic release of gold and foreign exchange from the internal reserve according as a reduction was brought about in those liabilities of the central bank against which a minimum reserve had to be maintained. An adverse balance of payments caused a need for gold and exchange as international currency for the settling of external obligations, but in the absence of new credit creation it also caused an automatic reduction in the central bank's liabilities; and to release still more of the reserve its liabilities could, of course, be further reduced by a deliberate policy of credit contraction. In addition, the lowering of the reserve requirement and the upward revaluation of the reserve, as a result of currency depreciation, served to release some of the gold and foreign exchange previously included in the minimum reserve, at least to the extent that it was not required as reserve against an increasing volume of notes in circulation or of notes and deposits of the central bank.

The principal purposes which the minimum reserve requirement was designed to serve were those of maintaining confidence in the currency at home as well as abroad and setting a limit to the expansion of credit. In discussing the evolution of the different methods of regulating note issues, it was shown in Chapter 2 that, although changes and adjustments were made from time to time and in various ways in order to meet the need for increased elasticity in the monetary circulation, care was usually taken by legislators, as far as circumstances permitted, to avoid unduly weakening the security of note issues and shaking public confidence, or facilitating the creation of unsound economic conditions.

The concept of adequate security for the note circulation was historically and psychologically associated with adequate metallic cover, but the proportion of metallic cover which was considered adequate tended to decline. The limited or unlimited inclusion of foreign exchange in the legal reserves of many countries in recent times was in turn associated with its convertibility into gold or, in any case, with its more or less similar function as foreign purchasing power. While the psychological background was undoubtedly an important factor in the development and maintenance of the system of minimum reserves, there was and still is also an economic basis for confidence in a currency which has a substantial minimum backing of international currency.

This does not imply that a currency with little or no direct and specific backing of gold and foreign exchange is, or should always be, subject to mistrust and liable to depreciation relative to other currencies. The country concerned may have concentrated its gold and exchange reserves in a State exchange fund instead of in the central bank, and may thus have a substantial indirect backing for its currency; or, as in the case of a creditor country, the net foreign assets of its nationals may, although in a more remote sense, be regarded as an indirect reserve, or at least as an ultimate reserve. Moreover, a currency may, even in the absence of direct or indirect backing of gold or foreign exchange, continue to enjoy the confidence of the public because of faith in a strong Government or in the productive capacity of the country or in the maintenance of equilibrium in the country's balance of payments with or without exchange control.

In general, however, it can be said that a direct backing of assets which constitute international purchasing power does represent, from the point of view of the public, a more intelligible and acceptable cover than an indirect backing of such assets held by an exchange fund, and certainly a more tangible and relevant cover than an ultimate reserve of foreign assets held outside the central bank and the Treasury; that gold and liquid foreign assets freely convertible into other currencies represent a more suitable reserve than non-liquid foreign assets or liquid foreign assets with restricted convertibility; that the existence of a substantial reserve is much to be preferred to a negligible reserve or none at all, and that although a legal minimum reserve is immobilized for immediate use, it is nevertheless in hand and available when the worst happens.

The foregoing arguments refer rather to the desirability of acquiring and maintaining an adequate reserve of international currency for use in an emergency, than to any need for prescribing a legal minimum reserve. The absence of a legal minimum does at least have the advantage of making the reserve fulfil its function as such more fully and freely; and it should not detract from the general purpose of a reserve to maintain confidence in the currency, provided the currency is backed by a reserve which, in the opinion of the public, is more or less adequate to tide the country over a crisis. The main point to be established here is that, whether a minimum reserve is prescribed by law or not, a currency which has at its disposal a substantial reserve of gold and liquid foreign assets, as a buffer against an adverse balance of payments, is prima facie in a stronger and sounder position than one which has as collateral cover only domestic securities, bills and advances. Such domestic assets can in any case not be utilized for the settlement of international accounts. In other words, they may represent suitable collateral cover from the point of view of adjustments in the internal monetary circulation, but they cannot fulfil the function of a reserve for the purpose of maintaining the external value of the currency.

The case for a legal minimum reserve really rests on its ultimate function of compelling the central bank to aim at maintaining such reserve, and thus of setting a limit to the expansion of currency and credit and the development of unsound economic conditions; and it does at least serve to strengthen the hands of the central bank against undue pressure from the Government. It is true that on various occasions in the past the strict maintenance of minimum reserves did have the effect of enforcing unwarranted deflation, but this was the result rather of undue rigidity of technique and policy than of the principle of the legal minimum. The restrictionist function of the legal minimum is aimed merely at preventing over-expansion of credit with a view to avoiding price inflation, excessive speculation, over-production, unbalanced production, and disequilibrium in the balance of payments. In short, the expansion of credit may not only have domestic repercussions, but also a direct bearing on the external position of a country in that it may bring about an adverse balance of payments through a relatively increased demand for foreign exchange.

As stated previously, there is still a substantial number of countries which have, in general, adhered to the principle of legal minimum reserve requirements, and which evidently believe that such requirements still have a useful economic function to fulfil as a restraining influence and a disciplinary instrument, namely, Switzerland, the Netherlands, Belgium, Portugal, Mexico, South Africa, Rhodesia, Zambia, Nigeria, Jamaica and Thailand.

Conclusion

It was shown that, with a view to regulating the note issue and safeguarding the value of the currency, the central bank was originally required almost everywhere to maintain a minimum reserve against its note issue or, as became more general during the twenties, against both its note and deposit liabilities; that, as a means of economizing in the use of gold and promoting the stabilization of currencies after World War I, foreign exchange was admitted along with gold as part of the legal minimum reserve to be held by the central bank in a large number and variety of countries; that, in order to introduce greater elasticity into the monetary system, formal provision was made in many countries for the temporary suspension of reserve requirements in an emergency; that, under the stress of the great depression of 1930–3, minimum reserve requirements were reduced or indefinitely suspended in some countries as a further means of promoting monetary flexibility; that during World War II the indefinite suspension of reserve requirements was also resorted to by certain other countries which were involved in that war, and which, with a few exceptions, did not subsequently revert to any reserve provisions; that since 1945 a further number of countries, including the United States, have relieved their central banks of the obligation to maintain minimum reserves, while many of the new post-war central banks were established without any specific reserve provisions; and that in the case of some of the central banks which still had to comply with reserve requirements, the legal minimum was reduced.

It is evident, therefore, that there has been a strong and persistent trend towards the abolition or indefinite suspension or relaxation of reserve requirements, and this was, no doubt, closely associated, whether as cause or effect, with the unprecedented increase in the note and deposit liabilities of central banks, which can, in turn, be attributed not only to the huge costs and other repercussions of two world wars and the rapid increase in world production and trade, but also to the modern concept of optimum flexibility in monetary management and the desire to avoid any strict discipline in monetary affairs. This trend towards increased monetary flexibility was permitted, in the first instance, by the general abandonment of the gold and gold-exchange standards during the thirties, and was also reflected in the International Monetary Fund Agreement of 1946, which was designed to create more effective machinery for international collaboration and co-operation in monetary management, as well as to provide for the extension of credit facilities in foreign currencies to member countries, subject to certain conditions and depending upon the quotas of the countries concerned. This represented a substantial potential addition to the foreign resources of member countries during periods of deficit in their balance of payments. A further and more direct provision for increased international liquidity was made with the introduction by the International Monetary Fund of the new system of Special Drawing Rights to a total amount of $9·5 billion over the three years 1970–2.

Thus, there would appear to be substantial justification for the conclusion that in recent times the world monetary situation has, in general, afforded too much rather than too little scope for flexibility, and that this development in itself may be regarded as at least one of the basic factors underlying the persistent inflation which has, in varying degrees, prevailed throughout the world.

References

1 *Monthly Review of the Federal Reserve Bank of New York*. July, 1945.
2 Commonwealth Treasurer in Parliament: Speech on new Commonwealth Bank Bill. Australia, 1945.
3 *Federal Reserve Bulletin*. February, 1965. p. 230.
4 *Federal Reserve Bulletin*. February, 1968. p. 124.

CHAPTER SIX

The Bank of Rediscount and Lender of Last Resort

Introduction

Like the custody of bank reserves, the functions of rediscount and lender of last resort developed out of the special position of the bank which was granted the complete or residual monopoly of note issue in its country. The centralization of metallic reserves in such a bank of issue further increased its capacity to create credit, and thus to rediscount and act as lender of last resort. These interconnected functions were, in fact, essential features in the development of such banks into full central banks.

The function of lender of last resort was historically associated with that of rediscount, since it was through the latter function that the former came to be fulfilled. The rediscount function preceded that of lender of last resort, and in many countries it remained the custom, except in abnormal circumstances, for the central bank to rediscount for individual banks as a matter of convenience to them, and not only when they had exhausted all other available sources and methods for the replenishment of their funds. The central bank may also be regarded as performing the function of lender of last resort when it is called upon to grant accommodation to the Government or to the public in times of monetary stringency; and by buying securities or bills of exchange in the open market and making more credit available at such times on its own initiative, it can eliminate or reduce the need for rediscount by banks and other financial institutions. The functions of rediscount and lender of last resort do not, therefore, always represent one and the same thing, but for reasons of general convenience and their historical association they can best be treated in the same chapter.

Origin and Scope of Rediscount

Originally the term 'rediscount' applied only to trade bills brought to the central bank by commercial banks, discount houses or bill brokers who were temporarily in need of funds and could not supplement their cash in any other manner, or at least not in more convenient or advantageous ways, than by rediscounting bills with the central bank.

In former days the bill of exchange was extensively used as a means of financing both domestic and foreign trade. It was to the banks a safe, self-liquidating asset which served, together with call loans to the money market, as a secondary cash reserve. Its liquidity was enhanced by the development of discount markets in London and several other centres, as well as by the existence of central banks which assumed the function of rediscounting such bills when called upon to do so, subject to certain conditions and terms.

In these circumstances the older central banks, as a matter of general credit policy, adopted the practice of granting accommodation to banks or other financial institutions only in the form of rediscounting trade bills or other self-liquidating paper, and laid down relatively stringent conditions regarding the quality and maturity of the paper eligible for rediscount. The underlying principle of this practice, which was first given some definite shape by the Bank of England about 1830, was that if the central bank normally dealt only in prime, self-liquidating paper based on goods in various stages of production and distribution, it would tend to give such paper special attraction and to set up a relatively high standard of elasticity and security requirements for banks as well as operators in the discount market, where there was one.

The real object of rediscount by the central bank was that no sound and genuine business transaction should be restricted or abandoned merely on account of a shortage of bank cash, and it was originally considered that, as such transactions would or could ordinarily be represented by bills of exchange, it would be sufficient and appropriate if rediscounting were confined to genuine bills of a total currency corresponding more or less with the time taken to complete the transaction.

Prior to 1914, the Bank of England and some of the central banks of Continental Europe regularly followed the policy of rediscounting only trade bills of relatively short maturity, except in cases of emergency when their requirements were temporarily toned down to meet the demand for accommodation. This was also the case with the Federal Reserve Banks when they commenced operations in 1914, since their powers of rediscounting were severely restricted under the original Federal Reserve Act. During the war of 1914–18 and the post-war period, however, the abnormal conditions compelled all central banks to relinquish some of the restrictions and to widen the basis of rediscounts as well as of collateral loans, or, where legal restrictions had been imposed on rediscounts and loans, their powers were enlarged by amendments to their statutes. Under these conditions central banks increasingly granted accommodation to commercial banks, discount houses and bill brokers also in the form of rediscounts of Treasury bills and loans against Government securities.

Subsequently the wider basis of rediscounts and collateral loans tended to remain, not only on account of the enormous expansion of the credit structure caused by war debts, but also because of changes in the methods of financing trade and in the structure of the money market. There was a growing tendency towards commercial credits on open account and bank advances on current account,* as a result of which the bill came to be used

* According to the League of Nations' *Monetary Review* of 1938–9 (p. 111), 'the development of the overdraft has been due partly to a general demand on the part of various trades that the buyer should make arrangements with a bank instead of giving a bill, and partly to a desire of the debtor to save the interest on the whole currency of the bill by paying only for a debit balance which may fluctuate from day to day'; and as additional

less and less in domestic trade; and owing to the increased financing of foreign trade by means of bank advances and settlements with sight drafts or telegraphic remittances, the foreign bill also came to be employed on a declining scale. On the other hand, with the increased debts and expenditures of Governments a larger use was made of Treasury bills, and commercial banks increasingly adopted Treasury bills as a secondary reserve, in view of the fact that this kind of credit instrument was also eligible for rediscount with the central bank and that it came to surpass the ordinary trade bill* and the bankers' bill in the discount market.

In these circumstances the supply of bills of exchange no longer served as an adequate basis for obtaining central bank credit, and rediscounting in the strict sense was increasingly applied to Treasury bills. Moreover, there was a growing tendency on the part of banks and operators in the discount market to seek accommodation from the central bank in the form of short-term collateral loans rather than rediscounts. The reason for this was that such accommodation was frequently required only for some days over a month-end or year-end or a holiday period, and that a loan involved less work and inconvenience for both borrower and lender, particularly in the case of loans against long-term Government securities which could be left in the custody of the central bank for that purpose. Furthermore, in several countries other credit institutions than commercial banks and discount houses came to borrow directly from the central bank at times.

As a result of these developments, such accommodation as has been extended by most central banks to commercial banks and other credit institutions has increasingly taken the form of loans

---

reasons for the general decline in the use of the bill are mentioned 'increased self-financing by industry' and 'the tendency towards the elimination of the wholesale merchant as intermediary, through the process of the integration of trade and industry'.

* In the United States an extensive use is made of promissory notes which are discounted by the banks and are also negotiated in the discount market. These promissory notes, which mostly have only the name of the maker thereon, are known there as 'commercial paper', in contrast to the genuine trade bills which are called 'trade acceptances'.

against eligible bills of exchange and promissory notes, Treasury bills and Government or other gilt-edged securities, as compared with formal rediscounts of eligible paper. For this reason it has become necessary to use the term 'rediscount' in a broader sense, i.e. embracing all forms of central bank accommodation to such institutions. In this sense, rediscounts constitute an entity distinct from advances to the Government (central or provincial), and also from discounts or advances to business enterprises and the general public in countries where such dealings are still undertaken by the central bank.

In Great Britain the process of rediscounting has been indirect in the sense that it became the custom for the banks to call up their loans to the discount market rather than rediscount with the Bank of England themselves, thus leaving it to the discount houses and bill brokers to seek accommodation from the central bank in times of monetary stringency. From this point of view, the London discount market served as a link between the Bank of England and the commercial banks. During World War II, however, circumstances caused the traditional barrier between the Bank and the other banks to be set aside. A new open-market technique was developed which 'allowed direct operations in bills between banks and the Bank of England and wholly by-passed the discount market',[1] and which virtually superseded the old rediscount procedure until the end of 1951.

In other countries, the more general procedure of rediscounting has been for the commercial banks to rediscount directly with the central bank, although the latter has also been prepared to rediscount for operators in the money market where there is one, as in the United States, France, Germany, Holland, Sweden, Canada, Australia and South Africa, and for special credit institutions which prefer, or are compelled by circumstances, to obtain accommodation directly from the central bank. In the United States, however, the operations between the bill market and the central bank are not referred to as rediscounts, but as sales of acceptances to a Federal Reserve Bank at the latter's buying rate for such paper.

Function of Lender of Last Resort

The central bank's function of lender of last resort developed out of the rediscount function and was primarily associated with the latter. It implied the assumption of the responsibility of meeting, directly or indirectly, all reasonable demands for accommodation from commercial banks and other credit institutions, subject to certain terms and conditions which constitute the discount-rate policy of the central bank.*

According to Hawtrey,[2] the Bank of England did not easily or willingly assume the responsibilities of the lender of last resort and was at the end of the eighteenth century found to give accommodation grudgingly. Thus, while the Bank performed the function of rediscount, it was prepared to do so only to a limited extent. It was only by a gradual process that the tradition that 'the Bank should never refuse to accommodate any eligible borrower became established'. In the crises of 1847 and 1857 the Government had to exercise some pressure on the Bank, and to encourage the latter to lend freely it promised legislation indemnifying the Bank if as a result thereof it failed to comply with the gold cover provisions of the Bank Act. In the crisis of 1866 'the Bank took the initiative in approaching the Government' and 'accepted the responsibility of unstinted lending'. Even after 1866, however, there was still some lingering doubt in the minds of the Bank's directors as to the full extent of the Bank's duties in this respect.

It was only after the publication of Bagehot's *Lombard Street*, in 1873, that the responsibilities of the Bank of England as the lender of last resort were 'unequivocally recognized';[3] and it was Bagehot himself who coined the expression 'lender of last resort'. After its final recognition by the Bank of England, this function was also assumed by similar banks of issue in other countries, and it came to be regarded as a *sine qua non* of central banking. It was thus automatically accepted by the many new central banks which were created in the twentieth century. There was, for example, no argument about it when the Federal Reserve Banks were established in the United States. Moreover, within its first two years (1921–3) the South African

* See Chapter 9.

Reserve Bank was called upon to face the responsibilities of lender of last resort when one of the biggest banks became involved in serious difficulties, and it did so unflinchingly and successfully.

Significance of Rediscount

The real significance of rediscount (in the broader sense) lies in the fact that it increases the elasticity and liquidity of the entire credit structure. It provides the commercial banks and other credit institutions with additional or alternative means* for the conversion of certain of their earning assets into cash, when their cash reserves are adversely affected and tend to fall below the statutory or traditional minimum, or when they find it necessary or desirable to increase their cash resources for the one or other purpose. It serves, therefore, to assure them that, to the extent that they have suitable paper to offer to the central bank for rediscounts or collateral loans, they can maintain their liquidity and thus their ability to meet withdrawals of deposits or legitimate demands for domestic accommodation or foreign exchange, even in the event of a crisis which virtually brought about a freezing of the discount and security markets.

While the credit-creating capacity of the central bank is not unlimited, being governed in the long run by such factors as the gold and exchange reserves and the balance of payments of the country, it is nevertheless a fact that the central bank, on account of its sole right of note issue and its custody of the banks' cash reserves, has a considerable capacity to extend accommodation at any particular time. The privilege of issuing legal-tender notes enables the central bank to meet heavy demands for currency, and the centralization of bank reserves gives it greater lending powers generally.

In general, the provision of rediscount facilities by the central bank promotes economy in the use of bank cash and makes it possible for the banks individually as well as collectively to conduct their business with smaller cash reserves than if they

* i.e., apart from and in contrast to the realization of bills and securities in the open market or the sale of foreign exchange to the central bank.

were to depend only on their own resources and on such money-market facilities as were available.

At certain times of the year or of the business cycle, there is a heavy strain on the cash reserves of the banks. For example, at the month-end, currency is drawn for monthly pay-rolls or monthly debt settlements which may coincide with the weekly wage payments or a holiday season, while at the end of the year or half-year or quarter these currency withdrawals coincide with tax or other payments which result in at least a temporary flow of funds from the commercial banks to the central bank as the Government's banker. In countries where agriculture plays a relatively important part, the strain on the banks is increased during the principal harvesting and crop-moving seasons when increased cash payments are made; and it is still further increased in times of intense business activity owing to larger pay-rolls and the expansion of bank credit and deposit liabilities. Moreover, the highly strained cash position as a result of a combination of these factors at any time will be aggravated by an adverse turn in the country's balance of payments. Apart from these factors which tend to affect the cash ratio of all commercial banks, the individual bank has always to reckon with the possibility of a sudden loss of cash due to large debit balances in the inter-bank clearings.

In the absence of a central bank, therefore, each of the commercial banks would have to aim at carrying adequate cash reserves to meet such emergencies, whereas with a central bank to fall back upon in case of need a smaller cash holding would suffice. Where there are organized money markets, and particularly where there are international money markets (as in London and New York), the banks ordinarily have wider scope for the conversion of assets into cash. There are, however, times when the money market as a whole is strained, and it is at such times that the central bank can be called upon to perform, directly or indirectly, its function of lender of last resort. The full acceptance of this responsibility by the central bank works, other things being equal, in the direction of encouraging the commercial banks to maintain relatively stable cash ratios; and this is of great importance to the central bank in performing its general function of credit control.

It is essential, on the other hand, that the increased elasticity and liquidity which rediscounting by the central bank affords to the credit structure, should not be abused. For example, banks should not attempt to economize in cash reserves to such an extent that, even in times of average or normal business activity, they require accommodation from the central bank during a large part of the year. Otherwise, it would be tantamount to their using rediscounts as permanent capital, and they would not have much in hand for meeting abnormal demands and conditions. Moreover, the central bank itself should aim at maintaining a position of great strength and liquidity in normal times in order not only to cope with unusual seasonal demands for credit, but also to deal effectively with emergencies and periods of general financial strain. Thus, while the central bank should have wide rediscounting and lending powers, it should in normal times be restrictive rather than liberal in its qualitative requirements, so that a safe margin would be available for abnormal times.

Furthermore, it must be emphasized that, while a central bank should definitely regard it as an important part of its duty to help banks in distress and act as lender of last resort, this does not imply that banks have an irrevocable right to unlimited accommodation from the central bank under all circumstances. In the United States, for example, where this question was debated and analysed more intensively than anywhere else owing to the existence of thousands of independent unit banks, it was laid down that, 'in extending credit accommodation to a member bank, the Federal Reserve bank is required to consider the general character and amount of the loans and investments of the member bank and whether it has been extending an undue amount of credit for the speculative carrying of or trading in securities, real estate, or commodities or for any purpose inconsistent with the maintenance of sound credit conditions'; and it was explained officially that 'under the law a bank is not entitled to credit from a Federal Reserve bank merely because it has eligible and acceptable paper, if the conduct of the bank's business has been such as to endanger its depositors or to promote the development of unsound credit conditions'.[4]

The imposition of restrictive conditions for rediscounts as a means of applying qualitative control of credit has also been adopted, in one form or another, by various other central banks. Moreover, restrictions on rediscounts, in the form of quotas or ceilings for the commercial banks or other credit institutions, have been employed by certain central banks as an instrument of quantitative credit control. These measures will be discussed in a later chapter. The point to be established here is merely that many central banks have found it necessary to adopt the attitude more specifically that the banks generally do not possess an absolute right to any amount of central bank credit at any time, even if they have at their disposal an adequate supply of eligible paper for the amount involved. In short, while the function of lender of last resort has been maintained as a general rule, central banks have shown an increased tendency, in the interest of credit control, to impose certain conditions for rediscounts depending upon the prevailing circumstances. It must, however, be borne in mind that the scope for such restrictive conditions is limited by the obligation which many central banks have to assume as a matter of general monetary policy, namely, to maintain, without undue penalty, the liquidity of certain credit instruments, such as Treasury bills, bankers' acceptances, agricultural bills, or export bills.

Discounting and Lending Powers

In the case of the Bank of England, no restrictions were imposed under its charter on its powers of discounting or rediscounting bills or making collateral advances. When it began to assume the responsibilities of lender of last resort, however, it decided to follow a policy of restricting its discounts and advances to certain types of paper only, and varying its rate of discount according to the demand for currency or credit, the state of business activity and the balance of payments. In due course this practice became a tradition and was followed by other countries where central banks came into being, with some modifications depending upon local conditions, until it was generally recognized as an essential feature of central banks that they should deal in certain types of paper only, that their discounts and advances should not extend beyond a certain period, and that they should not make unsecured advances.

The charters or laws of all the other central banks imposed varying restrictions on their discounting and lending powers, but the older central banks generally enjoyed wider powers than were found to be necessary prior to World War I.

When the establishment of a system of central banking in the United States was finally decided upon in 1913, it was considered necessary to restrict by law the Federal Reserve Banks to those functions and powers which the recognized central banks of Europe were actually exercising. In other words, it was decided to bring the central banking law of the United States into conformity with strict central banking practice rather than central banking law in Europe. The Federal Reserve Banks were, therefore, set up largely as banks of rediscount, with power to rediscount for the commercial banks which became members of the Federal Reserve System and to buy in the open market, from banks, firms, corporations or individuals, bankers' acceptances and bills of exchange of the kinds and maturities eligible for rediscount, with or without the endorsement of a member bank. Their powers of rediscounting for member banks were limited strictly to bills and promissory notes endorsed by the member banks' customers as well as by the member banks themselves.

Moreover, it was laid down that, in order to be eligible, such bills and notes must have arisen out of transactions actually related to agricultural, industrial or commercial purposes, and the proceeds from such paper must have been used for producing, purchasing, carrying or marketing goods, and not for financing fixed investments or investments of a purely speculative character or for relending operations. Furthermore, eligible paper was not to have a maturity exceeding ninety days, except in the case of agricultural paper arising out of the activities of farmers in connection with the production, marketing and carrying of agricultural products and the breeding, raising, fattening and marketing of livestock. For agricultural paper the maturity allowed was six months.

It was soon found, however, that under abnormal conditions (such as during a great war or a severe and prolonged depression), the restrictive provisions of the Federal Reserve Act did not allow of sufficient scope for the creation of central bank credit. Accordingly, in 1916, the Federal Reserve Banks were authorized to make advances, for periods not exceeding fifteen days, to member banks against their promissory notes secured by Government securities or by paper eligible for rediscount, and to rediscount bankers' acceptances drawn to create dollar exchange. In 1923 they were also empowered to rediscount eligible agricultural paper for Federal Intermediate Credit Banks, and the maturity allowed for such paper was extended from six to nine months.

In 1932, under another set of highly abnormal conditions, a further expansion of the basis for Federal Reserve loans to member banks was found necessary, and it was provided that, in exceptional and exigent circumstances, and when a member bank had no further eligible and acceptable assets available to enable it to obtain adequate credit accommodation, Federal Reserve Banks could make advances, for any period not exceeding four months, to such a member bank on its time or demand notes secured by any collateral satisfactory to the Federal Reserve Banks. Moreover, in 1934 the Federal Reserve Banks were empowered to make loans, for periods not exceeding five years, to industrial concerns for working capital purposes either directly or through a financial institution, but it was laid down that these loans could be made only when credit was not obtainable on a reasonable basis from the usual sources.*

It will be observed that it was found necessary to increase considerably the Federal Reserve Banks' powers of rediscounting and lending. This brought the Federal Reserve Act more into line with the charters and laws of the older central banks. The experience of the Federal Reserve Banks thus demonstrated the great danger of placing undue restrictions on central banks based upon their policy and operations in normal times. While the original Federal Reserve Act largely conformed with the actual practice followed by the older central banks prior to World War I, it did not conform with their practice under the abnormal conditions of the war and post-war periods and the depression of the early thirties, since they were likewise called

* The granting of industrial loans was discontinued in 1959.

upon to loosen their requirements and expand their operations, in short, to make greater use of their powers * than was previously found to be necessary or desirable.

Most of the new central banks which were established after 1920 were given wider powers than those which the Federal Reserve Banks had at that time. The rediscounting powers of the former were based largely on those of the latter, but the former were given the right to deal directly with the general public in the same kinds of paper as were eligible for rediscounts and advances to the commercial banks. The discounting and lending powers of these new central banks occupied a position almost midway between the powers provided for in the Federal Reserve Act of the early twenties and those in the statutes of the older central banks. The new central banks, however, also found out in due course that their powers of lending were too restricted, particularly in times of financial crisis, and consequently their powers had to be extended, principally in the direction of increasing the variety of securities against which they could make advances.

The South African Reserve Bank, for example, was empowered in 1930 to make advances not only against trade and agricultural paper eligible for discount and Treasury bills or other Government securities with a maturity not exceeding six months, as was formerly the case, but also against long-dated Government and Municipal securities, one-name bills or promissory notes secured by documents of title representing staple commodities fully insured and having extensive and active markets, and non-speculative dividend or interest-bearing securities having a ready sale on the stock exchange. Moreover, the maturity of commercial paper eligible for discount was extended from 90 to 120 days. Finally, under the new law of 1944 the only restrictions imposed on the Bank in regard to collateral loans were that it may not

* In the case of some of these older banks the lending powers also had to be extended. The Bank of France, for example, was empowered in 1936 to discount or rediscount bills drawn against wheat in storage, or drawn by concerns affected by the social reform laws and bearing the guarantee of the Caisse Centrale des Banques Populaires, or drawn against the receipts of certain French exporters representing amounts blocked in or not yet transferred from countries with transfer restrictions.

grant loans against fixed property or its own stock or the shares of any banking institution.

Dealings with Public

While almost all the older central banks, and many of the newer ones, have the power to deal directly with business enterprises and the general public, they have come more and more to accept the principle that a central bank should not ordinarily engage in general banking business with private customers to any great extent, if at all.

This process started towards the end of the nineteenth century when the Bank of England began to restrict its direct credit transactions with commercial and other private customers. It was followed in due course by the Netherlands Bank and the Riksbank of Sweden, and also by some of the other central banks in Europe; and this development on the part of the older central banks probably influenced the United States in its decision to limit the Federal Reserve Banks, from the start, to dealings with the member banks, apart from their open-market operations in bankers' acceptances and Government securities. Furthermore, the Bank of France, which had continued to conduct a large banking business with private customers through its widespread branch system, began about 1930 to curtail its dealings with the public.*

The method of restricting the central banks by law, as in the United States, was also adopted by several other countries during the thirties. For example, the Bank of Italy was required, under the new law of 1936, to confine its discount business to rediscounts for banks and other credit institutions, and to liquidate its existing discounts for private persons within a certain period, although it was permitted to continue making advances

* According to M. Jean Bolgert, 'while around 1930 half of the bill portfolio (of the Bank of France) consisted of bills discounted on behalf of non-bank customers, the proportion had dropped by the eve of the Second World War to about a quarter and fell to below 10 per cent after 1945 and to less than 1 per cent after 1954'. *Eight European Central Banks* (B.I.S.), p. 145, fn .3.

against securities to private persons as well as to banks; the Bank of Mexico was specifically required, under the new law of 1936, to deal only with member banks; and in Ecuador the new law of 1937 restricted the direct dealings of the Central Bank with the public. In some countries legal restrictions were imposed when their central banks were reconstituted under a new name, as in West Germany, first in 1948 as the Bank of the German States and then in 1957 as the Bundesbank. Thus, the latter bank was authorized to grant credit only to banks and other credit institutions, although it was expressly permitted to deal with any company, firm or individual in foreign exchange and certain payment and collection transactions.

In a number of countries, however, the process took the form of creating a new central bank to take over the central banking functions from the existing institution which also conducted a large commercial banking business, and which could, therefore, continue to do so. Thus, in Greece it was decided in 1928 to create a new central bank, the Bank of Greece, rather than that the National Bank of Greece should discontinue its commercial banking activities. Other special central banks which were created for this purpose are the Central Bank of Costa Rica (1950), Central Bank of Paraguay (1952), Reserve Bank of Australia (1959), Central Bank of Egypt (1961), Central Bank of Iran (1961), Central Bank of Iceland (1961), Central Bank of Nicaragua (1961), National Bank of Ethiopia (1963), Central Bank of Brazil (1965) and Central Bank of Uruguay (1967).

In Australia, for example, where the Commonwealth Bank had for years combined its central banking functions with its activities as a trading bank, industrial bank, savings bank and mortgage bank, it was first decided in 1953 to create a separate Commonwealth Trading Bank but still under the control of the Commonwealth Bank, with the declared object of 'protecting the trading banks from unfair attack by the Commonwealth Bank when operating under a Government with socialist objectives'. In 1959, however, the final step was taken when the Commonwealth Bank was split into the Reserve Bank as the new central bank and the Commonwealth Banking Corporation, with a separate Board, which was to manage the Commonwealth Trading Bank, Commonwealth Savings Bank and Commonwealth Development Bank (including the Industrial Finance and Mortgage Bank Departments of the Commonwealth Bank). The motive for this change is apparent from the statement of the Australian Treasurer, in his Second Reading Speech in Parliament on the Reserve Bank Bill, that the Bank 'will no longer be directly associated with the conduct of retail banking business in competition with the private banks . . . and will take its place at the head of a banking system that will be freed from earlier sources of conflict'.

The distinct trend towards restriction of central bank dealings with the public, whether voluntarily or by law, can be attributed to the following factors. In the first place, the main reason why many old or new central banks had also conducted commercial banking business was the lack of banking facilities in their respective countries in the earlier stages of their existence, and the consequent need to develop a suitable banking structure for the promotion of both domestic and foreign trade, but as other banks became able to provide adequate banking services on satisfactory terms, there was obviously less necessity, if at all, for the central bank to offer such services. Secondly, it was found by many central banks that at times their commercial banking operations came into direct conflict with their functions as the bankers' bank, lender of last resort and controller of credit. Thirdly, it was increasingly recognized that under modern conditions the central bank required the active and whole-hearted support and co-operation of the commercial banks for the purpose of general or selective credit control; that such co-operation could be effectively obtained in the long run only if it refrained from competing directly with them in their ordinary banking business, except when compelled to do so in the national economic interest; and that if, for example, it was considered necessary at any time to expand central bank credit, such credit should rather be created through rediscounts and open-market operations.

Decline of Rediscounts

The function of rediscount (i.e. including collateral loans) suffered a considerable decline during the thirties and the forties. As a result of the creation of central bank credit in other ways and for special purposes, the banks were almost everywhere provided with sufficient cash for practically all requirements. In many countries this situation arose mainly from the deliberate adoption, after the abandonment of the gold standard, of a cheap-money policy which was implemented by the central bank through the direct extension of accommodation to the Government and/or the increased use of open-market operations as a means of maintaining the elasticity and liquidity of the credit structure. The creation of central bank credit was also promoted by the revaluation of gold reserves* at the higher price of gold in terms of depreciated currencies.

In the United States, apart from the effects of the inflow of gold and the revaluation of the gold reserves, the open-market operations of the Federal Reserve System virtually nullified the normal working of rediscounts. In 1934 the highest figure for month-end rediscounts was $83 million, in 1936 $9 million and in 1939 $8 million, while even under the stress of war conditions the figure never rose much above $200 million. The System's holdings of Government securities, on the other hand, increased from under $300 million at the end of 1928 to $2,430 million at the end of 1933, and $24,300 million at the end of 1945.

In Great Britain, during World War II, the Bank of England followed new methods which superseded the old rediscount procedure. At the end of 1939, for example, the Bank adopted the technique of buying short-dated Treasury bills from some of the banks which in turn purchased long-dated bills from the market. In one way or another, direct operations in Treasury bills between the banks and the Bank of England were conducted on various occasions during the war, while open-market operations, apart from direct subscriptions to Treasury bill issues and ways and means advances to the Government, were carried out by the Bank to the extent necessary to maintain the cash position of the banks in the face of a continuous increase in the note

* Central bank credit was created through revaluation in the sense that, apart from the liquidation or reduction of Government debt to the central bank in some countries and an allocation or transfer to an exchange stabilization fund in a few instances, the revaluation profit was credited to the Government and thus brought into the money stream.

circulation and in their deposit liabilities under war conditions, as well as to avoid the discount market having to rediscount with the Bank at its penal rates. Thus, the Bank of England's holdings of Government securities increased from £700 million on 6th September, 1939, to £1,720 million at the end of 1945, but were subject to fluctuations during the course of every year in somewhat the same manner as in the case of rediscounts in former times.

In a large number of other countries, as explained in Chapter 3, the central bank's holdings of Government securities and/or its advances to the Government increased considerably between 1929 and 1939; and in most of those which became directly involved in World War II, the creation of central bank credit for Government purposes was further resorted to on a large scale. In some countries, on the other hand, the strong cash position of the commercial banks was caused primarily by a net favourable balance of payments and the revaluation of gold reserves.

In short, whether additional central bank credit was created against Government debt or against gold and foreign exchange, it had the effect of maintaining, although in varying degrees depending on circumstances, the cash reserves of the commercial banks above the statutory or traditional minimum, and thus of eliminating the need for rediscounts with the central bank, except on rare occasions and in the case of individual institutions affected by special conditions.

After the war, however, there was a revival of rediscounts in some countries, due to the reorientation of monetary policy which will be discussed in a later chapter. This movement started in Western Europe during the years 1946–8, but it was not until 1951 that rediscounts again began to assume some importance in other parts of the world.

In the United States, for example, the month-end average of rediscounts by the Federal Reserve Banks, which had remained relatively low during the post-war period, rose to $350 million in 1951 and $700 million in 1952, while the daily average for the month of December increased from $657 million in 1951 to $1,633 million in 1952. Subsequently, however, their rediscounts once more showed a downward trend, although it must be mentioned that there were some months in 1969 and 1970 when the daily average again exceeded $1,000 million, for example, $1,086 million in December, 1969, and $1,432 million in July, 1970, before dropping to $607 million in September and $321 million in December, 1970. Their holdings of Government securities, on the other hand, stood as high as $62,142 million at the end of 1970.

In Great Britain, the arrangement under which the Bank of England supplied the needs of the money market at relatively low fixed rates was discontinued in November, 1951, and the old rediscount procedure under conditions of a flexible market was restored. Accordingly, rediscounts by the Bank of England for the discount houses at or above varying Bank rate reappeared at certain times of the year, although not to any significant extent, particularly in recent years. Thus, the year-end rediscounts between 1964 and 1967 ranged only from £25 million to £116 million, while the highest quarter-end figure in the following three years was £210 million for the first quarter of 1968, followed by £67 million for the second quarter of 1970, and trivial amounts at the end of 1968, 1969 and 1970. In short, the use of open-market operations again served to reduce the need of the discount market to rediscount with the Bank of England at penal rates.

Other countries where rediscounts have not, in recent years, played any noteworthy part in central banking operations, are Canada, Switzerland, the Netherlands, Belgium, Iraq, Venezuela and Kenya.

With regard to countries where the function of rediscount is still performed on a relatively substantial scale, although in varying degree from time to time and from country to country, mention can be made of France, West Germany, Italy, Sweden, Yugoslavia, Japan, India, Indonesia, Korea, Argentina, Chile, Australia, South Africa, Egypt and Tunisia. In some of these countries, however, rediscounts have also shown a declining trend relative to other operations of the central bank, and in some the rates and other conditions applicable to rediscounts have been used as an instrument of credit control, which will be discussed in a later chapter.

In conclusion, while the function of rediscount has shown a distinct declining tendency in the case of many central banks, this does not mean that its historical association with the function of lender of last resort has been completely relegated to the background. This association has indeed been adversely affected, in general, by the fact that the central banks concerned have increasingly adopted other methods of regulating the money supply, but there are still occasions when they find it necessary or desirable to have recourse to rediscounts as one of the means of dealing with an emergency. For example, in the United States where rediscounts have in recent times played a very minor role, there was, as mentioned previously, a relatively high level of rediscounts during some months in 1970, particularly in July of that year. The significance of this event was revealed in the Annual Report of the Board of Governors of the Federal Reserve System for 1970, as follows:

> 'In May and June, Federal Reserve authorities took several actions to assure that the System would fulfil effectively the oldest and most traditional central banking function – that of serving as lender of last resort and of alleviating liquidity squeezes. In that period United States money and capital markets were experiencing unusual strains ... In recognition that pressures might pyramid in the commercial paper market after a major railroad filed for reorganization in mid-June, the authorities supplemented their efforts to ameliorate market strains through open-market policy with other policy measures. It was made clear that the Federal Reserve discount window would be available to assist banks in meeting the needs of businesses unable to roll over their maturing commercial paper.'

References

1 *The Economist.* 19 July, 1941.
2 Hawtrey, R. G. *Art of Central Banking.* Cass, 1932. pp. 119–125.
3 *Ibid.* p. 126.
4 *Federal Reserve Bulletin.* October, 1937. p. 977.

CHAPTER SEVEN

The Bank of Central Clearance, Settlement and Transfer

Introduction

The function of central clearance and settlement was first developed by the Bank of England about the middle of the nineteenth century, after the other banks had for years followed the practice of keeping balances with the Bank owing to its being the principal bank of issue and the Government's banker. According to Sprague,[1] it was in 1854 that the plan was adopted of settling the differences between the various banks at the end of each daily clearing by transfers between their respective accounts at the Bank of England.

Thereafter it was gradually taken up by the other banks of issue which came to develop into central banks; and most of the new central banks accepted it as a matter of course and as an automatic function of a bankers' bank. In the case of some central banks, however, specific provision was made in their laws that they should perform the function of facilitating clearings between banks. For example, the Central Bank of Chile (1925) was required 'to act as a Clearing House for member banks in Santiago and other cities of the Republic in which it has branches'. The purpose of the reconstituted Reichsbank of Germany (1924) and of the National Banks of Austria and Hungary was stated in their laws to be, *inter alia*, 'to facilitate the clearance of payments'. In Australia, the Commonwealth Bank Act of 1924 provided that the settlement of balances between banks had to be effected by cheques drawn on and paid into the Commonwealth Bank. In various other cases the statutes also make a specific reference to clearing-house operations or clearing facilities, but usually only as a permissive authority and not as a statutory injunction.

A distinction must, however, be made between central banks operating in countries where the commercial banks themselves have established elaborate clearing-houses with constitutions and premises of their own, and those in areas where no such independent institutions have been set up by the commercial banks. In the former cases the central bank, apart from its being a member of the local clearing-house, ordinarily has to perform only the function of settling the differences between banks at the end of each clearing or at the end of the day, whereas in the latter it usually provides for clearing-house accommodation and supervision as well as for the settlement of balances.

Although not usually regarded as an important factor, central clearance and settlement has generally been accepted as a necessary or a natural function of a central bank. Shaw,[2] for example, maintained that a 'central bank will operate as the clearing-house for all its member banks as a mere matter of mechanism or of bookkeeping'. Kisch and Elkin[3] also regarded it as obvious for the central bank 'to set up an expeditious and economical machinery for the clearance of drafts and settlement of internal accounts', because 'as holder of the balances of the commercial banks a central bank is specially qualified for this duty'.

As examples of those who considered that it was an important function of a central bank, the views of Jauncey[4] and Willis[5] may be quoted. Jauncey held that 'clearing is the main operation of central banking', and said in another instance, with reference to the statutory provision which compelled all commercial banks in Australia to clear through the Commonwealth Bank, that 'internally, then, the bank has the most important feature of central banking'. Willis also expressed the view that 'the clearing function, with its ancillary elements, ... is among the most significant of central banking functions and is one for which only a very incomplete substitute may be found through resort to other expedients'. One may, however, fully endorse the view that a perfect system of clearance and settlement can only be obtained by centralizing such operations in the central bank, without subscribing to the view that it is one of the most significant functions of such a bank.

Meaning and Significance of Central Clearance and Settlement

As the commercial banks keep their cash reserves with the central bank and thus have deposit accounts with that institution, it follows that settlements between the banks can most easily and conveniently be effected on the books of the central bank. Over a period there is seldom a substantial difference between the amounts of cheques and drafts drawn on any bank and presented by other banks on behalf of their customers for payment, and that of cheques and drafts on these banks received by its own depositors; but the daily differences in the clearings between such banks may be considerable, and such differences can best be adjusted by means of debit and credit entries in their respective accounts with the central bank. Should the clearing go heavily against some banks at any time, to such an extent that their credit balances with the central bank fall below the minimum prescribed by law or maintained by tradition, they can rediscount with the central bank for a few days if they expect the clearing to swing in their favour again soon. In fact, apart from withdrawals of currency, this is one of the more general reasons for rediscounting.

While the process of effecting settlements between banks on the books of the central bank is a comparatively simple operation, it is one which is of great convenience to the banking community and of some significance in economizing the use of money in banking operations, especially where the central bank has branches in various parts of the country and also uses its branches for the purpose of local settlements. It thus tends generally to strengthen the banking system of a country.

Moreover, Willis[6] emphasized that a system of clearing, organized and solidified by the central bank, 'is not only a means of economizing cash and capital, but is also a means of testing at any time the degree of liquidity which the community is maintaining – a matter which it is essential for the central bank to know from day to day'. He even went as far as saying that 'the attitude adopted (throughout his book) has been that of treating clearances as a test of liquidity', and that 'the bank performs its characteristic function by determining what classes of goods are to be admitted to the field of exchange and the process of clearing indicates the extent to which the judgments which have thus been registered by the bank, have been sound, or at least in accordance with the judgments of other elements in the productive processes of the community'. This may indeed be overstating the case for the clearing process as a test of general liquidity in the community, but the process of central clearance and settlement does afford the central bank a valuable means of ascertaining the relative trends of the operations of individual banks.

Bank of England as Settlement Bank

In England there are independent clearing houses in London and in twelve provincial towns, in seven of which the Bank of England has branches. In London the Bank of England is a member of the London Clearing House, and the Clearing House as well as the clearing banks have accounts at the Bank of England. At the end of each day the debit or credit clearing balances of the banks are settled by means of payments to or from the Clearing House through the medium of their accounts at the Bank. In the seven provincial towns where the Bank has branches, its branch is a member of the Provincial Clearing House and keeps accounts for the Clearing House and the local branches of the member banks, while the daily differences are settled by payments to or from the Clearing House through the medium of such accounts. As regards the five towns where there are Provincial Clearing Houses but no branches of the Bank, differences are settled between the head offices of the banks in London in the same way as differences in the London clearings.

A more or less similar procedure, with modifications depending upon local circumstances, is followed in the United States, France, Holland, Switzerland, Sweden, Denmark, Japan, etc., where independent clearing houses are operated in the principal cities.

Special Functions of Some Central Banks in Europe

In those countries of Europe where the system of payments by cheque or transfer and of clearings between banks developed very slowly, the central bank was obliged, as Lemoine[7] said of the Bank of France, 'to follow, in agreement with the Government, a systematic campaign in favour of the operations of clearing and transfer'. According to statistics cited by him, the efforts of the Bank of France between 1919 and 1926 achieved the quadrupling of the number of clearing houses and the trebling of the turnover of the clearing houses and of the transfer of funds by the Bank. In fact, the lack of adequate transfer facilities in France has been submitted as one of the main reasons for the establishment by the Bank of France of a network of branches and agencies all over France.

This was also true of Germany, where the Reichsbank used its vast network of branches and offices for the purpose of promoting payments by transfer throughout Germany either free of cost, not only for banks and other financial institutions but also for members of the general public who had current deposit ('giro') accounts with the Reichsbank, or at a nominal charge for those who did not have 'giro' accounts. The transfer business of the Reichsbank grew to enormous dimensions, and almost 95 per cent of the total turnover in 1938 was effected without cash changing hands. Economy of cash was, in fact, one of the main reasons for the intense activity of the Reichsbank in the 'giro' business. Moreover, owing to the slow development of clearing facilities between banks, the Reichsbank established clearing houses at its head office in Berlin and at its branches in the principal towns.

When the Bundesbank was established in 1957, one of the purposes specified in its statute was to 'ensure the due execution by banks of payments within the country', which was interpreted as meaning that it was 'the Bank's duty to provide the necessary arrangements and services for the carrying-out of cashless money transfers and, if need be, to take corrective measures should the smooth running and efficiency of the system be impaired'.[8] According to a brochure issued by the Federal Association of Private Banks in 1961, 'a large proportion of Germany's internal cheque, bill of exchange and money transfer traffic passes through the hands of the Bundesbank and its 251 branches. In order to handle clearing operations with the maximum of simplicity, a number of procedures have been devised which have proved successful in practice (for instance the simplified cheque collection procedure).'[9]

In such countries as Holland, Belgium, Switzerland and Hungary, where the 'giro' system of transfer through the State postal and telegraph services was well developed and largely performed the function of the bank cheque, the central banks were not originally called upon to the same extent as in France and Germany to facilitate transfers for the general public. In due course, however, they also decided upon a more active policy in promoting payments by transfer either free of cost or at a nominal charge. In the Netherlands Bank, for example, the total turnover of transfer operations during the year 1938–9 consisted of 797,000 in number and 19,000 million guilders in amount. Moreover, the Swiss National Bank, in its efforts to extend the 'giro' system, took steps 'to link its own giro system with the postal cheque and postal transfer systems and the bank clearing system, thus also bringing together the payment streams concentrated in these systems and the sections of the economy which they serve'.[10]

Special Functions of Federal Reserve Banks

Before the establishment of a central banking system in the United States, where there are thousands of independent unit banks instead of a small number of large banks with branches all over the country as is now the case in most countries, a great deal of expense and delay was suffered in connection with the collection of cheques drawn on banks in other towns of the

United States. It was customary for the paying bank to charge an exchange commission on cheques drawn on it and presented for payment by a bank in another town. Sometimes, owing to lack of the necessary arrangements, for example, as between banks in the smaller towns, various banks had to be employed before payment was finally effected. This was known as 'routing of cheques'. The exchange commission charged by banks was justified by them on the ground that, in order to pay their 'out-of-town cheques', they had either to ship currency to distant points or maintain balances there.

Soon after the Federal Reserve Banks commenced operations, they sought to bring about radical reforms in the handling and collection of cheques, and also of bills and drafts. Within two years they organized a nation-wide system of cheque collection, based on payment of cheques at par. Through the twelve Reserve Banks and their branches, and through the reserve balances and accounts which each member bank had to keep with its Reserve Bank, the Federal Reserve System provided the requisite network for the speedy and efficient handling and collection of cheques all over the United States.

Under this nation-wide plan, a Reserve Bank or any of its branches accepts from the commercial banks cheques for collection at par in any of the towns within its area of operation or within that of any other Reserve Bank or branches thereof. The account of the collecting bank with its Reserve Bank or branch thereof is credited, while the account of the paying bank with its Reserve Bank or branch thereof is debited, without any charge whatever, although they may be situated three thousand miles apart, as between the Federal Reserve Bank of New York and that of San Francisco or between the Buffalo branch of the former and the Los Angeles branch of the latter. As between one Reserve Bank and another, settlement is effected through the medium of debits and credits in the inter-district settlement fund maintained by the Reserve Banks with the Board of Governors of the Federal Reserve System in Washington. Should there be any need for currency shipments owing to a strong tendency for funds to move in a certain direction, the Reserve Banks concerned arrange for such shipments and pay the cost thereof.

Under the Federal Reserve Act, the Reserve Banks were not

permitted to collect cheques on which the paying bank charged a commission. Some banks* have continued to charge such a commission and have, therefore, remained outside the system of cheque collection by the Reserve Banks at par, but the great majority have fallen into line therewith. According to Burgess,[11] it was estimated that 98 per cent of the cheques drawn in the United States were payable at par through the Federal Reserve System. In this connection, however, it must be said that it is not the practice to give immediate credit in respect of cheques accepted for collection, but that a system of deferred credit has been adopted, depending upon the time ordinarily taken for the collection and transfer of the proceeds.

Moreover, provision has been made for telegraphic transfers of funds through the Federal Reserve System to all parts of the United States, at par for member banks when the transfers are made for their own purposes, and subject to a small charge to cover the cost of the telegram when the transfers are made for them for the accounts of other banks or companies and individuals. The procedure followed in the case of telegraphic transfers, as to debit and credit entries on the books of the Reserve Banks and the inter-district settlement fund, is the same as for the collection of cheques. Facilities are also provided by the Reserve Banks to member banks for the collection of bills of exchange, promissory notes and drafts, and even interest coupons of municipalities and companies.

Burgess[12] emphasized that 'what the clearing house did for city checks the Federal Reserve System has done for out-of-town checks in providing a means of systematic handling and thus reducing expense, delay, and risk in collections', and that, 'since the Reserve System has cut in half the time required to collect checks, it has greatly reduced the "interest charge" which some banks make for the use of funds represented by uncollected checks'.

* At the end of 1970 all the 5,768 member banks and 7,331 non-member banks were on the par list, while 501 non-member banks had not yet joined the par collection system, but these were almost entirely small country banks (see *Annual Report of Board of Governors of the Federal Reserve System for 1970*, p. 240).

Position at Other Central Banks

Although the peculiar conditions prevailing in the United States and arising principally out of the existence of over 13,000 commercial banks are not repeated elsewhere, the clearance, settlement and transfer operations of the Federal Reserve Banks have had some influence on other central banks, particularly the newer ones which are based to some extent on the American model and most of which also have extensive areas of operation. They do not, however, have the problem of large numbers of unit banks, since they have predominantly the branch-bank system; and under the latter, of course, the collection of cheques is greatly facilitated by means of debit and credit entries between branches of the same bank, while the adoption of central clearance and settlement through the central bank has further facilitated and expedited the process.

Under the branch-bank system, provided the banks have a large and well-spread number of branches, the central banks are usually not called upon to accept from other banks cheques and bills for collection, but they can with great benefit provide facilities to the commercial banks, and through them to their customers, for transfers of funds at par between all important centres. This function is performed by many of the new central banks. As in the United States, they found exchange commissions being charged by banks for the collection or payment of cheques and for transfers of funds. In both cases the banks justified their action on the ground that they frequently had to incur the cost of actual currency shipments; and in the case of cheques, the banks of several countries submitted a further justification for the exchange commission on the ground not only that they incurred a risk of loss on dishonoured cheques, but also that, since most of their advances were made in the form of overdraft on current account, their practice of crediting their customers' accounts immediately with the proceeds of cheques caused them a loss of interest.

These banks differed, therefore, from the banks of the United States in three respects, namely, that they had a widespread network of branches instead of operating only in a limited area; that they gave immediate credit instead of deferred credit; and that they extended accommodation to customers mainly in the form of overdrafts rather than discounts of promissory notes and acceptances. In these circumstances, the central banks concerned could not inaugurate a nation-wide system of cheque collection at par. They could, however, by having branches in all the important towns of their countries, establish a system of transfers of funds at par for the general public between such towns by arranging to make transfers at par for the commercial banks and also for the public, should the commercial banks fail to provide them with this facility.

Conclusion

It is evident that all over the world central banks have helped in various ways to improve the processes of clearance, settlement and transfer in their respective countries, and that, although this function is mainly of a routine technical nature, it has proved to be of great value to the banking sector and the community as a whole, by facilitating and speeding-up nation-wide settlements and transfers and economizing in the use of cash.

References

1 Sprague, O. M. W., as editor of Dunbar, C. F. *Theory and History of Banking*, 3 ed. Putnam, 1918. p. 87.
2 Shaw, W. A. *Theory and Principles of Central Banking*. Pitman, 1930. p. 155.
3 Kisch, C. H. & Elkin, W. A. *Central Banks*, 4 ed. Macmillan, 1930. p. 144.
4 Jauncey, L. C. *Australia's Government Bank*. Cranley & Day, 1933. pp. 166 and 168.
5 Willis, H. P. *Theory and Practice of Central Banking*. Harper, 1936. p. 359.
6 *Ibid.* pp. 343 and 359.
7 Lemoine, R. J., in *Foreign Banking Systems*, Ed. Willis & Beckhart. Henry Holt, 1929. p. 550.
8 Schmidt, W., in *Eight European Central Banks*, Ed. Bank for International Settlements. Allen & Unwin, 1963. p. 60.

9 *The Banking System of the Federal Republic of Germany.* Federal Association of Private Banks, 1961. pp. 8 and 9.

10 Kull, W. in *Eight European Central Banks*, Ed. Bank for International Settlements. Allen & Unwin, 1963. p. 282.

11 Burgess, W. R. *Reserve Banks and the Money Market*, Rev. ed. Harper, 1936. p. 99.

12 *Ibid.* p. 105.

CHAPTER EIGHT
The Control of Credit

Introduction

Prior to the 1920s no specific reference had been made in central bank statutes to the control of credit. Thus, even in the case of the elaborate Federal Reserve Act (1913), no mention was made of it in the preamble as one of the purposes of the Federal Reserve Banks which were established to 'furnish an elastic currency, to afford means of rediscounting commercial paper, to establish a more effective supervision of banking in the United States of America, and for other purposes'. During the late twenties, however, the statutes of certain new or reconstituted central banks in Eastern Europe, presumably under the influence of the League of Nations Financial Committee, stipulated that they were to 'exercise control over currency and credit', as in Greece, or to 'regulate the money circulation and credit', as in Poland, or to 'provide for the monetary circulation and the control of credit', as in Roumania.

The statutes of some of the new central banks which were established during the thirties and thereafter also contained references to the control or regulation of credit as one of their purposes or duties. For example, the Bank of Canada (1934) was 'to regulate credit and currency'; the Reserve Bank of India (1935) 'generally to operate the currency and credit system of the country to its advantage'; the State Bank of Pakistan (1948) to 'regulate the credit system'; and the Bundesbank (1957) to 'regulate the money circulation and the supply of credit to the economy'.

Whether the statutes of central banks contained such specific references to credit or, as in many cases, merely to the regulation of the currency or the monetary circulation or the monetary system or the supply of money, the control of credit has for many years been generally accepted as a necessary function of the central bank, in view of the fact that credit came to play a predominant part in the settlement of monetary and business transactions of all kinds, and thus to represent a powerful force for good or evil. For this reason it also became the main function of the central bank in all countries of any economic importance, the function which embraced the fundamental questions of central bank policy and the one through which practically all the other functions were united and made to serve a common purpose.

Although general agreement already prevailed at an early stage on the need for credit control and the entrusting of such control to a central bank with special privileges and powers, there have been considerable differences of opinion, from time to time, concerning not only the kind or kinds of credit which should be controlled and the main purpose or purposes for which such credit should be controlled, but also the principal methods and instruments which should, separately or collectively, be employed towards that end and the extent to which credit, in general, could be controlled effectively.

Scope of Credit Control

Originally the control of credit by the central bank was generally regarded as applying only to commercial bank credit and its effect on the quantity of money. The main controversial issues were whether only the demand deposits of the commercial banks or their total deposits should be included with paper and metallic currency in the definition of 'money', and to what extent the quantity of money affected the price level and/or the volume of business activity.

As far as commercial bank deposits were concerned, the consensus of economic opinion was that time and savings deposits should be excluded from 'money' because at any given moment they did not figure in the amount freely and immediately available for use as means of payment. Thus, the only bank deposits which were taken into account were those 'subject to withdrawal by cheque or to transfer by order'.

This concept of *money* served, for example, as the basis of the 'quantity theory of money' as formulated by Irving Fisher[1] in 1911, and which claimed a close and direct relationship between the quantity of money and the price level. This theory, which in its original form was clearly too mechanical and unsophisticated, was nonetheless widely accepted as at least a useful approach to the explanation of changes in the price level. It was refined and extended in various ways and forms, giving rise to new monetary theories during the twenties and thirties. Apart from such questions as the effects of variations in the velocity of circulation of money and the pros and cons of different objectives of monetary policy which will be discussed later in this chapter, particular attention was devoted to the need for broader concepts of money and credit for purposes of the control required to achieve the desired objective.

The concept of *money* as consisting only of currency in circulation and net demand deposits with the commercial banks, and perhaps also the deposits with the central bank other than bank and Government deposits, was considered adequate as indicating the freely and immediately available means of payment, but not for purposes of broader economic analysis, such as that of price and business-cycle phenomena. Thus, some economists held that at least the time and savings deposits with commercial banks should be included, as they could be converted into demand deposits or currency on expiry of the relevant period or notice required. For example, according to Angell,[2] 'it can also be argued that changes in time deposits work on general economic conditions somewhat as do changes in demand deposits, but at one remove'; and Milton Friedman's[3] modern version of the quantity-of-money theory was based on 'a monetary total defined to include currency outside of banks and all deposits of commercial banks, demand and time'.

The wider concept of the *quantity of money* or *money supply* was, however, also found by many economists and central bankers to be too narrow a basis for theoretical or practical exercises under modern conditions. Their main reason was that during the past three decades a great number and variety of other banking institutions were established in all kinds of countries, in some cases by the commercial banks themselves directly or indirectly as a deliberate policy of diversification, and that not only could their savings and short-term deposits fulfil the same function of money or near-money as those of the commercial banks, but their operations could in certain instances also lead to the creation of additional deposits of a near-money nature. The result was that greater attention was devoted to the enhanced importance and influence of near-money, in general, as well as the money supply.

The need for the concept of 'money plus near-money' was clearly set out, for example, in the report of a South African Technical Committee in 1964. In short, the Committee's viewpoint was that the other deposit-receiving banking institutions 'taken together may even be able, like the commercial banking system, to *create* money or near-money, i.e. to increase simultaneously their loans, discounts and investments, on the one hand, and their deposit liabilities, on the other, by *more* than any given increase in their cash reserves. The greater the extent to which their deposit liabilities serve as money or close substitutes for money, the greater is likely to be the proportion of their loans, discounts and investments which return to them as short-term deposits and the greater, therefore, their ability to create liquidity'.[4]

The inclusion of near-money in respect of all banking institutions was, however, still not regarded by some as an adequate basis for monetary policy under modern conditions. This led, *inter alia*, to the concept of 'general liquidity' or 'the state of liquidity of the whole economy', which was reflected, for example, in the report of the Radcliffe Committee of Great Britain in 1959, as follows:

> 'Though we do not regard the supply of money as an unimportant quantity, we view it as only part of the wider

structure of liquidity in the economy. It is the whole liquidity position that is relevant to spending decisions . . . The ease with which money can be raised depends on the one hand upon the composition of the spender's assets and on his borrowing power and on the other hand upon the methods, moods and resources of financial institutions and other firms which are prepared (on terms) to finance other people's spending.'[5]

In this connection, mention should be made of the fact that during the twenties and thirties several writers from different countries had also stressed the importance of non-bank credit. For example, Walter Leaf[6] maintained that the banks 'have little or nothing to do . . . with the constant volume of credit which is kept afloat by the aggregate capital of the trading concerns of the country – the standing amount which all industrial and commercial businesses, from the producer to the retailer, carry on their books as an asset in the form of debts due to them'; Dunkman[7] considered that 'too much attention has been devoted to instruments of bank credit – deposits and notes – to the exclusion of commercial and private credit instruments'; and Von Mises[8] pointed out that bills of exchange and other credit instruments were used as media of exchange along with deposits, notes and coin.

There is no doubt that all forms of credit have a bearing, in one degree or another, on the prevailing and prospective monetary situation in any country, and should, therefore, be taken into account in the determination and execution of monetary policy, but the question is to what extent the various forms of credit can be effectively controlled by the central bank with the legal powers and other means at its disposal.

Commercial bank credit should normally be both the easiest and the most natural form of credit to be controlled by the central bank. By tradition or law the central bank everywhere has developed close relations with the commercial banks in the performance of its functions as the bank of issue, the Government's banker, the custodian of reserves, the bank of central clearance and settlement and the lender of last resort, and the longer the central bank has been in operation the closer the relationship has become. Moreover, as the institution entrusted with the control of credit as well as currency, the central bank was granted various powers over the credit operations of the commercial banks, since these operations, like those of the central bank itself, exercised a direct influence on the money supply. This obviously made commercial bank credit the prime and essential target for credit control, and it was considered that, other things being equal, this should constitute an adequate basis.

As mentioned earlier, however, the monetary situation in many countries has, in recent times, been complicated by the proliferation of other banking or credit institutions which have tended to impinge more and more on the commercial banks' terrain and whose deposits have come to include a substantial proportion of near-money. This led, for example, the South African Technical Committee[9] to conclude that 'the near-banks can no longer be considered as innocent intermediaries which merely channel genuine saving into real investment, but must be viewed as institutions whose activities have appreciable monetary significance'. It may be added that this viewpoint was adopted by the South African authorities and that the central bank was empowered in 1965 to impose its measures of credit control on any or all classes of banking institutions, instead of only on commercial banks.

The need for the central bank to spread its net of credit control has also been felt in other countries where the increased competition from other credit institutions has made it more difficult for the commercial banks to carry out any policy of general or special credit contraction laid down by the central bank without losing further ground to these institutions, whose operations have in any case assumed sufficient proportions to frustrate the credit policy of the central bank at certain times. The recent tendency, therefore, has been for those central banks whose powers of credit control are still limited to commercial banks, to seek the necessary authority to apply the powers also to certain other credit institutions.

Thus, the least that has come to be widely accepted as essential for the purpose of credit control is bank credit *in general*, i.e. not only commercial bank credit but also other kinds of bank credit which have a monetary significance. Moreover, the consensus of opinion is that such bank credit also falls directly within the range or sphere of influence of the central bank.

On the other hand, it is certainly true that bank credit is not the only form of credit which can be used for the purchase of commodities and services; that the other forms of credit which, at least to the extent that they are not based on *created* bank credit, are derived directly from capital and which may for the sake of convenience be called 'capital credit', play an important part in the financing of trade, industry, agriculture, construction activities, etc.; and that in so far as such 'capital credit' manifests itself in a net addition to the effective demand for commodities and services at any particular time, it should have the same effect as bank credit on prices and on the volume of production and trade. There is no doubt, however, that 'capital credit' would not generally lend itself to direct control by the central bank or the Government in any relatively free-enterprise economy. It can, of course, be claimed that the operation of such credit must manifest itself through the banking system in one way or another, but from the viewpoint of the banks it is more of a formal and passive nature, and the position is further complicated by the fact that many different financial institutions (insurance, finance and trust companies, pension funds, etc.) are involved in both the 'capital credit' and 'equity capital' markets, and in varying degrees from time to time.

While 'capital credit', like equity investment, must be regarded, in the absence of general economic control, as falling outside the direct scope of central bank control, the central bank can exert an important indirect influence on the demand for and supply of such credit, for example, through its discount-rate and open-market policies. Furthermore, it can and should develop closer relations with the financial institutions concerned through periodical exchanges of views with their leading representatives, with a view to convincing them that all financial institutions ultimately have a common interest in the maintenance of sound credit conditions and thereby increasing its potential power of moral suasion over them whenever the occasion demands corrective action.

This conclusion also applies to the Radcliffe Committee's

concept of 'the state of liquidity of the whole economy'. It has served a useful purpose in drawing attention to the importance of liquidity outside the banking sector in the determination of monetary policy, but it is generally regarded as too indefinite and intractable a basis for practical application. As King[10] said, 'it is hard to see how such a concept (of general liquidity) could become the criterion for detailed action in practice'.

With regard to bank credit, which is generally accepted as being both essential and responsive to central bank control, the central bank has nevertheless to cope with certain difficulties and limitations.

The least that the central bank requires for its function of credit control, is to be endowed with adequate statutory powers over the relevant activities of not only the commercial banks but also other banking or credit institutions concerned, and to establish the requisite relations and means of communication which will secure their wholehearted and intelligent co-operation in the carrying out of its credit policy to the best of their knowledge and ability, as legal powers alone have not always proved to be sufficient. In recent times great progress has been made in both these directions. Thus, central banks have been granted wider powers in many countries, and in some of them these powers have been extended to cover certain credit institutions other than commercial banks, for example, in West Germany, Italy, Great Britain, France, Mexico and South Africa.

As far as voluntary and regular co-operation is concerned, the older central banks have naturally found it easier, with the aid of tradition and money-market developments, to manifest their leadership of the monetary and banking system in their respective countries, but many of the new central banks have also succeeded in creating favourable conditions for the exercise of their moral influence. In this connection it may be added that, according to experience in various countries, the central bank's moral influence has depended not only on its record of sound judgment, sense of public duty and general ability, but also on the legal powers at its disposal. It can be expected, therefore, that the trend will continue to be in the direction of increasing and extending the central bank's powers of credit control.

Apart from the central bank's legal position and prestige,

however, the question is to what extent the banking institutions concerned can control credit themselves in line with the directives or requests of the central bank. For example, in countries where the practice is for the banks mainly to grant overdraft limits or lines of credit to their customers, instead of fixed loans, the initiative lies with the customers until the banks decide to reduce the limits, but at any particular time there will be an amount of unused facilities which may be drawn upon and over which the banks have little, if any, control. Another limitation is that, while the banks may be able to determine the immediate distribution and use of their credit in accordance with the policy of the central bank, they cannot effectively control its ultimate use. The deposits which are, for example, created from the extension of credit for certain productive purposes can, through the medium of third, fourth or fifth parties, be applied to other productive purposes, or to consumption, or even to speculation in commodities, securities or real estate. In general, the personal element in credit control has proved to be a difficult and elusive force to contend with, owing to the action, reaction and interaction of human factors which cannot always be accurately determined or completely neutralized.

The practical limitations of the control of bank credit and the money supply will be further dealt with in the discussion of the objectives of credit control.

Methods of Credit Control

The principal methods or instruments which have been devised and employed, separately or collectively, by central banks for the control or adjustment of credit are:

1. The lowering or raising of their discount and interest rates with a view to lowering or raising money rates generally and encouraging the expansion or contraction of credit;
2. The buying or selling of securities or bills of exchange in the open market with a view to putting additional funds into the market or withdrawing funds therefrom and thus expanding or contracting the supply of money as well as bank cash;

3. The lowering or raising of the minimum requirements in respect of cash reserves and/or liquid assets to be maintained by the commercial banks or banking institutions generally, as an alternative or additional means of expanding or contracting their capacity to create credit;

4. The rationing of central bank credit or imposition of ceilings on total bank lendings as another method of controlling the volume of credit;

5. The issue of directives to banks concerning their lending and investment operations, in order to assist the central bank in securing a better qualitative distribution of credit;

6. The regulation of the terms and conditions under which credit repayable in instalments may be granted for purchasing or carrying consumers' durable goods, as a means of exercising some direct control over the volume of outstanding consumer credit;

7. The regulation of margin requirements in connection with purchases of Stock Exchange securities, as an instrument for exercising some direct control over the volume of credit used in the security markets;

8. The imposition of advance deposits to be made by importers with the central bank, in order to restrict imports at times of deficit in the balance of payments; and

9. The use of moral suasion and publicity to achieve the desired objectives.

The foregoing methods of credit control which have come to be employed in different combinations instead of one at a time, and which have varied in relative importance not only from time to time but from country to country, depending on the prevailing international or internal conditions and the current trend of monetary policy, will be discussed separately in detail in Chapters 9 to 12.

Objectives of Credit Control

The traditional objective of credit control was the stabilization of exchange rates through the medium of a monometallic or bi-metallic standard. The gold standard, for example, under which exchange rates could fluctuate only within narrow limits (the so-called 'gold points'), was maintained for this purpose almost throughout the world from 1873 to 1914 when it was suspended in practically all countries directly or indirectly involved in World War I. It was restored, in one form or another, in many countries after Great Britain returned to the gold standard, in 1925, at the pre-war gold parity. The main reason for this action was the general belief, which was strengthened by the economic disruptions associated with considerable fluctuations in exchange rates for some years after the war, that exchange stability was of paramount importance for the maintenance of international confidence and the conduct of international trade on the largest possible scale, which in turn was considered to be one of the prime requisites for the maximum economic welfare of the world.

Gold Standard

The maintenance of stable exchange rates under the gold standard was, however, accompanied at times by strong upward or downward trends in internal and world price levels and by an almost regular series of alternations of expansion and contraction of business activity. As a result of this, the desirability of aiming deliberately at the stabilization of the price level and/or the smoothing out of the business cycle was discussed from time to time, particularly in academic circles. Some attempts were actually made to achieve this, notably the one by the Federal Reserve System of the United States during the five years 1923–8; but, in general, these attempts were qualified by the accepted principle that the banking and financial conditions of a country should conform primarily to the requirements of more or less fixed rates of exchange with other countries. In other words, the levels of commodity prices, production and trade in a country were regarded as subservient, in the final instance, to the necessity for maintaining exchange rates in accordance with a recognized set of international rules. Thus, if circumstances rendered it necessary that something should give way, it should be prices and business activity first and exchange rates last.

While prior to 1914 the gold standard was neither a perfect regulator nor a completely automatic mechanism, it did nevertheless operate with much greater efficiency and freedom than during the period after its post-war restoration. There is much to be said for the view that the successful functioning of the gold standard in the former period was accompanied by more favourable international political conditions and coincided with an approximate equilibrium of economic forces in the world at large, but it did not necessarily mean that this state of affairs was only the cause and not also the effect of the efficient operation of the gold standard and the universal acceptance thereof as a regulatory and disciplinary instrument.

The only legitimate criticism which can be made against the functioning of the international gold standard during the period 1873–1914, is that too much reliance was placed on its beneficently automatic operation and too few and half-hearted attempts were made at managing the gold standard and neutralizing the effect of gold movements. The downward trend of prices in the first half of the period and the upward trend in the second half were, in no small measure, the result of too close adherence to rigid gold-reserve ratios and too great dependence on the available monetary gold stocks and the current gold production.

During the years 1925–31 when the gold standard again served as an international standard, the general conditions were definitely unfavourable for any approximately automatic operation even of the gold-bullion standard as opposed to the former gold-specie standard. There were the huge burdens of domestic war debts, the transfer difficulties and repercussions of international war debts and reparations, the increased economic nationalism with its numerous trade restrictions, the increased intervention and participation of governments in business and finance, and the various schemes for the artificial limitation of output. There were also frequent and large international movements of short-term funds.

Moreover, Great Britain had restored the gold standard in 1925 at the old parity which proved to be too high under the anti-deflationary trends of the economic and social policies which were followed at the time, while such countries as France and Belgium had resorted to excessive devaluation of their currencies, thereby causing further dislocation in international trade. Finally, some attempts were made at adjustment and management of the gold standard to meet the changed and changing world situation, but these experiments were half-hearted and incomplete when the abandonment of the gold standard in Great Britain in 1931 was precipitated by the general withdrawal of short-term funds from London. Many countries followed immediately, and the last to abandon the gold standard was the so-called 'gold bloc' in Western Europe, in 1936.

It can be concluded, therefore, that too little attention had been paid to the devising of measures for increasing the elasticity and adaptability of the mechanism of the gold standard, according as the economic structure became more rigid and complex. Moreover, insufficient efforts were made to secure international co-operation in the administration of the gold standard for the purpose of pursuing broader objectives than the stabilization of exchange rates.

Stabilization of Prices

As a result of the general abandonment of the gold standard and the return of considerable fluctuations in exchange rates, on the one hand, and the deflationary pressures prevailing during and after the Great Depression of 1930–3, on the other hand, greater prominence was given, in both academic and banking circles, to the question of controlling bank credit and the money supply with the object of stabilizing the general price level. There were many who expounded the view that price stabilization was to be preferred to the stabilization of exchange rates if the one was at any time found to be incompatible with the other, on the ground that the stabilization of domestic, if not international, prices would be most conducive to the national economic welfare.

Their point of view was based, in the first instance, on the fact that changes in the price level caused important changes and disturbances in the economic relationships within a country (e.g. between creditor and debtor, between producer and consumer, and between employer and employee) as well as between countries, which might in turn bring about serious and prolonged maladjustments, with dire economic and social consequences to all the countries concerned. Stabilization of the price level, on the other hand, would thus at least eliminate such disturbances and maladjustments. Moreover, they argued that the maintenance of stable exchange rates placed a country at the mercy of the monetary policy of other countries, inasmuch as inflationary or deflationary movements in, for example, one or two leading countries would ordinarily be transmitted to all countries which maintained fixed rates of exchange with them, whereas the stabilization of internal prices accompanied by adjustments in exchange rates to the extent necessary for that purpose, would render a country independent of the monetary policy of other countries. This was actually adopted for a time as the official policy of Sweden* when it followed Great Britain in abandoning the gold standard in September, 1931. During the thirties, such countries as Great Britain and the United States also followed a monetary policy aimed *inter alia* at stabilizing prices, but only after they had been reflated to an appropriate level.†

The advocates of a policy of price stability as a primary objective held that central banks had it in their power to control the general price level by bringing about the requisite decrease or increase in the quantity of money according as price indices showed or were estimated to show an upward or downward trend, with a view to promptly offsetting such trends. It was assumed, for example, that there was a close and consistent relationship between the quantity of money and the price level, particularly in the sense of the former being the cause and the latter the effect, and that central banks were always able to bring about the contraction or expansion of the quantity of money

* See Chapter 13.

† According to the British Empire Currency Declaration of July, 1933, 'the Governments of the British Commonwealth should persist by all means in their power . . . in the policy of furthering the rise in wholesale prices, until there is evidence that equilibrium has been re-established, and thereupon they should take whatever measures are possible to stabilize the position thus attained'; and about the same time President Roosevelt declared that 'the United States seeks the kind of dollar which a generation hence will have the same purchasing and debt-paying power as the dollar value we hope to attain in the near future'.

immediately and to the exact extent desired. In practice, however, neither of these assumptions has been found to be valid.

Before proceeding further, it should be mentioned that there are still economists who believe not only that price stability is a desirable objective of monetary policy, but also that it can be practically attained through appropriate control of the money supply. Friedman,[11] for example, 'took it for granted, in line with a long tradition of a near-consensus in the profession, that a stable level of prices of final products was a desirable policy objective', and considered that it could be achieved by 'increasing the quantity of money at a steady rate designed to keep final product prices constant', whether it is to be 5 per cent per annum 'with an eye primarily to short-run considerations' or 2 per cent 'on long-run considerations'.

While the existence of some degree of relationship between the money supply and the price level must obviously be conceded, the point to be made here is that there is no practical scope for the close and consistent correlation which would be necessary as a basis for a deliberate policy of price stability. In the first place, as stated previously, money is not the only medium that is used for the purchase of commodities, nor is it used only for the purchase of commodities or services. For example, an increase in the money supply may be accompanied by a decline in the level of commodity prices and a rise in the prices of securities and real estate; or a decrease in the money supply may be accompanied by a rise in commodity prices and a decline in the prices of securities and real estate. Lewinski[12] gave an example from Poland, where the quantity of money in circulation was halved between 1913 and 1925, while the index of wholesale prices rose by 35 per cent. The Stock Exchange index and the prices of real estate, however, showed a considerable decrease. Moreover, in the United States, during the years 1923–9 when a considerable expansion of bank credit and money took place, the level of commodity prices registered only minor fluctuations but the prices of securities and real estate showed a sensational rise.

Another factor is the variable velocity of the circulation of money which is largely the resultant of human reactions, not only to monetary and economic phenomena but also to political phenomena and world developments generally. Ordinarily it tends to increase during periods of expanding business activity and rising prices, and to decrease during periods of declining business activity and falling prices. Sometimes these tendencies may be capable of being reversed by sharp changes in money rates, and not at other times. Sometimes also an increased velocity of circulation may be capable of being offset to a large extent by a contraction of bank credit, and a reduced velocity by an expansion of bank credit; but it has happened on various occasions in different countries that a contraction of bank credit was largely nullified by a further increase in velocity and an expansion of bank credit by a further reduction in velocity.

Experience has shown that various non-monetary factors can exert a great influence on commodity prices. Thus, not only climatic and crop conditions, wars, political or industrial upheavals, but also changes in production methods or in fashions and waves of distrust and pessimism or confidence and optimism are liable to affect prices, sometimes even in a direction contrary to the movement of bank credit. There are economists who, although they acknowledge the powerful influence of non-monetary factors on prices, nevertheless hold that they can be neutralized by monetary action. At critical times, however, there are usually such complicated and divergent non-monetary factors at work that their potential impact on the price level cannot always be precisely determined and their effects cannot be wholly countered by monetary measures. In attempting to do the impossible in such circumstances, central banks may set in motion other forces which may do more harm than good.

In short, there would appear to be little prospect of credit control by itself being completely effective in stabilizing the price level, except under favourable circumstances and for limited periods.

With regard to the question whether, assuming that credit could be controlled effectively enough to stabilize prices, it would be economically advantageous to do so, the answer is not so simple as might appear at first sight. It is self-evident that the maintenance of a stable purchasing power of money must be a great advantage, but at various times there might be other considerations of policy which might be more conducive to the general economic interests of the countries concerned.

It must be borne in mind that price plays a very important part in economic life as a mechanism for facilitating adjustments and is a necessary instrument, in certain circumstances, for correcting wrong trends and restoring equilibrium. As Gregory[13] and Hayek,[14] for example, pointed out, experience has proved that recurrent dislocations and grave disharmonies can emerge in the economic structure even when prices are stable. For example, the relatively stable level of commodity prices in the United States from 1923 till the beginning of 1929 was accompanied by a sensational boom in the stock and real estate markets, an inflation of bank credit and a tendency towards overproduction, and was followed by a severe slump not only in security and real estate prices but also in commodity prices. Moreover, a stable level of commodity prices does not prevent the occurrence of changes in individual price-relationships which tend to bring about disturbances of their own. In other words, a stable price level is no guarantee of economic equilibrium and of a normal and steady growth in economic activity.

Business-Cycle Control

During the twenties and thirties the prevailing conditions also aroused greater interest in other objectives of monetary policy than stable exchange rates or a stable price level. Some, for example, considered that the monetary authorities should aim in particular at the elimination or at least smoothing out of cyclical fluctuations in business activity and employment which they did not in any case regard as purely the resultant of price movements, and that this could be achieved by means of the appropriate credit control.

Hayek,[15] for example, in his exposition of the monetary theory of the trade cycle which held changes in the money supply primarily responsible for cyclical fluctuations, expressed the view that 'if it were possible . . . to keep the total amount of bank deposits entirely stable, that would constitute the only means of getting rid of cyclical fluctuations'. But since such stability 'would be obtained at the price of curbing economic progress', he felt that it should be left to the bankers 'to weigh carefully the relative advantages and disadvantages of granting credits on an increasing scale'.

As in the case of price stabilization, however, the practical limitations of credit control in adverse circumstances also apply to the objective of business-cycle control. Moreover, experience has not shown the existence of any consistent correlation between the quantity of money and the business cycle. Changes in the money supply do frequently have a fairly close relationship with cyclical fluctuations in business activity, although not necessarily or primarily as 'cause'. There are times, however, when there is no such relationship and when changes in the velocity of the monetary circulation constitute the determining factor; and such changes may also operate as the effect of changes in business activity. While there are still adherents of the purely monetary theory of the trade cycle, it is generally recognized that cyclical fluctuations are caused by the action and interaction of various economic and non-economic forces.

On the other hand, although the business cycle cannot be regarded as purely or predominantly a monetary phenomenon, there is no doubt that the credit policies and operations of banks, by their very nature, play an important part in economic fluctuations. Their operations may not usually be the prime causal factor, but they may at times constitute a substantial contributing factor. The least that can be said is that an expansion of bank credit can promote a boom, or that an undue contraction of bank credit can deepen a depression, which was originally set in motion by other forces; and similarly, other things being equal, that a contraction of bank credit can retard a boom, or that an expansion of bank credit can promote a recovery from depression.

From this point of view, therefore, the central bank should aim at being able to determine not only the particular stage and relative trend of the business situation, but also the extent to which bank credit is responsible for the situation at any time as compared with the operation of non-monetary factors, since the relation between the two is important for the purpose of formulating the appropriate credit policy. The central bank can, directly or indirectly, exercise considerable influence on the volume of bank credit, and although, as stated previously, it cannot always neutralize the effects of non-monetary factors by means of a suitable adjustment of the money supply and of interest rates, it can at least achieve something in the desired direction.

In fact, this attitude towards credit policy had already been taken by the World Economic Conference of 1933 which recommended, *inter alia*, that central banks should endeavour to adapt their measures of credit regulation as far as their domestic position permitted, to any tendency towards an undue change in the state of general business activity, and that an expansion of general business activity of a kind which clearly could not be permanently maintained should lead central banks to introduce a bias towards restriction into their credit policy, while an undue decline in general business activity should lead them to introduce a bias towards relaxation. In practice, however, the problem has always been that of determining when a 'tendency towards an undue change' has actually begun to take place and, therefore, when and to what extent corrective action should be taken. There is, for example, the danger that by acting too soon or too much the central bank might create unnecessary economic disturbances.

It must also be mentioned that the depression of 1930–3 and the subsequent period of relative economic stagnation which prevailed in many countries, formed the background of another theory, namely, that changes in money incomes rather than in the quantity of money constituted the primary cause of economic fluctuations, and that, while the stability of money incomes could not be achieved by credit control alone, there were certain other official measures which could effectively supplement monetary policy for that purpose. Keynes,[16] for example, who stressed in particular the importance of disequilibrium between saving and investment in connection with cyclical fluctuations in money incomes and business activity, considered that equilibrium between saving and investment could best be attained, apart from the appropriate monetary action, through State control of investment or compensatory fiscal measures. This trend which, in one form or another, came to exercise a great influence on economic thinking and official policy in many countries, will be further discussed in Chapter 14.

In fact, it must be admitted that such measures as fiscal policy and compensatory Government action, and perhaps also some form of investment control, would be needed to supplement monetary policy in any attempts to control the business cycle. Under the modern economic organization, however, the business cycle has become a highly complex phenomenon; and although the oscillations of business activity have consistently been found to be cyclical and rhythmical, they have not been uniform in type or regular in duration. There has usually been something different about every business cycle, due to changes in fashions and in methods of production and distribution, changes in political ideologies and in international relationships, changes in human reactions, etc. In general, therefore, the most that could be achieved by the joint action of the central bank and the Government would be to reduce the amplification of economic fluctuations as far as possible in the prevailing circumstances.

Full Employment

While employment, and particularly the avoidance or countering of undue unemployment, was naturally included as an important aspect of business-cycle control, mention should be made of the emphasis which was laid at one stage on 'full employment' as an objective of monetary policy. This was the result not only of the persistent unemployment which had prevailed in many countries during the thirties, but also of the fear of mass unemployment which might arise from general demobilization after the end of World War II. Thus several countries individually declared, in official documents[17] during 1944–5, that the basic objective of their general economic policy would, in future, be that of maintaining full employment (United States and Australia), or a high and stable level of employment and income (Great Britain, Canada, Sweden and South Africa); and that all available instruments of monetary, fiscal and other economic action would be applied towards the achievement of such objective.

General Economic Stability and Growth

After the war the trend of monetary policy developed in the direction of a combination of certain objectives rather than any one of the previous primary objectives, as none of them had consistently proved to be compatible with the maintenance of a sound and stable economy.

Canada had, in fact, already adopted the principle of multiple objectives in 1934, when the Bank of Canada was established 'to regulate currency and credit', and not only 'to control and protect the external value of the national monetary unit' but also 'to mitigate by its influence fluctuations in the general level of production, trade, prices and employment so far as may be possible within the scope of monetary action'. This combination of objectives, which must be viewed against the background of floating exchange rates and economic stagnation after the Great Depression, was generally regarded as too comprehensive and of too conflicting content for practical purposes. Nevertheless it did draw attention to the various economic factors, internal and external, which had to be taken into account by the monetary authorities, i.e. to the extent that they could be reconciled with each other at any particular time, and it did acknowledge the limitations of monetary action.

With regard to the post-war situation, apart from the problems of demobilization and readjustment, there was considerable anxiety in monetary circles about not only the continuance of the inflation which had unavoidably occurred during the war, but also the recurrence of severe disruption of exchange rates and world trade unless a new international monetary system was brought into operation. This led to the establishment, in 1946, of the International Monetary Fund which was designed to provide the necessary machinery for international monetary collaboration and co-operation, 'to promote exchange stability' and 'maintain orderly exchange arrangements among members', and 'to facilitate the expansion and balanced growth of international trade, and to contribute thereby to the promotion and maintenance of high levels of employment and real income and to the development of the productive resources of all members as primary objectives of economic policy'.

Thus, after a long interval of managed currencies and substantial fluctuations in exchange rates, the principle of exchange stability through a formal international monetary system was restored in the major part of the world. Provision was made, however, for movements in exchange rates between member countries within a maximum limit of 1 per cent on either side of their respective gold parities (which was wider than the 'gold points' under the gold standard), and also for orderly adjustment of exchange rates in the event of a fundamental disequilibrium in the balance of payments of a member country. Moreover, the International Monetary Fund Agreement sought to combine international exchange stability with the maintenance of high levels of employment and real income as 'primary objectives of economic policy', i.e. not only of monetary policy.

As far as the monetary authorities of member countries were concerned, the net result was that the objective of monetary policy also became, in effect, that of *general economic stability*, i.e. in the ideal sense of orderly and balanced economic growth within the limitations set by the magnitude and adaptability of a country's available human, natural and financial resources and by the prevailing world conditions, and within the framework of international exchange stability (subject to orderly adjustment of exchange rates in certain circumstances). In the United States, for example, the objective of Federal Reserve policy has frequently been described as being that of 'a balanced and sustainable rate of real economic growth'.

With regard to international exchange stability, it can be claimed that, considering the serious disruption and disequilibrium caused by the long and costly war, a substantial measure of success was achieved by the International Monetary Fund during its first twenty-five years. There were indeed many changes in gold parities prior to August, 1971, in the form of devaluations as well as revaluations. The most important devaluations were those of sterling by 30 per cent in 1949, which was followed, wholly or partly, by many countries, and by a further 14 per cent in 1967, and the devaluation of the French franc by 11 per cent in 1969, while the principal revaluations were those of the West German mark and the Dutch guilder by about 5 per cent in 1961, and a second revaluation of the mark by 9 per cent in 1969. It must be emphasized, however, that these adjustments were effected within the framework of the International Monetary Fund.

The first real breakdown in the international exchange machinery occurred when the United States dollar, which had served as the main reserve currency, was declared to be inconvertible into gold* in August, 1971, and the practice of allowing exchange rates to float in certain circumstances, which had been followed by West Germany and the Netherlands from May of that year, became more general. By the end of 1971, however, the machinery was restored after a number of realignments of either gold parities† or so-called central exchange rates had been agreed upon, as reflected, for example, in the devaluation of the United States dollar by about 8 per cent and the revaluation of the West German mark (for the third time), the Swiss franc and the Japanese yen. The fact that the existence of floating exchange rates over a wide and important area was allowed to last only four months was a clear indication of the great significance attached to international monetary co-operation and the maintenance of exchange stability.

The system of fixed parities, however, was again disturbed in the middle of 1972, when Great Britain found it necessary to let sterling float, at a lower level, although an assurance was given that sterling would return to a fixed parity as soon as conditions warranted it. This was followed by a new international monetary crisis in February–March, 1973, the outcome of which was the floating also of the Swiss franc, the Italian lira and the Japanese yen, the devaluation of the US dollar by a further 10 per cent, the revaluation of the West German mark by a further 3 per cent, and the decision of the European Economic Community countries with the exception of Great Britain, Italy and Ireland, to keep their currencies interlinked within narrow margins, but to float jointly against the US dollar. The result was the recurrence of a fairly general situation of floating exchange rates, which represented another serious set-back for the International Monetary Fund's objective of maintaining international exchange stability but which, it is hoped, will again prove to be only of a temporary nature.

* i.e., for central banks and Treasuries which had previously been the only parties entitled to convertibility.

† To achieve greater flexibility in exchange rates, provision was made for the widening of the limits on either side of the exchange parities from 1 to 2¼ per cent.

As regards the other objective of internal economic stability, due account must be taken of the fact that, while no general economic depression has occurred at any time since the war and a relatively rapid rate of growth of world production and trade has been attained, with only moderate recessions in the volume of business activity from time to time, there has been a persistent world-wide inflation of prices of commodities and services, albeit to a greater extent in some countries than in others and during some periods than during others. This inflationary trend which has been so strong that it has come to manifest itself in some measure even during periods of economic stagnation (so-called 'stagflation'), has had various harmful effects, such as distorting the allocation of resources and thereby reducing the rate of real growth; disturbing relationships between the different economic groups in the community, benefiting some at the expense of others; and encouraging anticipatory counteraction in view of the expectation of continued inflation.

The persistent inflationary pressures have been attributed by some either to 'cost-push inflation' or to 'demand-pull inflation' as the primary factor, but whether the former or the latter was the initial factor in any country, the final result has been that both have come to operate nearly everywhere, the one constantly reacting to the other. The real question, however, is what the basic causes of the inflationary pressures have been. In the first place, mention can be made of the greater emphasis which has been placed on growth rather than stability, and the consequent bias towards monetary expansion. This naturally led to rising wages and prices, due to the increased demand for labour, commodities and services and the increased supply of money and credit to meet the financial requirements of growth. Furthermore, the process of inflation has been stimulated by the tremendous increase in Government debts, whether for economic or social and political reasons, as reflected in the increased holdings of Government securities by central banks and commercial banks, i.e. the so-called 'monetization of Government debt'. Other contributing factors have been the increased bargaining power of organized labour and the continual pressure from the general public for a higher standard of living and higher standards generally.

Moreover, it must be stressed that the inflationary trend continued to prevail even at times when many countries claimed to be following anti-inflationary or disinflationary monetary and fiscal policies, and the process has not yet been stopped. This can be interpreted as showing not only the strength of the forces underlying the inflationary trend, but also the technical limitations of credit and fiscal controls or the dilatory and inadequate application of the countermeasures or the premature abolition or relaxation of such measures owing, for example, to the fear of serious unemployment.

Conclusion

While the existence of technical and other limitations in regard to the scope of credit control must be accepted as unavoidable in the modern complex economic organization, it is clear, nevertheless, that central banks should constantly strive to control credit to the extent that they can do so, with a view to protecting or furthering the economic interests of their respective countries. The least that the central bank should be able to achieve in any economic situation, is to exercise a substantial influence, in the appropriate direction, on bank credit, the money supply and interest rates; and although these factors, as explained previously, may not be the only decisive ones involved, they are certainly always, albeit in varying degrees, important contributing factors. Moreover, while all the aforementioned methods and instruments of credit control have not been found to be applicable and effective in all types of countries, or in the same degree at all times in the same country, the central bank of practically any country should, subject to such local adaptations and improvizations as may prove to be necessary in the prevailing circumstances, now be able to devise methods which it can employ with some degree of effectiveness towards achieving the desired objective of monetary policy.

With regard to the implementation of credit control, the experience of many central banks has indicated the importance and utility of certain guidelines. In the first place, the central bank should aim at being able to assess approximately the extent to which bank credit is responsible for a given economic situation at any time as compared with the operation of non-monetary factors, since the relation between the two is very important for the purpose of formulating the correct credit policy.

Secondly, the central bank should aim at being able to determine the particular stage of the business cycle at any time, with a view to deciding not only when to act but what to do and how far to go. The question of correct timing is, as usual, of vital importance. On the one hand, there is always the temptation to delay the application of restrictive monetary counter-measures in view of their almost inevitable, though temporary, adverse effects on the internal economy; and, on the other hand, there is a danger of taking action too early and causing unnecessary disturbances in the economy.

Thirdly, the central bank should strive to secure the active and continuous co-operation of the commercial banks as well as other banking institutions for the more effective execution of its monetary policy, since experience has shown that it cannot rely only on its legal powers and weapons. It should also endeavour to increase its moral influence over other financial institutions and the business community generally. With its leadership of the financial structure well established and willingly accepted and its actions and warnings heeded by businessmen, because by experience they have found it to be in their interest to do so, the central bank has more than half its battle won.

Fourthly, owing to the much wider sphere of Government operations under modern conditions and the increased economic importance of the public sector generally, the central bank now more than ever needs the co-operation and support of its Government. Monetary policy has proved everywhere to have only limited scope as an instrument for the maintenance of 'general economic stability and growth', which has come to be widely accepted as the principal objective of national economic policies. It needs to be supplemented by, and co-ordinated with, fiscal measures designed to secure appropriate adjustments in the level of public investment and current expenditures as well as in the incidence of taxation on private investment and consumption. In short, it is no longer a question of what monetary policy can achieve by itself but what it can do in conjunction with fiscal policy.

Fifthly, the central bank must always keep a watchful eye on the state and trend of the country's balance of payments and monetary reserves, in view of their internal as well as external implications. In particular, a persistent downward trend in the reserves might indicate the existence of a disequilibrium in the balance of payments of the kind requiring timely measures to correct a situation of excess demand, if a depreciation of the external value of the national currency is to be avoided. It is only when the disequilibrium is 'fundamental', in the sense that its correction exclusively by means of restrictive monetary, fiscal and other domestic measures would produce an excessively high rate of unemployment and unduly curb economic growth, that a devaluation of the currency should be considered.

Finally, in line with the objective of general economic stability, monetary and fiscal policies should not only be directed towards the maintenance of stable exchange rates, as agreed with the International Monetary Fund, but also, to the extent that these objectives can be reconciled with each other, towards the minimization of fluctuations in business activity and the general price level, i.e. the avoidance at least of the extremes of booms and slumps and of inflation and deflation.

References

1 Fisher, Irving. *Purchasing Power of Money*. Macmillan, 1922. pp. 17–21.
2 Angell, J. W. *The Behaviour of Money*. McGraw-Hill, 1936. p. 11 fn.
3 Friedman, Milton *The Optimum Quantity of Money and Other Essays*. Aldine, 1969. p. 47.
4 *Report of the Technical Committee on Banking and Building Society Legislation*. South Africa, 1964. par. 27, p. 10.
5 *Report of the Committee on the Working of the Monetary System*. London, 1959. par. 389, p. 132.
6 Leaf, Walter, in *Banking*, Rev. ed. Ed. Sykes. Butterworth, 1935. pp. 92–3.

7 Dunkman, W. E. *Qualitative Credit Control.* Columbia U.P., 1933. p. 37.
8 Von Mises, L. *The Theory of Money and Credit.* Cape, 1924. pp. 52 and 61.
9 South African Technical Committee, *op. cit.* par. 28, p. 10.
10 King, W. T. C. 'More about the Radcliffe Report'. *South African Bankers' Journal.* October, 1959. p. 312.
11 Friedman, *op. cit.* pp. 47–8.
12 Lewinski, J. S. *Money, Credit and Prices.* King, 1929. pp. 21–3.
13 Gregory, T. E. *The Gold Standard and its Future*, 3 ed. Methuen, 1934. p. 163.
14 *See* Hayek, F. A. *Prices and Production.* Routledge, 1935.
15 Hayek, F. A. *Monetary Theory and the Trade Cycle.* Cass, 1933. pp. 190–2.
16 Keynes, J. M. *Treatise on Money.* Macmillan, 1930. Vol. I, pp. 172–84; *General Theory of Employment, Interest and Money.* Harcourt, Brace, 1936. p. 164; *London Times.* January, 1937.
17 British White Paper on Employment (1944); United States Full Employment Act (1945); Canadian White Paper on Employment and Income (1945); Australian White Paper on Full Employment (1945); Report of Swedish Post-War Economic Planning Commission (1944); South African White Paper on Outlines of Post-War Reconstruction (1944).

CHAPTER NINE

Discount-Rate Policy

Evolution of Discount-Rate Policy

The Bank of England was the first to develop the discount rate as an instrument of credit control. It used its discount rate (better known as Bank rate) for this purpose for the first time in 1839, and again in connection with the crises of 1847, 1857 and 1866.

During this period the Bank gradually developed in the direction of accepting the position of being the 'lender of last resort', and such methods as credit rationing and shortening the currency of eligible bills, which were previously adopted as a means of protection in a crisis, were clearly difficult to reconcile with the duty and responsibility of the lender of last resort. This responsibility implied that the Bank had to meet all reasonable demands for accommodation in an emergency, and that it had, therefore, to protect itself and safeguard its gold reserve by raising its rates of discount and interest with a view to confining the demands for accommodation to those which were most urgent and necessary, and so reducing the ultimate demand for credit.

From its experience with the crises mentioned above, the Bank derived two lessons which became part of its traditions and were subsequently adopted by other central banks as a *sine qua non* of discount-rate policy. The first was that the central bank should not wait too long before applying a restrictive credit policy, since the trend of credit expansion could not easily be reversed after it had gained sufficient momentum. In 1847 the Bank raised its rate too late and too slowly to be promptly effective; and in 1857 and 1866 it again proved to be tardy in using Bank rate for checking credit expansion until there was an actual outflow of gold.

The second lesson was that a financial panic could, in certain circumstances, easily be brought about by a fear of inability to obtain the required banking facilities, and that it could be promptly allayed by the assurance that all legitimate requirements would be met at a rate. In 1847 and 1866 the Bank did not actually find it necessary to avail itself of the authority to increase its fiduciary note issue beyond the limit imposed by the Bank Act. The mere fact that money would be available, if required, proved to be sufficient to relieve the tension and cause the panic to subside.

In the meantime important changes had taken place in the nature of the Bank rate. In 1845 the practice of the minimum rate was introduced and an elastic credit policy* was adopted. In that year it was announced by the Bank that the published rate would be applicable only to first-class bills† of a given maximum currency, while in the case of other bills the rate would vary with their currency and their quality.[1] The principle of an elastic or fluctuating Bank rate, as well as of differential rates with Bank rate as a published minimum, was maintained and became part and parcel of Bank-rate policy.

Other accepted features of Bank rate were that it should normally be above the market rate, since the Bank was to be the ultimate source of credit to be exploited only when all outside sources had been tapped and since Bank rate, therefore, served the purpose of a penalizing rate; and that while Bank rate might lead the market rate upwards either as a general warning or for the specific purpose of credit contraction, it should ordinarily be content with following the market rate downwards.

The Bank's policy of normally fixing Bank rate above the market rate meant in practice that the Bank did not get much

* For example, the rate varied from 2½ per cent in 1844–5 to 10 per cent in 1857 and 1866.

† Bearing at least two good names, one of which had to be a London acceptor.

discount business except in emergencies, and also that its own customers had a legitimate grievance. Accordingly, in 1878 the Bank announced that it would no longer consider itself bound to adhere to its published rate when discounting for its own exclusive customers, but would discount for them at or near market rate.[2] This was not, however, tantamount to a revival of competition, as the Bank's customers were limited in number. At the same time it was understood by the discount market that it could rely upon the Bank for accommodation not only in times of crisis, but also on any occasion of temporary stringency or strain.

The Bank's position as the central institution of the British financial structure was now firmly established, and its functions of leadership and regulation of the money market were more generally understood and recognized. In 1890, for example, when the failure of Baring Brothers created a serious emergency, the Bank raised its rate to 6 per cent; and realizing the potential repercussions of such a failure, it also undertook, in co-operation with other English banks and financial houses, to guarantee the payment at maturity of all obligations of the failing house, as a result of which the Bank succeeded in allaying public alarm and averting a general panic. With regard to the crisis of 1907, which was brought about by the financial panic in the United States and showed the vulnerability of London as an international financial centre with a free gold market, the raising of Bank rate from 4½ to 7 per cent within a week proved to be effective in meeting the emergency and restoring equilibrium within a relatively short period.

During this period the Bank resorted to various other methods in the performance of its regulatory functions, such as borrowing from the London market, raising its buying and selling prices for gold within certain limits, and arranging for or accepting credits from France and Russia. In general, however, Bank rate was relied upon as the main instrument of regulation.

The experience of the Bank of England with its discount-rate policy, and the theory underlying it, were widely discussed in the other countries of Europe about the middle of the nineteenth century.

In 1857 the Bank of France began to adopt the Bank of

England practice of raising the rate of discount for the purpose of stopping a drain on its gold reserve, but it deliberately followed a policy of making a minimum of changes and keeping such changes within a relatively narrow range. Between 1844 and 1900 it changed its rate only 111 times, compared with 400 changes in the rate of the Bank of England; and between 1901 and July, 1914, the alterations in their rates numbered 10 and 66 respectively.[3] Moreover, in times of emergency the former did not raise its rate as high as the latter usually did. In the crisis of 1907, for example, the Bank of France raised its rate from 3 to 4 per cent, while the Bank of England advanced its rate from 4½ to 7 per cent within a week. In 1866 their rates had ranged between 3 and 5 per cent, and between 3½ and 10 per cent respectively, and in 1873 between 5 and 7 per cent and between 3 and 9 per cent respectively.

In 1877 the Bank of France also adopted the policy of charging a premium on gold when it was called upon to deliver gold in redemption of its notes. As Conant[4] said, 'this means of protecting its gold reserve has been treated by the bank in some measure as a substitute for raising the rate of discount in a monetary pressure, and while it protects the gold of the bank it has none of the advantages upon the money market which follow the different policy of the Bank of England.'

In general, the Bank of England stood at the one end, with the greatest frequency and the widest range of changes in rates of discount, and the Bank of France stood at the other end, with the smallest frequency and the narrowest range. In between these two came the Reichsbank, Netherlands Bank, Riksbank of Sweden, National Bank of Belgium, etc., with varying degrees of frequency and range.

The Reichsbank, in particular, followed the fluctuating rate policy of the Bank of England, with high rates at times, rather than the relatively uniform rate policy of the Bank of France. According to Loubet,[5] the Reichsbank changed its discount rate 84 times between 1875 and 1900 compared with 167 in the case of the Bank of England and 25 in that of the Bank of France. Moreover, its rate was as high as 9 per cent in 1866, 8 per cent in 1870, and 7½ per cent in 1907.

The record frequency of changes in the rate of the Bank of

England prior to 1914 may be attributed mainly to the following two factors. In the first place, London had developed into the world's financial centre, with a free gold market and a well-developed discount market, discounting and accepting bills drawn in any part of the world and affording opportunities for the investment of foreign short-term capital. Under these conditions the Bank of England as the central institution was rendered highly vulnerable and sensitive to complications and disturbances anywhere in the world, and was subject to large and sudden demands for accommodation and export of gold. Secondly, the gold reserve of the Bank of England was, as a rule, comparatively small in relation to the size of the British credit structure and the huge volume of business and financial transactions conducted through London. The general opinion in England at the time was, however, that the advantages derived from London's position as the world's financial centre and a free gold market far outweighed the disadvantages connected therewith.

Theory Underlying Discount-Rate Policy

The theory underlying the use of the discount rate as the principal instrument of credit control under the gold standard was, briefly, that changes in the discount rate of the central bank would bring about more or less corresponding changes in local money rates generally, and that such changes in money rates would, through their operation on the supply of and demand for money and credit and on the international flow of capital, have the effect of re-adjusting the domestic levels of prices, costs, production and trade, and correcting any disequilibrium in the balance of payments.

A definite trend in the outflow of gold from any country would indicate lack of equilibrium in its economy, and would aggravate the ultimate difficulties if allowed to continue unchecked. This disequilibrium would ordinarily be reflected in either (1) maladjustment between imports and exports of merchandise whether caused by relatively high domestic costs of production discouraging exports and encouraging imports, or by a tendency towards heavy buying and stocking of imported goods owing to the increasing domestic demand, or (2) excessive outflow of capital due to investment in foreign countries or withdrawal of foreign balances or flight of capital caused by fears regarding the currency and other factors, or, in the case of debtor countries, cessation of the inflow of new capital.

Whatever the nature of such disequilibrium, the most prompt and effective corrective under the gold standard was found to be a substantial rise in money rates and contraction of credit, with the following results: liquidation of commodities and securities, contraction of domestic demand, decline in investment and speculative activity, lower prices, lower wages, etc. This course of events in the country concerned would normally have the effect of encouraging exports and discouraging imports, while the higher money rates would tend directly to attract foreign capital and to discourage the withdrawal of foreign balances or the remittance of foreign bills to that country for discount. In due course, the period of time depending upon various circumstances, the operation of these factors would restore equilibrium. If the corrective measures were maintained long enough, they would not only stop the outflow of gold but even reverse the flow and bring about recovery of the gold lost, which would in turn relieve the credit stringency, reduce money rates, and revive general business activity.

On the other hand, a continued inflow of gold of large dimensions would tend to sow the seeds of disequilibrium through its operation on the credit structure of the receiving country. It would have the effect of cheapening money and encouraging the further expansion of credit, trade, production, investment and speculation, which would in turn tend to raise the domestic level of prices and costs and to encourage investment in foreign countries, until an adverse balance of payments was established and gold began to flow out again.

For its successful application, therefore, the theory underlying discount-rate policy required, firstly, that the discount rate of the central bank should have a prompt and decisive influence on money rates and credit conditions within its area of operation, particularly when it was desired to raise money rates and contract credit; secondly, that there should be a substantial measure of elasticity in the economic structure in order that prices, wages, rents, production and trade might respond to changes in money rates and credit conditions; and thirdly, that the international flow of capital should not be hampered by any arbitrary restrictions and artificial obstacles.

Relationship between Official Discount Rate and Money Rates

A close relationship between the trend of the official discount rate and that of at least short-term money rates could be established by means of an active and well-organized money market working on a narrow margin and depending upon the central bank for accommodation in times of heavy seasonal strain or intense business activity, as well as by means of traditional conventions and general recognition of the leadership of the central bank.

In Great Britain both these factors operated in the past to make Bank rate effective, although in general discussion much more stress was laid on the former than on the latter factor. The Bank of England was generally described as the regulator and controller of the London money market, where operations were conducted on such a scale and organized so finely that dealers and brokers were 'forced' into the Bank with every appreciable change in credit conditions, whether originating from the side of supply or demand. The Bank was always ready to grant the necessary accommodation to the market, even in cases of acute stringency. If, however, it considered that the demand for accommodation arose not from a temporary seasonal emergency but from some disequilibrium in the economic structure, whether caused by internal or external forces, it would raise its rate much or little, or for a second and third time in quick succession, depending upon its interpretation of the extent of the disequilibrium and upon the reaction of the money market and also other markets or other countries. As in the case of other prices, the marginal theory applied to the discount rate in such circumstances, Bank rate for the marginal discounts determining the rate for discounts as a whole.

As mentioned previously, Bank rate was usually higher than

the market rate of discount in London and somewhat in the nature of a penalizing rate, the Bank of England being the supplier of credit resorted to only after all outside sources had been tapped. But as soon as a credit strain developed and the market had to seek accommodation from the Bank, the market rate of discount for bills eligible for rediscount at Bank rate was forced up to the level of that rate; and this process was, of course, repeated in the case of other types of bills for which the Bank quoted higher rates, depending upon their currency and quality.*

While the relationship between Bank rate and the market rate of discount was determined primarily by money-market conditions, that between Bank rate and other money rates was based largely on traditional conventions and recognition of the leadership of the Bank. In accordance with these conventions, the clearing banks in London followed the practice of providing for an agreed margin between Bank rate and the rate of interest which they paid for deposits subject to seven days' notice. Their deposit rate was generally fixed at 1½ per cent below Bank rate. The call rate in turn was usually fixed at ½ per cent above the deposit rate, as the banks required some margin of profit for themselves between the rate paid on deposits and that charged by them on their call loans to the market. With regard to the rate charged by the banks on advances to their customers, a margin of 1 per cent above Bank rate was ordinarily maintained, subject to a minimum of 5 per cent.

These conventions were not of the nature of hard-and-fast rules. There were occasions on which deviations from the conventional practice took place, but in general there definitely prevailed a strong tendency to observe the traditional relationships between Bank rate and the rates quoted by the clearing banks for deposits, call loans and advances; and as the call loans from the banks to the discount market usually represented the greater part of the funds employed by the latter, the call rate had some influence on the market rate of discount.

In short, as a result of the narrow margin on which the London money market worked and with the aid of traditional conventions, the Bank of England was placed in a position to fulfil

* For short-term collateral advances to the market the Bank charged ½ per cent above Bank rate.

its function as the regulator of the money market and the controller of credit with a substantial measure of success. At various times, however, owing to large foreign balances or for other reasons, the money market was in a highly liquid state, and the Bank had to resort to some form of open-market operations in order to withdraw funds from the market and make its rate effective.

Furthermore, prior to 1914 the economic structure of Great Britain had an appreciable degree of elasticity which permitted of prices, wages, rents, production and trade responding to changes in money rates and credit conditions; and there were no arbitrary restrictions on the international flow of capital and the readjustment of international money rates.

Whatever success the Bank of England had with its discount-rate policy in those days was also of great significance to the world as a whole. London was the world's clearing house and the only real international money market at the time, as a result of which the monetary as well as the general economic tendencies in Great Britain were, through the medium of stable exchange rates under the international gold standard, transmitted in due course and in varying degrees to practically all other parts of the world.

With regard to other countries, the relationships between the official discount rate and money rates generally were different in scope and degree from those in Great Britain, as the monetary and banking conditions outlined above were peculiar to that country and to London as its financial centre. In those countries which had central banks at that time the discount rate was used as an instrument of control; and it was, in one way or another, part of their policy to take an active part in rendering the monetary and credit conditions in their respective countries more responsive to changes in the discount rate. In general, however, their discount-rate policy did not prove as effective a weapon as in the case of the Bank of England.

In the first place, none of the other countries had such an active and well-organized money market. There was, for example, no real discount market in these countries. The commercial banks discounted bills for their own customers and the central bank rediscounted bills for the commercial banks, besides discounting for their own customers, as was particularly the case with the Bank of France and the Bank of Italy. The rates of these central banks could be used as a means of raising money rates generally whenever the commercial banks within their areas of operation were forced by circumstances to rediscount with them; but changes in money rates in their countries did not usually have such prompt effects as in Great Britain, since their economic structure was less elastic and their credit organization less sensitive.

Secondly, while certain conventions in respect of interest rates were in vogue in some of those countries, they were not so pronounced or semi-automatic as in Great Britain. Nor was the psychological reaction on the part of trade, industry and the public such an important factor as in Great Britain.

Thirdly, the other central banks had less necessity than the Bank of England for the use of the discount rate as a means of protecting their gold reserves. On the one hand, they had relatively larger reserves at their disposal, taking into account the volume of business and financial transactions in their countries and their less vulnerable position in general; and on the other hand, many of them also resorted to other methods of protecting their gold reserves. The central banks of Germany, Holland, Belgium and Denmark, for example, followed a policy of holding foreign exchange as their first line of defence of exchange rates. Writing about the Netherlands Bank, De Jong[6] said that 'the effect of the foreign bill policy in stabilizing the Bank rate cannot, of course, be expressed in exact figures', but 'by way of illustration it may be mentioned ... that, whereas the official discount rates of the Bank of England and the German Reichsbank had been altered during the years 1894 to 1913 (inclusive) ninety times and seventy-three times respectively, the Netherlands Bank's discount rate for bills had been changed only thirty-six times in the same period'.

Discount-Rate Policy since 1914

After 1914 there were again various occasions on which the central banks of different countries employed the discount rate as a major instrument of credit control; but in general its importance as such tended to decline absolutely as well as relatively to other methods of control.

The Bank of England, for example, maintained its rate at 5 per cent, except for a period of nine months in 1916–17, throughout World War I and for a year after the cessation of hostilities. It was raised to 6 per cent in November, 1919, and then to 7 per cent in April, 1920, in an attempt to check the post-war inflation which had been steadily gaining momentum. After deflation had set in, the Bank began in April, 1921, to lower its rate in stages of ½ per cent at a time to 3 per cent by July, 1922; but with the first signs of a general revival of business activity it was raised to 4 per cent in July, 1923, while the further rise to 5 per cent in March, 1925, was connected *inter alia* with the contemplated return to the gold standard. Except for a few months during the second half of 1925, the rate was kept at 5 per cent till April, 1927, when as a result of a moderate recession it was reduced to 4½ per cent and maintained there until the expansion of business activity, combined with heavy speculation in New York and an outflow of capital from London, caused an increase in the rate to 5½ per cent in February, 1929, followed by a further rise to 6½ per cent in September of that year.

The turning point was marked by the Wall Street crash in October, 1929, when Bank rate was promptly lowered to 6 per cent, and then to 5 per cent by the end of the year. With the development of a serious trade depression and easier monetary conditions, the rate was further reduced in four stages to 3 per cent by May, 1930, and to 2½ per cent in May, 1931. In July, 1931, however, it was raised to 4½ per cent in two stages on account of the financial crisis in Central Europe, followed by a further rise to 6 per cent in September, 1931, when Great Britain was forced to suspend the gold standard as the result of a flight from sterling and a substantial loss of gold. In February, 1932, the Bank could again begin to lower its rate, first to 5 per cent and then in five stages to 2 per cent by June, 1932.

It will be observed, therefore, that, as compared with sixty-six changes between January, 1901, and July, 1914, the Bank of England altered its rate only thirty-four times between 1919 and 1932; and of these thirty-four changes ten occurred in 1931 and

1932, the last six consisting of reductions in stages from 6 to 2 per cent. Moreover, the highest rates reached during this period were 7 per cent from April, 1920, to April, 1921, 6½ per cent from September to October, 1929, and 6 per cent from September, 1931, to February, 1932, thus also showing a declining trend.

During the period 1919–32 the Bank of France altered its rate only seventeen times, but the Federal Reserve Bank of New York made thirty-four changes in its discount rate, as in the case of the Bank of England, although they did not always occur at the same time or in the same degree. With regard to the Reichsbank (which had maintained its rate at 5 per cent between December, 1914, and July, 1922, and thereafter raised it in various stages during the hyperinflation period to 30 per cent by August, 1923, and 90 per cent between September and December, 1923, and which was also compelled by a financial crisis to raise its rate in three stages from 5 to 15 per cent in June–August, 1931), there were thirty-six changes in its discount rate between 1919 and 1932, which represented the highest number of rate changes of any central bank during that period.

After 1932, however, official discount rates were, with few exceptions, used in conjunction with other methods to maintain a cheap-money policy; and notwithstanding a costly and devastating war over a large part of the world, the discount rates of most countries directly or indirectly involved stood at the same or a lower level *after* the war than during the cheap-money period which preceded it. Except for two brief periods during August–October, 1939, when as a result of disturbances preceding and following the outbreak of war in Europe the rate of the Bank of England was 4 and 3 per cent respectively, it was maintained unchanged at 2 per cent from June, 1932, to November, 1951, while the Federal Reserve Bank of New York kept its discount rate at 1 per cent, the lowest figure in history for any central bank, from August, 1937, to January, 1948. The Bank of France, which had reduced its rate from 3 to 2 per cent in 1939, lowered it further to 1¾ per cent in 1941 and 1⅝ per cent in January, 1945; the National Bank of Belgium reduced its rate from 2½ to 2 per cent in 1940 and 1½ per cent in January, 1945; the Reserve Bank of New Zealand lowered its rate in various stages from 4 per cent prior to the war to 1½ per cent in 1941, and the Bank of Canada from 2½ to 1½ per cent in 1944; and the Netherlands Bank and the Riksbank of Sweden, after raising their rates at the beginning of the war, lowered them again to 2½ and 3 per cent respectively in 1941, the latter being further reduced to 2½ per cent in February, 1945. The Swiss National Bank, moreover, kept its rate unchanged at 1½ per cent since November, 1936.

In many countries the maintenance of cheap money, with primary reliance on wartime physical and fiscal controls to restrain inflation, was continued after the war, whether regarded as a necessary element of post-war reconstruction or of a long-term policy of full employment and social security. During the late forties, however, a gradual revival of discount-rate policy began to take place in some countries, owing to the persistence of inflation and the evident inadequacy of non-monetary controls.

The Bank of Japan and the National Bank of Belgium were the first to raise their discount rates, namely, the former from 3·29 to 3·65 per cent in October, 1946, and to 5·84 per cent by October, 1951, and the latter from 1·5 to 2·5 per cent in November, 1946, and to 3·5 per cent by August, 1947. During the years 1947–50 official discount rates were also raised in France, Italy, West Germany, Spain, South Africa, Netherlands, Sweden, Denmark, Finland, Canada, Greece and Ecuador, as well as in the United States although in this case the increase was only from 1 to 1·25 per cent in January, 1948, and to 1·75 per cent by August, 1950. The Bank of England, on the other hand, did not change its rate until November, 1951, namely, from 2 to 2·5 per cent, with a further increase to 4 per cent in March, 1952. In 1953–4 some central banks decided to lower their rates, for example, to 3 per cent in England, West Germany and France and 1·5 per cent in the United States; but from the beginning of 1955 there was again a general upward trend which finally raised the bank rates of Japan and England to 8·395 and 7 per cent in May and September, 1957, respectively; and also to 7 per cent in New Zealand, 5 per cent in France, Netherlands, Sweden and Austria, 4·5 per cent in Belgium and South Africa, 4 per cent in Spain and India, and 3·5 per cent in the United States. As an exception, however, the bank rate of West Germany which had reached its high point of 5·5 per cent in May, 1956, was reduced in three stages to 4 per cent by September, 1957.

With regard to the more recent record of official discount rates, the Bank of England changed its rate twenty-eight times between the end of 1958 and the end of 1971, with a low point of 4 per cent from January, 1963, to February, 1964, and a peak of 8 per cent from November, 1967, to March, 1968, and again from February, 1969, to March, 1970; the Federal Reserve Bank of New York twenty times, with low levels of 2½ per cent from November, 1958, to March, 1959, and 3 per cent from August, 1960, to July, 1963, and a high point of 6 per cent from April, 1969, to November, 1970; the Bundesbank of West Germany twenty-two times, with a low point of 2·75 per cent from January to September, 1959, and a peak of 7·5 per cent from March to July, 1970; the National Bank of Belgium twenty-seven times, with a low point of 3·5 per cent from December, 1962, to July, 1963, and a peak of 7·5 per cent from September, 1969, to October, 1970; the Bank of Japan twenty-three times, with low points of 5·48 per cent from June, 1965, to September, 1967, and 4·75 per cent at the end of 1971, and a high point of 7·3 per cent from December, 1959, to August, 1960, and again from September, 1961, to October, 1962; and the Bank of France fourteen times, with a low level of 3·5 per cent from October, 1960, to November, 1963, and again from April, 1965, to July, 1968, and a peak of 8 per cent from October, 1969, to August, 1970.

It is evident, therefore, that during the past twenty years many central banks have again resorted to a fairly frequent and extensive use of the discount rate, although certain factors tended to limit its effectiveness as an instrument of credit control, despite the relatively high rates imposed at times in some countries. Before discussing these factors, however, mention should be made of the different background of official discount rates not only in the United States but also in countries without organized money markets.

Position of Federal Reserve Banks

When the Federal Reserve Banks of the United States commenced operations in 1914, they tended strongly towards adopting an active discount-rate policy, with the aid of open-market operations when necessary for the purpose of making their rates effective, as the Bank of England had been doing up to that time; but they lacked a money market which would be responsive to changes in credit conditions and in official discount rates.

Realizing its importance as a basic factor in the technique of credit control in a major country, the Federal Reserve Banks took an active part in promoting the establishment of a well-organized money market in New York, with four different sections: the market for bankers' acceptances; the market for commercial paper; the market for short-term Government securities; and the call-loan market. They were particularly interested in the development of the markets for bankers' acceptances and short-term Government securities and rendered this possible by declaring themselves ready at all times to buy such acceptances and securities from any bank, discount house or bill dealer,* and by quoting favourable rates for such paper. In due course subsidiary money markets were established in some of the other Federal Reserve Bank centres, such as Chicago, Boston and San Francisco, while that of New York developed into an international money market of great importance, representing a good second to the London market and exerting at times a profound influence on the latter.

The position of the official discount rate in relation to certain money rates in New York was, however, different from that in London, due mainly to different conditions. Thus, in the case of the rates charged for call loans or for the accommodation extended by member banks to their business customers, or the rates paid on deposits, there were no conventional relationships of the types prevailing in London. In particular, the call rate in the latter applied primarily to loans from banks to the discount

* The Reserve Bank also bought acceptances from bill dealers subject to re-purchase by the dealers within fifteen days, for the purpose of tiding them over temporary pinches in the market.

market and was, for obvious reasons, usually between the bank deposit rate and the market discount rate, whereas in New York it was related principally to loans from banks to the Stock Exchange, whether for their own account or 'for account of others', and was for that reason not always closely associated with other money rates, as it depended largely on the volume of speculative activity on the Stock Exchange.

Another difference was that the British banks did not directly approach the Bank of England for accommodation but called up their loans to discount houses and bill brokers, who were then forced to sell bills to the Bank or borrow from it, whereas in the United States the member banks dealt directly with their Reserve Banks. Moreover, the discount rate of the Bank of England was a minimum rate applied only to first-class bills, equivalent in general to bankers' acceptances in the United States, whereas the discount rate* of a Federal Reserve Bank applied to the promissory notes of bank customers endorsed by the borrowing member banks, or to the short-term collateral notes† of the member banks themselves.

In general, the Federal Reserve Bank of New York succeeded in establishing a fairly close correlation between the trends of its discount rate and those of the open-market rates for commercial paper and bankers' acceptances; but while its discount rate was, as that of the Bank of England, above the market rate of discount for bankers' acceptances, it was not as a general rule above the market rate for commercial paper (i.e. promissory notes dealt with in the open market).

Burgess,[7] however, pointed out that the commercial paper which a member bank brought to a Reserve Bank for rediscount was different from open-market commercial paper, since it had a bank endorsement, carrying with it the assumption by the

* Apart from the discount rate the Federal Reserve Banks quoted a buying rate for bankers' acceptances dealt with in the open market, and this rate was naturally lower than the discount rate and frequently as low as the market rate for the purpose of assisting and maintaining a bill market. The Federal Reserve Banks also quoted rates, with various margins above the discount rate, for advances to member banks against security other than eligible paper or Government securities or for advances to the public against Government securities.

† Based on eligible paper or Government securities.

member bank of the risk of non-payment. From his outline one was encouraged to conclude that, if due allowance were made for the value of the bank endorsement on such commercial paper, the discount rates of the Reserve Banks could not really be regarded as having been below the market rates of the paper discounted. Burgess admitted, on the other hand, that 'it is a fair question whether a slightly higher discount rate – more in the nature of a penalty rate – might not have been better', since 'access to the Reserve Banks may have been a little too easy'.

In fact, the absence of the practice of a penal rate of discount was submitted by various economists during the twenties and thirties as one of the important factors which militated against the effectiveness of discount-rate policy in the United States. For example, Beckhart[8] stated that 'the consensus of opinion among students of the subject here (United States) or abroad is that the Bank rate should rule higher than the market on each of the several types of paper discounted by the system'; and according to Gregory,[9] 'an important section of American opinion holds that the rate charged by the Reserve Banks should be a penal rate: that, in other words, the rate should be kept above the rates ruling, not only in the open market, but also above the rates ruling at the commercial banks for "over-the-counter" discounts'. Gregory's own conclusion was, however, that 'it is the tendency of reserve rates to follow, rather than to precede, market rates which should be criticized, rather than the tendency of reserve rates to be below market rates'.

During the thirties and forties a passive discount-rate policy was followed by the Federal Reserve Banks, and greater emphasis was placed on other methods of credit control, such as open-market operations and variable reserve requirements, and on the tradition against continuous and large borrowing by the member banks irrespective of the rates. This trend has, in general, continued to prevail although, like many other central banks, the Federal Reserve Banks have again resorted to relatively frequent changes in their discount rates since the fifties.

Official Discount Rates in Countries Without Organized Money Markets

The majority of countries do not have organized money markets. There is a money market everywhere in the sense that at any given time there are always some institutions and individuals wishing to borrow money for one purpose or another and for short periods, and others seeking to lend money for those purposes and periods; but in many countries there are no market operators specializing in the mobilization of all surplus funds available for short-term financing of their particular lines. In such cases, the banks and similar financial institutions act as the primary intermediaries between short-term lenders and borrowers and, along with the Treasury which might be borrowing direct from the public on Treasury bills, virtually constitute the money market. Such a money market, however, while it does establish approximate relations between supply and demand in respect of various types of short-term surplus funds, is seldom active and mobile and does not effectively cover all sources of loanable funds, particularly those available only for very short periods. In other words, it is not finely balanced and does not ordinarily work on a narrow margin, as a result of which it generally is not automatically responsive to changes in the official discount rate.

It has already been shown that even organized money markets are not always responsive, owing to highly liquid conditions and sometimes other factors; but it can at least be said that, except under abnormal circumstances, they tend to be either automatically responsive or capable of being made responsive, with the aid of suitable open-market operations, to the discount-rate policy of the central bank. Without active money markets, however, central banks cannot usually rely on the one or the other.

In spite of these handicaps, the central banks of almost all such countries have, at one time or another, adopted the discount rate as an instrument of control in varying forms and degrees. In fact, the statutes of many of the newer central banks actually contain a provision to the effect that they must fix and publish the minimum or standard rate at which they will discount eligible bills of exchange, or the rates at which they will discount the various classes of bills. Most of them quote not only a discount rate for first-class trade bills (with a currency up to three or four months and bearing two good names), which is called the official or standard or bank rate, but also the same or a slightly higher rate for agricultural bills* (with a currency up to six or nine months and sometimes consisting of one-name promissory notes secured by warehouse receipts), or for collateral advances against bills, notes, and Government or Municipal securities. Moreover, in some cases special rates are quoted for discounts of Treasury bills or export bills. Some of them also publish separate rates for discounts and advances to the commercial banks as distinguished from the general public.

The significance of the discount rates of these central banks has been of a three-fold nature.

In the first place, in conjunction with the other rates based on it, the official discount rate indicated the rates at which the public should be able to obtain accommodation on the specified types of paper from the commercial banks as well as the central bank. Under their statutes most of these central banks had relatively wide powers of dealing with the public, and being situated in debtor countries, where there was intermittently, if not chronically, a tendency towards relatively high interest rates, they regarded it as part of their duty to ensure satisfactory banking services and reasonable rates to the community. With this object in view, many of them entered into direct dealings with the public to the extent considered necessary in the prevailing circumstances. In due course, however, the majority found it possible to contract or abandon their business with private customers, as the commercial banks came to render the same services and to quote the same rates as they did for the same kinds of paper, and to make use of central bank credit in order to supplement their own resources in case of need. In these countries, therefore, the scope for substantial deviations from the central bank's rates, after allowing for differences in the currency and quality of paper and the security for advances, was

* In some countries, however, lower rates are quoted by the central bank on agricultural than on commercial bills and loans, as a means of assisting and encouraging the producer.

limited in general to the types of accommodation which the central bank was prohibited from granting under its statutes, or from which it normally refrained as a matter of policy.

Secondly, where separate rates for the commercial banks are not published, the discount rate also represents the basis of the rates at which they can obtain central bank credit. In the case of some of these central banks, the commercial banks have to pay the full rates for discounts and loans as quoted by the central bank, while in other cases they are allowed a margin of ½ or 1 per cent below the published rates of the central bank, on the ground that the assumption by the borrowing bank of the risk of non-payment ordinarily gives the paper which it has presented to the central bank for rediscounts or collateral loans a higher value as compared with the paper presented directly by the public, or because the central bank relies primarily on the commercial banks for the distribution of central bank credit as and when required. In some cases, however, the central bank has reserved and also exercised the right, apart from raising its discount and interest rates whenever it considered that the monetary situation demanded credit contraction, to reduce or remove the margin which it formerly allowed the commercial banks, or even to impose a penalty over and above the relevant published rates, in order to emphasize more strongly to them the necessity for contraction of credit.

Thirdly, the discount rate of the central bank also has an important psychological value as an instrument of credit control in the developing or underdeveloped countries. As in the case of the more mature economies, it is at least a reflection of the central bank's opinion of the country's monetary and credit situation, and sometimes of the economic position generally. As Gibson [10] said, a rise in the discount rate may be regarded as 'the amber coloured light of warning of a robot system of finance and economics', while a fall in the discount rate may be looked upon as 'the green light indicating that the coast is clear and the ship of commerce may proceed on her way with caution'. The psychological value of the discount rate, therefore, depends largely on the prestige of the central bank and the degree of co-operation and support which it can obtain from the commercial banks and other credit institutions.

This co-operation can, for example, be secured by means of conventional relationships between the discount rate of the central bank and the rates quoted by the commercial banks for discounts, loans and deposits. It has already been shown that, partly because of the powers given to these central banks to grant direct accommodation to the public on certain classes of bills and securities, the commercial banks have been induced to quote approximately the same rates for the same types of accommodation. As regards other types of accommodation, however, conventional relationships appear to be the easiest means of obtaining the desired results. This view was also held by Copland[11] who, in referring to the situation in Australia, said that 'clearly the most satisfactory arrangement is a system under which the leadership of the central bank is recognized in a set of conventions through which the banks implement the banking policy desired from time to time by the central bank'.

Some of the newer central banks have succeeded in attaining a conventional relationship between the official discount rate and the commercial banks' rates for advances as well as discounts. In the case of the South African Reserve Bank, for example, the commercial banks decided at an early stage to change their overdraft rates whenever the Bank changed its discount rate, and invariably in the same direction, although not always in the same degree. Thus, when it raised its rate from 5 to 6 per cent on the 13th November, 1931, the banks raised their minimum overdraft rate from 6¾ to 7½ per cent on the 20th November, 1931, and when it lowered its rate from 6 to 5 per cent on the 7th October, 1932, they lowered their rate to 6¾ per cent on the 10th October, 1932. This relationship has been maintained throughout, although the margin between the two rates has in the meantime been increased, first to 2 per cent and then to 2½ per cent, with the acquiescence of the Reserve Bank.

In general, it may be said that, where conventional relationships between the discount rate of the central bank and the discount and advance rates of the commercial banks have been set up, the need for an active money market has not been so great or urgent for the purpose of central banking control through the discount rate. It is, however, of sufficient importance to the central bank operating in a country without an organized money market, to take the lead or at least assist in the development of such a market not only as a means of extending its control, but also as a means of mobilizing short-term loanable funds with a view to affording possessors of such funds an outlet for investment, on the one hand, and ensuring ordinarily more favourable terms for short-term borrowers, on the other.

This has been done in a number of countries with substantial success. In South Africa, for example, the Reserve Bank took the lead with the establishment of the National Finance Corporation, under an Act of Parliament in 1949, with certain special powers and privileges and with the participation of the principal banking and other financial institutions. The objects of the Corporation were to provide adequate facilities for the employment of temporarily idle funds as call money and to promote the development of a money market. This was followed, in due course, by the establishment of private discount houses and merchant banks, of which there were three and nine respectively at the end of 1972, while the National Finance Corporation continued to operate in the background.

Moreover, in Canada the central bank promoted the development of a money market by declaring itself prepared to grant temporary accommodation to money-market dealers at a rate which was related to the current rate for Treasury bills. In November, 1956, the Bank of Canada decided to fix its bank rate, for commercial banks as well as money-market dealers, at ¼ per cent above the latest weekly average tender rate for three-month Treasury bills. Since June, 1962, however, the bank rate has been dissociated from the Treasury bill rate, while the rate for the money-market dealers 'under securities purchase and resale agreements' has continued at ¼ per cent above the weekly Treasury bill rate, 'subject to the provision that the Money Market rate cannot go higher than Bank Rate'.[12]

In Australia the Reserve Bank also took the lead in the development of a money market, in 1959, by undertaking to extend credit facilities to nine authorized dealers in short-term money. For this purpose arrangements were made for a more or less regular issue of Treasury bills, as was done in Canada and South Africa, and this was likewise followed by the development of other forms of money-market activity.

With regard to those countries where the central bank has not been able either to develop a money market or to establish conventional relationships between its discount rate and other money rates, and where, moreover, the commercial banks are not accustomed to rely on the central bank for accommodation in one degree or another and are thus not obliged to follow increases in the official discount rate, the tendency has been to grant the central bank wider powers of direct control over the commercial banks, including the power to determine the actual or maximum rates of interest applicable to their various types of loans and deposits. This power, according to Kim,[13] was provided in 'many post-war central bank laws' since 'these central banks are (then) in a position to make sure that the rates of banking institutions conform to the changes of the Bank rate if such is deemed necessary'.

Decline in Significance of Discount Rate

It was mentioned earlier that the importance of the discount rate as an instrument of credit control tended, in general, to decline after World War I; that during the thirties and World War II as well as some years after the war, discount-rate policy was completely relegated to the background; and that although it staged a distinct revival since the late forties, its influence on its own was apparently subject to certain limitations. This can be attributed not only to radical changes in technical money-market conditions and in the economic structure generally, but also to the increased use of other methods of credit control because of their greater directness and adaptability in certain circumstances.

In the first place, banking methods and the stock-in-trade of money markets have undergone an important change since the twenties. With the increasing tendency towards commercial credits on open account and bank advances on current account, the bill of exchange came to be used less and less as an instrument for financing domestic trade; and owing to the increased financing of foreign trade by means of bank advances and settlements with sight drafts or telegraphic transfers, the foreign bill also came to be employed on a much smaller scale. The existence in many countries, due to amalgamations, of a small number of big banks with nation-wide branch systems, and liquid monetary conditions (whatever the cause) most of the time, further limited the volume of domestic and foreign bills offered for discount in the central money markets. Another important change was the predominance of Treasury Bills or other short-term Government securities as the stock-in-trade of money markets and as the secondary reserve of banks, owing to the tremendous increase in national debts and in the current financial requirements of Governments. These developments naturally brought about a radical change in the structure of the money market and increased the Treasury's influence over the market as compared with that of the central bank.

With regard to the London money market, the position was also changed, as Sayers[14] pointed out, by the development since the fifties of new money markets in London, in addition to the traditional discount market, namely, 'the Euro-dollar market, the local authorities market, and the inter-bank market' (i.e. between banks 'outside the clearing'), and by the competition of the clearing banks for large deposits at rates above the conventional agreed rate of interest for deposits at seven days' notice, owing to the increased competition of hire-purchase finance houses and the wider use of Treasury bills by companies with surplus funds. According to Sayers, 'this change in the London clearing banks has tended to accentuate the importance of the interest rates in the new money markets of London, and correspondingly to reduce the importance of the traditional structure of Bank Rate, Treasury bill rate and . . . overdraft and deposit rates'. In 1971 the Bank of England[15] entered into new formal arrangements with the clearing banks and the discount houses with a view, *inter alia*, to 'greater competition in the banking system as a whole', including the abandonment by the clearing banks of their collective agreements on interest rates, and 'because the authorities need to ensure that they have adequate influence over credit extended by the discount market, whether on the basis of funds borrowed from the banking system or of funds borrowed outside the banking system'.

This was followed in October, 1972, by the decision to discontinue 'the regular weekly Bank Rate announcement' and to introduce instead 'new arrangements for determining and announcing the level of its minimum rate for lending to the money market', namely, that 'the Bank's minimum lending rate will, until further notice, be the average rate for Treasury bills established at the most recent tender, plus half per cent rounded to the nearest quarter per cent above'. Although it was also mentioned that 'changes in the Bank's lending rate independent of the above formula are not excluded by the new arrangements', and although it is accepted that the Bank of England can, in one way or another, exercise an important influence on the Treasury bill rate as the basis of its minimum lending rate,* the new policy nevertheless represents a revolutionary step considering the significant role played by the Bank rate of the Bank of England in the evolution of discount-rate policy as an instrument of monetary policy and its extension over a large part of the world. It can be regarded as another factor confirming the decline in the significance of changes in the official discount rate, particularly in respect of the psychological influence associated there-with.

Furthermore, the relative position between London and other money markets has changed considerably since World War I. As Einzig[16] said, 'while before the War London's lead as a market for short-term loans was incontestable, since the War several rival centres have developed and have been making rapid progress at the expense of London'. New York developed an international money market of great importance, including an active discount market. Paris, Amsterdam and Zurich also succeeded in organizing discount markets, although restricted in their scope and turnover by various factors; and Stockholm, Brussels, Rome and Tokyo have likewise been developing their money-market organization. The London market, which formerly exercised a predominant and centralized influence over monetary conditions in the world, thus had to contend with the increasing competition of other money markets; and as a result of this decentralization there was at times serious confusion and overlapping in international financial affairs.

* At the end of 1972, for example, this rate stood as high as 9 per cent, and after being reduced in stages to 7½ per cent, it was raised again to 9 per cent in July, 1973, and further to 11½ per cent before the end of the month.

Moreover, political, monetary and economic complications in various countries, and frequently also exchange control, dislocated the international flow of capital and intermittent currency uncertainties caused the so-called 'hot money' to flee back and forth in search of refuge and safety. This was accompanied by increased rigidity in the structure and functioning of the capital market in most countries.

The field for discount-rate policy was further narrowed as a result of increased rigidity in the economic structure, in general. As stated previously, the efficient working of a discount-rate policy required, *inter alia*, a substantial measure of flexibility in the economic structure in order that prices, wages, production and trade might respond to changes in money and credit conditions. Since World War I, however, the trend has been definitely in the direction of economic rigidity, due mainly to the extension of Government activities and economic controls and the increased organization and bargaining power of labour. In this connection, Wagemann,[17] for example, had already in 1937 found it necessary to stress that 'the more an economy is regulated in prices, wages, transportation charges, and the more the Government extends its influence over business, the more the influence of interest declines'; and that 'the influence of interest also declines as the tax burden increases'. In the meantime the effects not only of a higher level of taxation on net interest earnings or payments but also of persistent inflation have tended further to limit the influence of interest rates on the economy as a whole, and on the monetary situation in particular.

The development of other methods of credit control (such as open-market operations, variable reserve requirements and credit ceilings or quotas), which were regarded as more direct in their incidence or more adaptable in their application in certain circumstances, naturally caused a further contraction of the influence of the discount rate. These methods will be discussed in the following chapters.

Conclusion

While it must be admitted that, under modern conditions of economic rigidity and complexity accompanied by high taxation and persistent inflation, the role of interest rates in the economy has declined and, accordingly, that there is less scope for an independent discount-rate policy than was originally the case, recent experience has shown that the discount rate of the central bank still has a necessary and important function to perform in conjunction with other measures of control. In short, changes in the official discount rate can contribute towards the maintenance or restoration of economic stability to the extent that it can bring about or facilitate corresponding changes in interest rates in general, either directly or indirectly, and that the changes in interest rates can operate to correct or counter wrong trends in the economy.

In the first place, changes in money rates tend to affect both the demand for and the supply of money and short-term credit in the desired direction. Increases in money rates, for example, have a deterring influence on the demand for credit and, at the same time, an inducement towards caution and restraint on the part of the banks and other financial institutions, and towards saving on the part of the public out of current income as well as the conversion of cash assets into time deposits and fixed-interest securities. It is admitted that increases in money rates do not necessarily induce increased saving in the *whole* of the community and also that they do not necessarily affect *all* borrowers, and particularly not those borrowers who expect to continue to make large profits and to whom, moreover, interest charges are not an important factor in their total costs. Some of these borrowers, however, are liable to be affected psychologically by an increase in the official rate, in the sense that such a step indicates the opinion of the monetary authorities on the state and probable trend of financial and economic conditions generally, and that it may be followed by further increases and also by other restrictive measures. The essential fact is that to whatever extent increases in money rates do deter certain borrowers for the time being and make certain people more conscious of the monetary advantage of current saving, the pressure of demand for goods and services will be relieved at a time when circumstances call for it. On the other hand, reductions in money rates tend to have the opposite effect, namely, to encourage the demand for goods and services and the expansion of economic activity generally.

Furthermore, substantial changes in money rates also tend to have a corresponding effect on long-term interest rates, although not usually at the same time or in the same degree. At times, they have been found to rise or fall together, being apparently affected by the same cause. In general, however, there is a time lag, the short-term rates being usually more sensitive and responsive than the long-term rates and thus more likely to change first. Their tendency to have automatic reciprocal reactions on one another arises from the fact that, as Hawtrey[18] said, 'long-term and short-term loans sometimes present themselves as alternatives both to borrowers and to lenders', and that 'the two rates are in competition with one another at various points'. Sayers[19] also held that 'any persistent and appreciable change in short-term rates is always associated with some change in long-term rates; and banking policy is thereby enabled to influence those business decisions which turn on the level of long-term interest rates, as well as on those rarer cases in which short rates are of direct importance'.

To the extent, therefore, that the discount rate of the central bank in any country can influence not only short but also long-term interest rates, it should have some effect, in the desired direction, on the volume of investment in respect of both equities and long-term credit.

In this connection Keynes had, in his *Treatise on Money** in 1930, pointed out that the traditional theories of Bank rate had concentrated largely on the influence of Bank rate 'as a means of regulating the quantity of bank-money' and 'as a means of protecting a country's gold reserves by regulating the rate of foreign lending', and had not clearly or adequately taken into account the influence of Bank rate on 'the rate of investment relatively to saving' and the repercussions of changes in the relation between saving and investment on prices, production, employment and wages. Subsequently, however, presumably under the influence of the relative economic stagnation which prevailed in many countries during the thirties, Keynes came to the conclusion that changes in interest rates by themselves were no longer capable of contributing materially towards the maintenance of equilibrium between saving and investment as a necessary condition of general economic equilibrium, and that, apart from

* Vol. 1, p. 185.

regulation of the quantity of money through open-market operations, this objective should be pursued through the medium of State organization of investment[20] or, failing this, compensatory planning of public works,[21] rather than through that of Bank-rate policy.

The former emphasis on control of short-term rates was attributed by Williams[22] to the fact that, in those days, 'short-term assets played the predominant role in banking changes and it was through them that adjustments were made to changes in the reserve position of the banks', the result of which was 'a high degree of sensitivity in short-term open market rates'. In recent times, however, 'as bank investments have increased, long-term interest rates have shown increased sensitivity to changes in bank reserves, and the emphasis in monetary theory has shifted to the need for controlling the long-term rates, as more effective for the control of investment, income, and employment than control merely of the short-term rates'. In short, reliance could no longer be placed merely on direct control of short-term rates and on such influence as changes in these rates might have on long-term rates and the volume of investment. Other methods of control were also required which had direct reactions on long-term rates and investment, and which were directly related to the general level of money incomes rather than to the quantity of money. For these reasons, attention was directed to open-market transactions in long-term securities as well as fiscal policy and investment control.

As regards the question whether or to what extent bank credit could be employed to play the part of capital in order to reduce long-term interest rates, it must be borne in mind that, in the long run, the function of capital could and should be performed only by savings of one kind or another, and that the supply of capital relative to demand must, therefore, be allowed to exert its influence on the level of interest rates. In short, interest on capital could not, in the long run, be determined by the supply of money, although it could be influenced temporarily by changes in such supply in order to offset disturbing factors.

Thus, within limits both as to time and degree, cheap money might be artificially maintained with the aid of central bank credit and with beneficial results to business activity as well as to State finance, for example, as part of a policy designed in times of deflation and depression to promote reflation and recovery. But the experience of many countries during the past forty years has shown the limitations and dangers of a cheap-money policy, either because at times it failed to encourage enterprise owing to distrust, fear and uncertainty regarding the future course of prices, costs and exchange rates, or to an increased desire for liquidity on the part of entrepreneurs, investors and speculators, or because at other times when it did serve to promote enterprise, it led in due course to abuse of credit, unsound investment, over-speculation, disequilibrium in the balance of payments and depreciation of currency.

In conclusion, although there has been a tendency, from time to time, to place greater emphasis on the availability than on the cost of credit as an instrument of monetary policy, the two are, in fact, complementary in that they tend to affect and reinforce one another in the desired direction. Moreover, it is surely logical and more intelligible to the banking and business community and the general public that, if circumstances in their country call for credit to be made scarcer or easier, by official intervention, it should also be made dearer or cheaper respectively, whether in anticipation of, or in response to, the natural effect of demand and supply.

References

1 King, W. T. C. *History of the London Discount Market.* Routledge, 1936. pp. 109–12.
2 *Ibid.* p. 295.
3 Palgrave, R. H. I. *Bank Rate and the Money Market.* Murray, N.Y., 1903. p. 151; Hawtrey, R. G. *A Century of Bank Rate*, 2 ed. Cass, 1962. App. I and IV.
4 Conant, C. A. *History of Modern Banks of Issue*, 5 ed. Putnam, 1927. p. 65.
5 Loubet, P. *La Banque de France et l'Escompte.* App. E. (Quoted by Andréadès, A. M. *History of the Bank of England.* King, 1924.)
6 De Jong, A. M., in *Foreign Banking Systems.* Ed. Willis & Beckhart. Henry Holt, 1929. p. 744.

7 Burgess, W. R. *Reserve Banks and the Money Market*, Rev. ed. Harper, 1936. pp. 225–7.
8 Beckhart, B. H. *Discount Policy of the Federal Reserve System*. Holt, 1924. p. 510.
9 Gregory, T. E. *Gold, Unemployment and Capitalism*. King, 1933. pp. 135 and 137.
10 Gibson, A. H., in *London Bankers' Magazine*. April, 1937.
11 Copland, D. B., in *Economic Journal*. December, 1937.
12 *International Financial Statistics*. I.M.F., September, 1971. p. 77.
13 Kim, B. K. *Central Banking Experiment in a Developing Economy*. Korean Research Centre, 1965. p. 133.
14 Sayers, R. S. *Modern Banking*, 7 ed. Oxford U.P., 1967. pp. 324–9.
15 *Bank of England Quarterly Bulletin*. September, 1971. pp. 309 and 314.
16 Einzig, P., in *Investors' Chronicle* (London). 23rd May, 1931.
17 Wagemann, E. *Wirthschaftspolitische Strategie*. Hanseatische Verlagsanstalt, 1937. pp. 313–15.
18 Hawtrey, R. G. *A Century of Bank Rate*. Cass, 1938. pp. 146 and 206.
19 Sayers, *op. cit.* p. 201.
20 Keynes, J. M. *General Theory of Employment, Interest and Money*. Harcourt, Brace, 1936. p. 164.
21 —— *The Times*, London. January, 1937.
22 Williams, J. H. 'The Implications of Fiscal Policy for Monetary Policy and the Banking System'. *American Economic Review*, December, 1941. pp. 2–4. (Reprint from *Proceedings of the American Economic Association.*)

CHAPTER TEN

Open-Market Operations

Evolution of Open-Market Operations

Prior to 1914 the Bank of England had, as stated previously, relied upon Bank rate as the primary instrument of credit control. At various times, however, when, owing to large foreign balances, or for other reasons, the London money market was in a highly liquid state, the Bank experienced great difficulty in making its rate effective and felt the need for some method which would enable it to reduce the liquidity of the market whenever it desired to raise money rates generally.

The method which was evolved in earlier days was that of withdrawing funds from the market principally by means of what were known as 'selling Consols spot and buying for the account'* and 'borrowing in the market'. By the former was meant that the Bank sold Consols (Consolidated Government stock) for cash and simultaneously repurchased them for the 'account', i.e. the date for the monthly settlement on the Stock Exchange; and thus, to the extent that Consols were sold spot and repurchased, funds were withdrawn from the market for the unexpired period of the monthly account. Borrowing in the market, on the other hand, meant that the Bank borrowed from

* According to King, this method was first adopted during the thirties of the nineteenth century. It was also frequently referred to as 'borrowing on Consols'. (*History of the London Discount Market*, p. 116.)

discount houses and bill-brokers against the pledge of Government securities. Whichever method was adopted, the net result was the same, namely, that the total volume of funds in the market was reduced and that the market rate tended to rise much or little depending upon the extent of the Bank's operations.

According to Sayers,[1] the Bank used the method of selling Consols spot and buying them back for time more extensively than that of borrowing in the market up to the end of the nineteenth century, but after that the position was reversed. While these two methods were the principal devices employed by the Bank for the purpose of withdrawing funds from the market, other methods were also used on various occasions, such as the outright sale of Government securities, borrowing from the commercial banks, and borrowing from special depositors (Governments of Japan, India and Argentina).

After discussing the employment of all these methods during the period from 1890 to 1914, Sayers[2] came to the conclusion that 'the Bank had, in an extremely hesitating and not very consistent manner, solved its problem of controlling market rate by adopting a number of devices for reducing the supply of money in the market', but that 'the solution of this problem was piecemeal rather than systematic, and in many ways it was unsatisfactory', and that 'the diversity of methods employed by the Bank alone suggests that it was not very happy about any of them'.

The only other central bank which undertook some form of open-market operations prior to 1914 was the Reichsbank, which, in addition to buying and selling foreign bills, used to offer Treasury bills for sale in the open market at times with a view to absorbing surplus cash and preventing a too rapid fall in the market rate.[3]

When the Federal Reserve System was established in 1913, it was also intended that the Federal Reserve Banks should use open-market operations as a supplement to discount-rate policy; and they were accordingly authorized to buy and sell, in the open market, bonds and notes of the United States Government, and also bills, notes, revenue bonds and warrants with an unexpired currency of not more than six months, issued in anticipation of the collection of taxes or of the receipt of assured revenues by any

State, county, district, political sub-division, or municipality in the United States.

During World War I and for some time thereafter, the open-market operations of the Bank of England, the Reichsbank and the Federal Reserve System were, as in the case of their discount-rate policy, governed mainly by the requirements of war finance or post-war readjustment; i.e. apart from the creation of central bank credit through collateral loans against Government securities, they increased their own holdings of Government stocks or Treasury bills.

In 1920 the Bank of England and the Federal Reserve Banks again began to employ open-market operations merely as a supplementary instrument with the object of making their discount rates effective. In due course, however, they came to adopt such operations at times as the principal method of credit control, and sometimes as an independent instrument, i.e. without any change in their discount rates; and this trend was, in general, also followed by the other central banks which began to participate in open-market operations.

The increased use and importance of open-market operations can be attributed, on the one hand, to the decline in the influence of discount-rate policy owing to the changes and limitations discussed in the previous chapter, and the consequent need for another and more direct method of credit control, and, on the other hand, to the wider scope and need for open-market operations as a result of the considerably increased volume and variety of Government and other gilt-edged securities which were created in many countries, and in times of peace as well as war.

Meaning of Open-Market Operations

In the wider sense, open-market operations may be held to cover the purchase or sale by the central bank in the market of any kind of paper in which it deals, whether Government securities or other securities, or bankers' acceptances or foreign bills.

In Great Britain, United States and several other countries, however, the term 'open-market operations' came to be applied only to the purchase or sale of Government securities, both long and short term, and also only to the outright purchase or sale thereof. The principal reasons for this narrower interpretation would appear to be that the markets for Government bonds and Treasury bills in these countries were sufficiently broad and active for all the purposes of open-market policy; that the central bank rather than the market took the initiative in outright purchases or sales of Government securities; and that such operations, therefore, reflected the deliberate credit policy of the central bank (whether such policy was followed by the central bank in subservience to the requirements and objectives of the State or solely in accordance with its own aims and objectives). On the other hand, in the case of purchases of Government securities under 'sales contracts' or 'repurchase agreements', or of bankers' acceptances, the initiative was generally taken by the market. The readiness of the Federal Reserve Banks, for example, to buy such securities and acceptances at all times at or close to market rates was based on their desire to develop and maintain an active money market.

In countries, however, where the central bank also deals outright in Government-guaranteed securities or other securities, because of an inadequate supply of Government securities or for other reasons, such transactions should appropriately be included under 'open-market operations', since their effects on the monetary situation are the same as in the case of operations in Government securities. This also applies to purchases or sales of foreign exchange by the central bank, but as other aspects of monetary policy are involved in such transactions, they are discussed elsewhere, namely, Chapters 5 and 13.

Theory of Open-Market Operations

Briefly stated, the theory of open-market operations, as a special form of creation or cancellation of central bank credit, is that purchases or sales of securities by the central bank tend directly and immediately to increase or decrease the money supply and the cash reserves of the commercial banks; that an increase or decrease in the supply of bank cash and, therefore, in the credit-creating capacity of the commercial banks, tends still further to increase or decrease the quantity of money; and that changes in the quantity of money tend not only in themselves to bring about the desired adjustments in the domestic levels of prices, costs, production and trade, but also through their effect on changes in money rates and credit conditions which, in turn, tend to operate in the direction of the desired adjustments.

Thus, like discount-rate policy, open-market operations aim at the desired expansion or contraction of money and credit and of general economic activity. But while the former depends only on its indirect influence on money and credit through primary changes in money rates and secondary repercussions on long-term interest rates or yields, open-market operations are designed to have a direct and immediate effect on the volume of money and credit as well as on interest rates generally to the extent that operations are conducted in both short- and long-term securities. Open-market operations, therefore, potentially represent a more direct as well as a more comprehensive instrument of credit control.

With regard to the technique of open-market operations, the initial impact of such operations is on the deposits of the commercial banks with the central bank as well as on the customers' deposits with the commercial banks. By selling securities, for example, the central bank would reduce, other things being equal, the bankers' deposits by an equivalent amount, as the buyers of these securities would usually* be either commercial banks or customers of commercial banks, and as payments for such purchases would be effected through debits to the bankers' accounts with the central bank; and by selling securities the central bank would also reduce, other things being equal, the amount of customers' deposits with the commercial banks to the extent that such customers acquired the securities sold by the central bank. Conversely, when the central bank bought securities, the result would be reflected in credits to the bankers'

* Exceptions arise when customers of the central bank other than the commercial banks buy some of these securities and pay for them out of their deposits with the central bank. This would reduce the other deposits of the central bank and make the reduction in bankers' deposits less than what it would otherwise have been.

accounts and, therefore, in an increase in the commercial banks' cash reserves, and also in an increase in the customers' deposits with the commercial banks.

In short, the theory of open-market operations was based on the assumptions, firstly, that the quantity of money as well as the cash reserves of the commercial banks would be increased or decreased in accordance with the extent or aim of the central bank's open-market operations; secondly, that the commercial banks would seek to increase or decrease their discounts, loans and investments in accordance with the increase or decrease in their cash reserves; and thirdly, that the scope or demand for bank credit would increase or decrease in accordance with the increase or decrease in the potential availability of credit and the lowering or raising of money rates.

Scope of Open-Market Operations

While it must be admitted that normally there are at least strong tendencies in the direction of the foregoing assumptions, important qualifications have to be made in respect of deviations from the normal. In the first place, the quantity of money and the commercial banks' cash reserves do not always increase or decrease even approximately in proportion to the purchase or sale of securities by the central bank, as one or more counter-forces might be operating simultaneously. For example, the outflow of capital or a net unfavourable balance of payments for any other reason, or withdrawal of notes for increased currency requirements or for hoarding purposes, or a net transfer of Government funds to the central bank, might neutralize partly or wholly the effect on the supply of money and bank cash of a purchase of securities by the central bank or might accentuate the effect of a sale of securities; and a net favourable balance of payments or the return of notes from circulation or from hoards might offset partly or wholly a sale of securities by the central bank or might accentuate the effect of a purchase of securities.

Secondly, commercial banks do not always increase or decrease their discounts, loans and investments in proportion to the increase or decrease in their cash reserves. In other words, changes in the credit base and, therefore, in the volume of credit that could be created would not always bring about corresponding or proportionate changes in the volume of credit that was actually created. There are various circumstances of a monetary, economic or political nature which might deter commercial banks from employing increased cash reserves fully if at all, or from contracting credit when their reserves were reduced. In some countries, such as Great Britain, France, Netherlands and Canada, the banks traditionally tend to aim at maintaining approximately a constant cash ratio in respect of their demand or total deposit liabilities, i.e. apart from any variable cash reserve requirements* which might be imposed on them at times by the central bank, but in many countries, including the United States, the banks usually tend first to reduce or repay their indebtedness, if any, to the central bank in case of an increase in their cash reserves. There are also certain technical factors which must be taken into account by all commercial banks. For example, while under normal conditions and with a customary cash ratio of, say, 10 per cent, one additional unit of bank cash could serve as a basis for ten units of bank credit, one unit of cash could, in the event of an increased demand for foreign exchange or larger withdrawals of note and metallic currency resulting from the expansion of bank credit, command only one unit of foreign exchange or local currency. Moreover, unless the banking system as a whole adopted a policy of credit expansion, the expanding banks would tend to lose part of their cash to the non-expanding banks through the clearing settlements between the banks and might thus be compelled to contract again.

Thirdly, it is not just a case of commercial banks refraining at times from the full employment of their increased cash reserves, but also one of a lack of willing or deserving borrowers. While an increase in the credit base would tend to lower money rates, the scope or demand for credit would not always increase in accordance with the reduction in money rates. In times of economic or political uncertainty, entrepreneurs might not be prepared to undertake great risks† even if their bankers offered them

* See Chapter 11.

† As Leonard Ayres said, 'that willingness to take risks (i.e. present risks in the hope of making future gains) can be legislated out of being, but it

increased accommodation at moderate rates. Thus, owing to the risks involved, there might be either a lack of borrowers as such or a lack of borrowers who were credit-worthy applicants and required credit for purposes which were acceptable to banks under the prevailing circumstances. Conversely, when money rates rose owing to a decrease in the credit base, the increase would not always result in a reduced demand for bank accommodation or in reduced opportunities for the employment of bank credit; or if such a reduction did take place it would not always be in accordance with the rise in money rates. The prospects of business and speculation might appear sufficiently attractive for entrepreneurs, investors and speculators to induce them to make still greater use of credit notwithstanding the higher rates.

It is clear, therefore, that the scope of open-market operations by the central bank might be limited at times by the simultaneous operation of various counterforces, in respect of not only the supply of money and bank credit but also the demand therefor. The question is whether and to what extent the central bank could offset the effects of the counterforces concerned at any time by suitably adjusting its open-market operations, i.e. by purchasing or selling securities in a greater or lesser measure than would otherwise have been considered necessary. The primary problem, of course, would be that of gauging accurately the extent and duration of all the actual or potential disturbing factors, and this in turn would depend not only on the experience and skill of the central bank in this field, but also on the degree of complexity of the prevailing economic conditions and trends. It is evident that various central banks have at times succeeded in neutralizing the effects of disturbing factors, to a large extent at any rate, but it is also obvious that it would be virtually impossible to do so effectively at all times and for all purposes. Thus, while there is no doubt that central banks should aim at offsetting, as far as possible, the impact on the desired money supply of whatever counterforces might be

---

cannot be legislated into being', and 'it can be induced, and encouraged, and facilitated, but it cannot be ordered or coerced into existence', for the reason that 'it must be the product of conditions and circumstances that are both favorable to business enterprise, and reliably stabilized'. (*American Bankers' Association Journal*, May, 1938.)

operating at any time, it should be borne in mind, as pointed out in Chapter 8, that in attempting to do the impossible in difficult circumstances they might set in motion other forces which might do more harm than good.

The scope of open-market operations naturally depends also on the breadth and activity of the markets in both short and long-term Government securities, if not also certain other securities; the relative importance of these markets in the financial structure as a whole; and the volume of the requisite securities at the disposal of the central bank for market dealings. Until recent times the Bank of England and the Federal Reserve Banks of the United States were the only central banks which had all these facilities and which could, therefore, make the most extensive and regular use of open-market operations. A number of other central banks have in the meantime succeeded in developing reasonably active markets in Government securities and acquiring sufficient securities for exercising a substantial influence on these markets and the monetary situation, in general. Furthermore, some of the central banks which had at times to cope with excessive liquidity, due, for example, to a favourable balance of payments position, but did not possess the requisite securities for withdrawing funds from the market when they desired to contract credit, even resorted to acquiring the power to issue their own securities or financing the repatriation of foreign debts of their Governments for conversion into local securities or having the whole or part of their loans to the Government converted into marketable securities.

Open-Market Operations in Great Britain

As mentioned earlier, the Bank of England at first employed open-market operations as a supplementary instrument with the object of making Bank rate effective, i.e. at times when the Bank deemed it necessary to bring market rates closer to Bank rate or to adjust market conditions to a change which it was about to make in Bank rate. For example, in the last week of January, 1931, after sterling had been weak in terms of various currencies for months in succession and the Bank's gold reserve had dropped to almost £140,000,000, and after market rates had been below the Bank rate of 3 per cent by at least 1 per cent for many months, the Bank suddenly intervened in the market with a policy designed to bring market rates more into touch with the existing Bank rate. It not only sold Government securities with a view to withdrawing loanable funds from the market, but it also sold Treasury bills in the market at rates considerably in advance of market rates for fine commercial bills. These operations resulted in the immediate adjustment of market rates to the higher level dictated by the Bank's intervention. The rise in money rates proved effective so far as the foreign exchanges were concerned, and the rates on New York and Paris moved away from their respective gold-export points.[4]

Between 1932 and 1951, however, the main purpose of the Bank's open-market operations was, as explained in Chapters 8 and 9, to maintain cheap money, firstly as part of an expansionist and reflationary policy in view of the Great Depression of the early thirties and its aftermath of economic stagnation, and secondly, to assist in the financing of war expenditure and post-war reconstruction. The use of Bank rate as a positive instrument of credit control was resumed towards the end of 1951, but although relatively frequent and sometimes drastic changes in Bank rate have been made since that time, the general tendency would appear to have been to regard open-market operations not only as a means of helping to make Bank rate effective whenever considered necessary, but also as the principal and consistent method of control because of their direct expansionist or contractionist influence on the supply of money and bank cash. In other words, changes in Bank rate were apparently found necessary to make open-market operations more effective, instead of the reverse as had originally been the case.

Another objective of the Bank's open-market policy was to avoid disturbances in the money market as a result of movements of Government funds or seasonal movements generally. In this connection, a more systematic and consistent technique was evolved as compared with the hesitating and half-hearted manner in which such operations were undertaken prior to 1914. The Bank, for example, almost regularly acquired Government securities (stock or Treasury bills, mostly the latter) during

December in order to offset the heavy withdrawals of currency for the Christmas holiday and shopping disbursements, and disposed of them in January with the return of notes from circulation. It also conducted such 'stabilizing' operations in connection with the movement of Government funds, acquiring securities during periods of heavy tax payments or at other times when funds flowed into the Government accounts at the Bank and disposing of them when heavy disbursements were made by the Government for interest payments or for other purposes. The object of these purchases and sales* was, of course, to prevent, as far as possible, the market and its rates being disturbed by temporary withdrawals and accruals of funds on account of the financial operations of the Government. Moreover, the Bank adopted a similar practice in respect of the 'ironing out' of the seasonal autumnal drain. On some occasions, however, it refrained from neutralizing a particular seasonal movement apparently because of its desire to see a corresponding change in market rates.

The policy of neutralizing disturbing movements was also applied to offsetting the inflow and outflow of gold and foreign exchange resulting from what appeared to be temporary or artificial trends in the balance of payments, particularly in connection with the large-scale movements of fugitive capital. Prior to 1932, the Bank did this on its own account as part of its policy of insulating the internal credit structure from external forces as far as possible and avoiding changes in market rates and in Bank rate which were not essential for purposes of control and regulation. It bought securities when gold flowed out of the country and sold them when gold flowed in again. When, however, in its opinion the prevailing conditions demanded that the outflow or inflow of gold should have its particular effect on the credit base either wholly or partly, it did not offset the particular

* These transactions did not necessarily represent actual purchases or sales in the market, but frequently consisted, on the one hand, of Treasury bills being acquired by the Bank directly from the Treasury by tender or otherwise, and, on the other hand, of Treasury bills maturing which were not renewed by the Bank. This is generally acknowledged as one of the great advantages of Treasury bills in connection with central banking operations, of which open-market operations in the literal sense constitute only one phase.

movement of gold or did so only partly according to circumstances. After the Exchange Equalization Account was brought into being in 1932, the Bank performed these operations mainly on behalf of the Account, which was managed by the Bank for account and subject to the control of the Treasury. The new procedure therefore was that, through the Exchange Equalization Account, the effects of gold and capital movements on the credit situation were to be offset, as a general rule, by the sale of an equivalent amount of Treasury bills when gold or exchange was purchased by the Account, and by the purchase or redemption of bills in the case of an outflow of gold or sale of exchange.*

Another phase of open-market operations was that of supporting Government credit in connection with the issue of new loans or the conversion of old loans, particularly the raising of the large loans needed during the two world wars and their subsequent conversion or consolidation which could not have been concluded successfully at moderate rates without the active assistance and co-operation of the Bank, including the provision of the requisite increase in the credit base and the money supply.

The net result of all the Bank's operations in Government securities was that its total holdings (including some securities guaranteed by the Government) increased from about £370 million at the end of 1932 to about £4,100 million at the end of 1970, i.e. an increase of £3,700 million which was reflected in an increase of about £3,200 million in the Bank's note issue and about £600 million in its deposits. Thus, the bulk of the Bank's acquisition of Government securities† was associated with the increase in its note circulation, but the concomitant increase in its deposits was nevertheless of great significance, since such deposits consisted mainly of bankers' deposits.

* The functions of the Exchange Equalization Account will be further discussed under 'Exchange Control' in Chapter 13.

† In this connection it should be mentioned that a part of the increase in the Bank's holdings of Government securities arose from the fact that, during 1939, the whole of the Bank's existing gold reserve of £327 million was transferred to the Exchange Equalization Account, in exchange for Government securities which took the place of the gold as cover for that amount of the note issue.

It must, however, be emphasized that changes in the Bank's holdings of Government securities do not always represent the results only of open-market operations, but are frequently connected with changes resulting from other operations of the Bank, such as those in respect of ways and means advances to the Government, Treasury bills acquired directly from the Government or from other central banks, Treasury bills maturing without being renewed, transfer of securities to other central banks and extra-budgetary funds, transactions with the Exchange Equalization Account, etc. In short, the Bank's open-market operations and its other transactions are dovetailed and constitute variable complements in its overall credit policy, and the extent of the open-market operations, therefore, depends upon the effects of the Bank's other transactions which in turn depend upon a variety of circumstances.

It may be added that, in recent years, the Bank's open-market operations have apparently not proved to be sufficiently effective, even in conjunction with substantial changes in Bank rate, since the Bank has found it necessary to make increased use of other methods of credit control, such as variable reserve requirements and credit ceilings which will be discussed in the following two chapters.

Open-Market Operations in the United States

The open-market policy of the Federal Reserve System, on the whole, aimed at the same objectives as in the case of the Bank of England, but with important differences in degree or emphasis and in the scale of operations.

Open-market operations were on various occasions undertaken for the purpose of making the discount rates of the Federal Reserve Banks effective or preparing the ground for changes in their rates. This was apparently their primary function during the twenties when an active discount-rate policy was followed. During the thirties and forties, however, open-market operations were designed to maintain cheap money and the official discount rate was kept at a very low and almost constant level. Although substantial changes in the discount rates of the Federal Reserve

Banks, as in the case of many other central banks, were resumed during the fifties, their open-market operations remained the principal instrument of monetary policy and served various purposes.

In the first place, such operations were frequently carried out, as in Great Britain, with the object of supporting Government credit in connection with new issues or conversions, and generally maintaining orderly conditions in the market for government securities. In the latter connection, for example, attention was directed by the Board of Governors, in their annual report for 1939, to the direct influence of open-market operations on conditions in the capital market. Referring to the decline in the prices of United States Government and high-grade corporate bonds on the outbreak of war in Europe, the report stated that, 'in undertaking large-scale open-market operations in September, 1939, the System was guided principally by the following considerations: (1) By helping to maintain orderly conditions in the market for United States Government securities the System can exert a steadying influence on the entire capital market, which is an essential part of the country's economic machinery, and disorganization in which would be a serious obstacle to the progress of economic recovery ... (2) The system also has a measure of responsibility for safeguarding the large United States Government portfolio of the member banks from unnecessarily wide and violent fluctuations in price'. In varying degrees, depending upon the prevailing circumstances, both these factors continued to influence the open-market operations of the Federal Reserve System.

Moreover, it became a regular part of open-market policy to avoid disturbances in money-market conditions as a result of movements of Government funds or seasonal movements. In September, 1937, for example, the Federal Open Market Committee* issued a statement that 'in view of the expected seasonal demands on the banks for currency and credit during the coming weeks the Committee authorized its Executive Committee to purchase in the open market from time to time sufficient amounts

* Consisting of the Board of Governors of the Federal Reserve System and five representatives of the Federal Reserve Banks in order to coordinate the open-market operations of the twelve Federal Reserve Banks.

of short-term United States Government obligations to provide funds to meet seasonal withdrawals of currency from the banks and other seasonal requirements', and that 'reduction of the additional holdings in the open market portfolio is contemplated when the seasonal influences are reversed or other circumstances make their retention unnecessary'.

With regard to gold movements, purchases or sales of securities were made at times to offset the effects of an outflow or inflow of gold, but these transactions did not represent a regular phase of open-market policy and were usually undertaken only in the case of exceptional movements of gold. Thus, a somewhat similar procedure as in the case of the British Exchange Equalization Account was adopted in December, 1936, for the purpose of insulating the internal credit structure from gold movements, through the medium of the Stabilization Fund and the Inactive Gold Account operated by the Federal Treasury, which bought all the imported or locally produced gold with the proceeds of Treasury bills and sterilized it for all practical purposes. In September, 1937, however, $300,000,000 gold was transferred from the Inactive Gold Account to the Federal Reserve System in the shape of an equivalent amount of gold certificates which were issued to the Federal Reserve Banks, while the latter credited the Treasury accounts with the proceeds thereof; in February, 1938, it was announced that gold acquired by the Treasury would be included in the Inactive Gold Account only to the extent that such acquisitions in any one quarter exceeded $100,000,000; and in April, 1938, it was decided, for reasons of monetary policy associated with the trade recession, to abolish the Inactive Gold Account and desterilize all the gold still held by that Account.

The principal phase of open-market policy in the United States, either in conjunction with discount-rate policy or independently thereof, was that of counteracting extreme trends in the business situation by buying securities during periods of declining activity and selling securities during periods of expanding activity. As far back as 1923, the following principle was adopted by the Federal Reserve Board, namely, 'that the time, manner, character, and volume of open-market investments purchased by Federal Reserve Banks, be governed with primary regard to the accommodation of commerce and business and to the effect of such purchases or sales on the general credit situation'.[5]

Burgess[6] emphasized in 1936 that 'open market operations found their major use as one of the most effective instruments of the Reserve System in its effort towards creating monetary conditions which would favour economic stability', and that 'Federal Reserve policy had been a compensating influence directed towards greater business stability', but that 'the effectiveness of operations clearly depended on general economic conditions'.

The following brief survey of the Federal Reserve Banks' open-market operations between 1930 and 1970 serves as an indication of the enormous extent as well as the varying objectives of such operations.

Firstly, with a view to counteracting the deflation and depression which set in after the 'Wall Street Crash', the Federal Reserve Banks increased their holdings of Government securities from $523 million to $848 million between the end of 1929 and that of 1931; but as this did not have much effect, they decided in 1932, like the Bank of England, to follow in more determined manner a policy of cheap money and reflation and increased their holdings to $2,439 million by the end of 1933. As late as September, 1937, the Board of Governors[7] still referred to the purpose of the open-market operations as being 'to maintain at member banks an aggregate volume of excess reserves adequate for the continuation of the System's policy of monetary ease for the furtherance of economic recovery', and to 'the System's policy of maintaining a condition of monetary ease' as 'a policy that has been actively pursued since the early months of 1932'.

During the years 1939–40, however, their holdings of Government securities were reduced by $380 million to $2,184 million as one of the means of counteracting the large increase in the member banks' cash reserves consequent upon the inflow of capital and gold. With the entry of the United States into the war at the end of 1941, the open-market policy was again reversed, and by the end of 1942 the Federal Reserve System held almost $6,000 million in Government securities, which were still further increased to $11,600 million at the end of 1943 and $24,000 million at the end of 1945. The objective of these operations was, of course, as in the case of the Bank of England and various other central banks, to facilitate the financing of the war effort and the maintenance of cheap money.

After the war there was at first a declining tendency in the System's total holdings of Government securities until a level of $18,300 million was reached in June, 1950. But whereas its holding of Treasury Bills, certificates and notes was reduced from $23,300 million at the end of 1945 to about $12,700 million in June, 1950, due mainly to the substantial net budget surplus during this period, its bond portfolio increased from $947 million to $5,600 million respectively. This increase is to be attributed to the fact that the System considered itself obliged, as an essential part of the Government's monetary and debt-management policies, to continue to support long-term Government bonds at relatively low yields. After the outbreak of the Korean war in the middle of 1950, however, there was again a large increase in the System's total holdings, namely, to $24,700 million at the end of 1952.

This was followed by an almost continuous annual increase to over $62,000 million at the end of 1970, i.e. an increase of over $37,000 million or 150 per cent in 18 years. There were the usual alternating phases of restrictive and expansionary monetary policies during this period, depending upon the prevailing economic conditions and trends and the objectives of official economic policy, but in general the System's open-market operations would appear to have shown a distinct bias towards monetary expansion, with a view to maintaining a minimum average rate of economic growth and avoiding severe unemployment, even at the cost of persistent disequilibrium in the country's balance of payments.

It may be added that, although the most extensive use was made of open-market operations in the execution of the monetary policy of the Federal Reserve System, it was found necessary, as in the case of the Bank of England, to employ other instruments of credit control, not only to reinforce a policy of monetary contraction but also to support one of monetary expansion. With regard to the latter, for example, the Board of Governors reported that 'during 1970, as usual, the Federal Reserve relied mainly on open market operations in encouraging growth in the monetary aggregates and easier credit market conditions. But it also used other monetary policy instruments as the stance of policy was adapted during the year to emerging sectoral, liquidity, and balance of payments problems'.[8]

Open-Market Operations in Other Countries

It is only in recent times that the question of open-market operations by central banks attained some measure of prominence in countries outside of Great Britain and the United States.

As stated previously, the Reichsbank had also, prior to 1914, undertaken open-market operations at times with a view to absorbing surplus cash and preventing a too rapid fall in the market rate. With its reorganization in 1924, however, the Reichsbank was prohibited from conducting open-market operations, except in trade bills and foreign exchange; and it was not till 1933 that it was again specifically given the power to do so. Sarow,[9] for example, bewailed the circumstance that 'the Reichsbank found it a severe handicap that in the credit crisis of 1931 open-market operations were still forbidden'.*

Under the amendments of 1933, the Reichsbank obtained the right to buy and sell certain specified securities,† 'with a view to regulating the money market', and to include such securities as cover for the Bank's note issue; and, in the annual report of the Reichsbank for that year, it was stated that those amendments were intended to give the Bank 'an increased freedom of movement with regard to the requirements of modern times, *inter alia* by means of the open-market policy'. Such open-market operations were promptly undertaken for the purpose of exercising general control over the money and capital markets, and supporting the credit of the State in connection with the conversions and

* Mildred Northrop, after referring to the Reichsbank's 'readiness to abandon bank rate in periods of emergency' (prior to 1933) as proof that 'the Reichsbank itself considered its discount policy an inefficient tool of central bank control', said that 'this attitude was conditioned . . . in part by the inability of the German bank rate to lean upon open market operations'. *Control Policies of the Reichsbank, 1924–33*, p. 306.

† Securities issued by the Government or by any German State or municipality or by certain Government credit institutions.

new loans for carrying out the policy of National Socialism, such as the financing of the labour creation programmes.

After the initial stimulus had been administered by open-market operations, the Reichsbank proceeded to place its credit at the disposal of the German economy in the form of re-discounts to the commercial banks and other financial institutions, rather than in the form of direct open-market operations.

The Bundesbank, which was established in 1957 as the new central bank of West Germany, was also specifically authorized, 'for the purpose of regulating the money market', to buy and sell 'in the open market' a wide variety of securities, namely, eligible trade bills, Treasury bills and bonds issued by the Federal Government, certain Federal Special Funds or the States, as well as 'other bonds admitted to official stock exchange dealings'. In practice, however, the Bank preferred to deal mainly in Federal Treasury bills and Treasury bonds with a maturity not exceeding two years, and as there was an inadequate supply of such securities available during its earlier years, it arranged for the conversion of some of its equalization claims* on the Federal Government into the desired marketable securities which were required from time to time to reduce the liquidity of the banking sector resulting from a favourable balance of payments. Another important feature was that, in principle, the Bundesbank sold money-market securities only to the banks and certain public agencies and also bought securities only from such institutions, and this meant that in the main only bank liquidity fell within the scope of the Bank's open-market operations.[10]

With regard to France, Margaret Myers[11] said that in the decade following 1857, 'when the Bank of France changed its discount rate frequently in imitation of the Bank of England, the question was raised as to whether or not the Bank of France should also engage in open-market operations in the English fashion', and that 'the question was decided in the negative, not because it was thought that the Bank lacked the necessary auth-

* These claims, as explained in Chapter 3, arose from the currency reform of 1948 and the conversion, into so-called 'Equalization Claims', of Government debt held by the banks, including the central bank at the time (the Bank Deutscher Länder which was subsequently reconstituted as the Deutsche Bundesbank).

ority, but because it would expose the Bank to risk of loss, and also to the suspicion of manipulating the market'. After 1918, however, the attitude of the Bank of France generally was that it did not have any real authority to conduct open-market operations, as it was not specifically empowered by its statutes to buy and sell Government securities for its own account.

In 1938 the position of the Bank of France was altered in that it was specifically empowered by decree of the President to undertake open-market operations in respect of Treasury bills and National Defence Bonds with a maturity not exceeding two years,* short-term bills of certain other public authorities, and bankers' acceptances. The decree emphasized that this power was granted to the Bank 'in order to influence the volume of credit and to regulate the money market'; and the Prime Minister, in his report to the President, justified it on the ground that 'capital movements which have affected the Paris market, in the course of recent years, have demonstrated the utility of giving the Bank greater freedom and a more effective power of intervention', and that open-market operations 'should render discount policy more effective on the money markets'. According to the annual report of the Bank of France for 1939, its interventions in the money market during that year 'effectively aided the lowering of money rates which had already become evident at the end of 1938, and ... made it possible to avoid abrupt reactions which, in a market left to itself, might have been precipitated on several occasions by the vicissitudes of international politics'.

In general, it would appear that open-market operations did not form an important part of the Bank's monetary policy, not only because of the absence of a sufficiently wide and active money market but also because the Bank could rely on its large and regular rediscounts for the commercial banks and other credit institutions and its use of credit quotas as instruments of credit control, together with its discount-rate policy. During 1971–2, however, according to the Annual Report of the Bank

* The Bank was prohibited from obtaining securities direct from the Treasury and was only allowed to operate in the open market. This was facilitated by the establishment of five discount houses, some of whom performed functions similar to those of the discount houses operating in the London market.

for International Settlements, 'there were extensive changes in the system of central-bank credit-granting to the banks in connection with the shift away from rediscounting towards reliance on techniques of open-market intervention'.

In Holland, the subject of open-market policy was discussed in 1936 when the renewal of the charter of the Netherlands Bank had to be sanctioned by the Legislature. Under the old charter, it was unable to conduct open-market operations, but under the new charter as amended in 1945 it was given the power to buy and sell Government bonds, Treasury bills and bankers' acceptances, and this power was also incorporated in the new Bank Act of 1948. Until 1952, however, there was little or no scope for 'an effective open-market policy'. As explained by its President in 1958, 'the Bank was faced with the problem how to maintain a sufficient portfolio of Treasury paper so as to enable it sufficiently to control the market', and 'it was only due to the willingness of the Treasury to convert part of its book debt to the Bank into Treasury paper that the Bank's portfolio could be sufficiently increased'.[12]

In Norway, where under the old law there was some doubt as to whether the Bank of Norway had the power to carry out open-market operations, an amendment was passed in 1936 with a view to making the position quite clear. It was specified that the Bank could buy and sell Government bonds or bonds of the Norwegian Mortgage Bank or other interest-bearing and readily negotiable securities. Provision was also made for a Securities Adjustment Fund, and for allocation to this Fund of a portion of the Bank's profits after payment of a 6 per cent dividend. Moreover, any profit or loss resulting from purchases and sales of securities was to be credited or debited to this Fund. The Governor of the Bank at the time explained that open-market operations constitute 'a necessary supplement to the means of the Bank in the carrying out of its credit policy', and that 'the intervention may act in conjunction with other means and intensify their effect'.[13]

In Sweden, owing to highly liquid money-market conditions and the relatively small amount of Government securities held by the Riksbank in 1938, the latter made arrangements with the National Debt Office under which Treasury bills or other

Government securities could be created,* as and when required, to be sold in the open market for the express purpose of absorbing an excess of liquid funds. As in various other countries, however, the problem was 'the absence of a money market which could be used as a channel of intervention', although 'from 1957 onwards' deliberate steps were taken 'to cultivate the money market and to use intervention as an instrument of credit policy'.[14]

In Switzerland the National Bank also found it necessary at times, as in 1949–50 and 1960–2, to arrange for special short-term securities to be issued by the Government for the purpose of absorbing the excess liquidity of the commercial banks caused by the inflow of foreign capital. These securities, called 'sterilization rescriptions', were issued only for account of the National Bank which had, therefore, to pay interest thereon itself until redemption. It may be added, however, that the Bank's legal authority for engaging in open-market operations was substantially increased in 1953.[15]

In Belgium the National Bank was expressly authorized in 1937 to buy and sell Treasury bills and long-term Government bonds in addition to trade bills, but the limits which were imposed on the Bank's purchases of Government securities hampered the carrying out of any extensive open-market policy. In October, 1939, however, the maximum limit for its holdings of Government securities was raised from 1,500 million to 5,000 million francs. The Treasury, moreover, assisted in the establishment of an open market by issuing three-months' Treasury bills on a public tender basis. In due course, however, the function of open-market operations came to be entrusted to the Fonds des Rentes, an autonomous body which was established in 1945 and on which both the Treasury and the National Bank were represented.[16]

In Hungary the National Bank was empowered in 1938 to make purchases and sales on the open market calculated to direct and regulate the money market and the capital market, and to undertake participation in an institution for the regulation of these markets.

In Denmark the National Bank had already, during the

* As these securities were to be specially created for the purposes of the Bank, it had to pay the interest on such securities itself.

thirties, conducted open-market operations not only in Government securities, but also in mortgage-bond certificates as a means of regulating the volume of money available for building activity in accordance with movements in the country's balance of payments.

Open-Market Operations by New Central Banks

The need for some form of open-market operations as a supplement to discount-rate policy and as an instrument of monetary stabilization was, under modern conditions, similarly felt by many of the new central banks which were established after 1920. The scope for open-market policy on the part of these banks was, however, limited by the existence not only of relatively narrow markets for Government securities, but, in many cases, also of statutory restrictions on their powers of dealing in Government securities.

These restrictions were imposed, as explained in Chapter 3, as a result of the unfortunate experiences which the older central banks had with Government paper during the 1914–18 war and post-war periods, and were intended to protect the new central banks against unsound demands from the State. In this connection, however, it must be pointed out that many of these restrictions were relaxed during the period from 1930 to 1933 under the pressure of the severe depression, and also since that time as a result of the increased needs of Governments or as a matter of public policy.

The South African Reserve Bank, for example, which was at first permitted to invest in Government securities, having more than six months but not more than two years to run, only up to the amount of its paid-up capital and reserve funds, was authorized in 1941 to hold Government securities of any currency, to a total amount equal to its paid-up capital and reserve funds plus one-third of its liabilities to the public. While this additional power was granted to the Bank at the time in order to facilitate the repatriation of Government securities domiciled overseas, it was retained in the new law of 1944 despite the fact that in the meantime practically the whole of the £75 million repatriated securities acquired by the Bank had been redeemed by the Government out of the proceeds of new local loans. Moreover, this limitation on its total holdings of Government securities which was the only restriction imposed by the new law on its dealings in securities, was finally repealed in 1961.

The Bank of Canada was at first limited to holding 'securities issued or guaranteed by the Dominion of Canada or any province, having a maturity exceeding two years from the date of acquisition by the Bank', only up to three times the amount of its paid-up capital; but by 1938 it was empowered to hold such securities up to 50 per cent of its outstanding note and deposit liabilities, provided that its holdings of securities not maturing within ten years did not exceed five times the amount of its paid-up capital and reserve funds. These remaining restrictions were, however, removed entirely during 1954.

As a result of the removal or reduction of restrictions on their holdings of Government securities, the newer central banks came to possess ample legal powers for dealings in these securities, but their scope for using these powers as an instrument of monetary policy was restricted by the lack of broad and active markets in such securities and in some cases also by an inadequate supply of marketable securities.

With regard to the former, the logical step was for the central bank to take the lead or at least assist in the development of a money market, particularly for Treasury bills and other short-term Government securities,* and also a market for longer-term Government securities (Government bonds). As mentioned in Chapter 9, a number of the newer central banks have succeeded in developing a money market for the purpose of improving the financial environment for their discount-rate policy, and special reference was made to the position in Canada, South Africa and Australia. The money market, however, could naturally also serve as an important, if not the principal, medium for open-

* The emphasis had to be placed on the market for short-term Government securities since in most of the countries concerned the trade bill and bankers' acceptance were not used to any great extent, and since such trade bills as were available for discount were usually discounted by the commercial banks directly for their customers and kept by them till maturity, except of course when rediscounted with the central bank.

market operations as a means of exercising a more direct influence on the money supply and the liquidity of the banks. In fact, many of these central banks, like the older ones, found it more convenient and effective, in general, to operate in the money market than in the Government bond market, not only because of the smaller risk of loss and disturbance in the event of a substantial upward trend in interest rates, but also because it was easier to develop the former. The problem was merely to arrange for a regular and sufficient issue of Treasury bills as a part of borrowings by the Government, and to promote the use of Treasury bills not only as a secondary reserve for the commercial banks but also as a liquid asset for other financial institutions and the business community.

In some countries, however, it was found necessary or advantageous for the central bank also to operate in long-term securities, in order to promote the development of a more active and orderly market in Government bonds which would at least help to extend its direct influence on the financial situation. With regard to the Bank of Canada, for example, Plumptre[17] was able to say in 1940 (i.e. only six years after its establishment) that its open-market operations 'serve in some degree to broaden the Canadian bond market'; that 'at least the Bank must be one more dealer in the market'; that 'it is probably more than this because the other dealers are inclined to give its daily price lists and its other activities more than ordinary attention'; and that the switching operations (trading of one type of Government bond for another) which the Bank was reported to undertake at times constituted 'a useful form of participation in the bond market because it keeps the Bank in touch with affairs, and meets the demands of other traders, without involving the Bank in any change in the aggregate of its security holdings or in the reserves of the commercial banks'.

In South Africa the Reserve Bank, which had previously taken the lead in the development of a money market, decided in 1952 to assist also in creating a more active market in Government securities generally by quoting buying and selling prices based on a pattern of rates for the various maturities to be fixed from time to time in accordance with the general trend of the supply–demand position in the gilt-edged market. In this connection, its general aim was reported to be both to establish appropriate relationships between the rates for different maturities and to maintain orderly conditions in the gilt-edged market whether the circumstances demanded an upward or a downward adjustment or relative stability, and thus to avoid unwarranted fluctuations. In 1970, however, a Commission[18] reported that 'hitherto full justice has not been done to open-market operations as a policy instrument in South Africa, because, amongst other things, of its comparatively rigid interest pattern and the fact that the secondary market in Government stock . . . is fairly limited'; that 'one of the reasons why the secondary market' in Government stock is not highly developed, is the fear on the part of potential dealers in this market that in the absence of a deliberate open market policy they may not succeed in making a market in such paper at all times'; and that 'an inadequate portfolio of Government stock is, in fact, one of the practical reasons why an open market policy has hitherto not been applied'. The Commission recommended, therefore, that 'the monetary authorities should initiate an active open market policy after thorough preparations to this end have been made'; and in August, 1973, it was finally announced[19] that the Reserve Bank proposed 'to extend its existing operations in the open market by entering the market more actively as a buyer and seller of Government securities when it deems it desirable to influence market conditions', and, in particular, 'to reinstate the Treasury bill as the most important money market instrument', for which purpose it would, as its primary form of accommodation to the discount houses (apart from overnight loans), discount Treasury bills on a buy-back basis at ½ per cent above the latest Treasury bill tender rate.

In Argentina, the question of undertaking open-market operations as a means of reducing or absorbing an excess of liquid funds was greatly facilitated by the fact that, at the time of its constitution in 1935, the Central Bank acquired a substantial amount of Consolidated Treasury Bonds.* When, therefore, in

* These bonds did not constitute a new Government issue, but were merely the result of the conversion of Treasury bills and other Government securities held by the Banco de la Nacion and the Caja de Conversion and transferred to the Central Bank on its establishment.

its first year of operation it desired to reduce the excessive liquidity that had arisen from the revaluation of gold and a favourable balance of payments, it succeeded in devising an ingenious method of dealing not only with the problem of liquidity* but also with that of laying the foundation of an open market. This method consisted of making three-months' paper, with no fixed interest, out of long-term and fixed-interest Treasury Bonds, by issuing Certificates of Participation in these Bonds. At first the Certificates were offered to the banks in amounts and at prices already fixed, but after a few months' experience the Bank decided to change this procedure and substitute that of fortnightly tenders and allotments to the highest bidders, which 'amongst other advantages allows oscillations of the money market to be closely followed'.[20] Moreover, the Certificates could be discounted at any time with the Central Bank at the minimum rate for rediscounts of bills bearing two signatures.

The Central Bank of Argentina also conducted open-market operations in Government bonds as a regulatory measure. In referring to the progressive increase in the quotations of Government bonds during 1941, as a result of an abundance of available funds in Argentina caused by the inflow of capital and the grain purchases of the Government, the Bank reported[21] that it 'intervened to regulate the market without running counter to its natural tendency and, in this case, prevented the rises from occurring abruptly which might have entailed the risk of disturbing reactions'. At other times again it made 'large purchases of securities which contributed to steady the stock market and to restore confidence in banking circles', such as 'at the outbreak of war, at the time of the fall of France and . . . when the United States entered the war'; and 'in all these cases the movement was of a temporary nature and the bonds acquired by the regulatory institution were soon absorbed once again by the market'.

Finally, mention should be made of those central banks which, owing to the lack of marketable Government or other suitable

* Another method of absorbing liquid funds was that of redeeming part of the foreign debt of the Argentine Government during 1936 and 1937, out of the proceeds of Government bonds and Treasury bills issued in Argentina and out of exchange profits; and this was again resorted to on a large scale during World War II.

securities, were authorized to issue their own negotiable securities for such open-market operations as were found necessary in the interest of monetary stabilization. In Guatemala, for example, the new law of 1945 provided that, for the purpose of stabilizing the money market, the Monetary Board could order the issue by the Bank of Guatemala of freely negotiable 'stabilization bonds' which the Bank could repurchase in the market before maturity if the circumstances warranted it. Similar powers were also granted, in the forties and fifties, to the central banks of Ceylon, Philippines, Korea, Ecuador, Costa Rica, Cuba, El Salvador, Chile, Mexico and Egypt. The South African Reserve Bank was likewise authorized in 1969, to 'issue its own interest-bearing securities for purposes of monetary policy and buy, sell, discount or rediscount, or grant loans or advances against, such securities'; but this power was not exercised as 'the use of Government stock in open market operations (was) to be preferred', for which the necessary arrangements as to sufficient volume and variety were to be made 'in a non-inflationary manner'.[22]

Conclusion

It was shown that, despite the limitations of open-market operations at times due to certain simultaneous counterforces, many central banks, old and new, exerted themselves to establish or extend, in one form or another, the employment of such operations as an instrument of monetary policy, and to devise ways and means of improving their ability to offset the effects of any disturbing factors; that, while open-market operations were usually employed in conjunction with other instruments of monetary policy, some central banks adopted it constantly, and some at least intermittently, as their principal method of credit control; and that certain central banks which had at times to cope with excessive liquidity, due to a favourable balance of payments position, but did not possess sufficient marketable Government or other suitable securities which could be sold in order to absorb the surplus funds and repurchased in order to relieve a credit stringency, even resorted to acquiring the power to issue their own negotiable securities for this purpose, or to financing the repatriation of foreign debts of their Governments for conversion into local securities, or having the whole or part of their loans to their Governments converted into marketable securities.

The main reason for this distinct trend in favour of open-market operations was the fact that, to the extent that they could be conducted effectively after allowing for any disturbing or limiting factors, such operations exercised a direct influence on the money supply and the liquidity of the banks in the desired direction, i.e. towards expansion or contraction or maintenance of the existing monetary position depending upon the prevailing circumstances and the current objectives of monetary policy. Although the money supply itself was not always the decisive factor, as explained in Chapter 8, it was nevertheless an important contributing factor, and any instrument which could help the central bank directly to control the money supply, was significant enough to be developed as far as possible.

The need for such a direct influence on the money supply and the liquidity of the banks was accentuated by the decline in the significance of discount-rate policy as an instrument of credit control, due to the fact that, as explained in Chapter 9, various factors tended to make the internal economy and the balance of payments less responsive to changes in interest rates. Moreover, other factors tended to limit the extent to which interest rates could be raised as an anti-inflationary measure.

Finally, experience has shown that central banks in all kinds of countries can, with advantage in one degree or another, employ open-market operations for any of the following purposes, separately or jointly as circumstances may permit or demand, namely, to reinforce changes in official discount rates and bring about the desired changes generally in short- or long-term interest rates or both; to absorb an excess of liquid funds or relieve an undue credit stringency; to insulate the internal credit structure from sudden and temporary movements in the balance of payments; to neutralize movements of Government funds and seasonal movements generally; and to maintain orderly conditions in the money and gilt-edged markets, in general.

References

1 Sayers, R. S. *Bank of England Operations, 1890–1914*. King, 1936. pp. 27–36.
2 *Ibid.* pp. 128–9.
3 Conant, C. A. *History of Modern Banks of Issue*, 5 ed. Putnam, 1927. p. 217.
4 *The Economist*. 31st January, 1931.
5 *Federal Reserve Bulletin*. May, 1923.
6 Burgess, W. R. *Reserve Banks and the Money Market*, Rev. ed. Harper, 1936. pp. 249–54.
7 *Federal Reserve Bulletin*. October, 1937.
8 *Annual Report of the Board of Governors of the Federal Reserve System for 1970*. p. 17.
9 Sarow, F. *Offenmarktpolitik zur Konjunkturregelung*. Duncker & Humboldt, 1927. Preface.
10 *See* Schmidt, W., in *Eight European Central Banks*. Ed. Bank for International Settlements. Allen & Unwin, 1963. pp. 73–6.
11 Myers, M. *Paris as a Financial Centre*. King, 1936. p. 29.
12 *Principal Memoranda of Evidence Submitted to the Radcliffe Committee of Great Britain*. H.M.S.O., 1960. Vol. I, p. 262.
13 *Monthly Report of the Bank of Norway*. February, 1936.
14 Lindh, S., in *Eight European Central Banks*. Ed. Bank for International Settlements. Allen & Unwin, 1963. pp. 324–6.
15 Kull, W. *Ibid.* pp. 292–3.
16 Janssens, V. *Ibid.* p. 41.
17 Plumptre, A. F. W. *Central Banking in the British Dominions*. Toronto U.P., 1940. pp. 233–4.
18 *Third Report of the Commission of Enquiry into Fiscal and Monetary Policy in South Africa*. 1970. pp. 170–3.
19 *Annual Report of the South African Reserve Bank for 1972–73*.
20 *Annual Report of the Central Bank of Argentina for 1936*. p. 6.
21 *Annual Report of the Central Bank of Argentina for 1941*. pp. 7–8.
22 *Third Report of the Commission of Enquiry into Fiscal and Monetary Policy in South Africa*. 1970. p. 171.

CHAPTER ELEVEN

Variable Reserve Requirements

Introduction

The employment of variable reserve requirements as an instrument of credit control is of relatively recent origin. The United States, which was the first country to introduce statutory provision for the maintenance by commercial banks of minimum credit balances with the central bank, based on fixed percentages of their demand and time deposits, was also the first to grant legal authority to the central bank to vary such reserve requirements, from time to time, within certain limits above the normal minimum reserve ratios. This power was initially granted to the Federal Reserve System in 1933 and extended in 1935, 'in order to prevent injurious credit expansion or contraction', the minimum reserve percentages not to be less than those existing at the time nor more than twice such percentages.

The principle of variable reserve requirements, which was devised as an alternative or additional means of enabling the central bank to expand or contract the available supply of bank cash, and thus the actual or potential volume of bank credit and money, came to be adopted, in one form or another, by all kinds of countries, from the mature to the under-developed economies. In most of these countries the central bank was granted specific legal authority to employ this instrument, with certain minimum and maximum limits, but there are some countries where the central bank has evidently preferred, or been satisfied, to perform this function by voluntary agreement with the commercial banks.

The evolution of the different methods and uses of variable reserve requirements can with advantage be traced and assessed from separate surveys of their development in a selected number of countries, in the chronological order in which they came to adopt this instrument of monetary policy.

United States

As stated earlier, the Federal Reserve System was authorized in 1935 to vary the requirements in respect of minimum reserve balances to be maintained by member banks with their respective Federal Reserve Banks, subject to the reserve percentages not being less than those existing at the time (namely, 13 per cent of net demand deposits for central reserve city banks, 10 per cent for reserve city banks and 7 per cent for country banks, and 3 per cent of time deposits for all member banks), nor more than twice such percentages (i.e., up to 26, 20, 14 and 6 per cent respectively).

This authority was exercised for the first time in August, 1936, when the reserve requirements were raised by one-half because of the fear that the large increase in the cash reserves of the member banks resulting from the heavy inflow of gold might be used as a basis of injurious credit expansion. As the Board of Governors[1] explained at the time, 'it is far better to sterilize a part of these superfluous reserves while they are still unused than to permit a credit structure to be erected upon them and then to withdraw the foundation of the structure'; and in the Annual Report of the Federal Reserve Bank of New York for 1936 it was stated that the principal effect of the increased reserve requirements was 'not to restrict the current availability of money, but rather to limit the potential expansion of credit which might ultimately be based upon the reserves held by the banks'. The immediate result of the increase of one-half in the minimum reserve requirements was that the excess reserve balances of the member banks were reduced from $3,100 million to $1,800 million; and this reduction brought the reserves 'within the scope of control through the System's open-market portfolio which consists of $2,430 million of United States Government securities'.

The excess reserves of the member banks, however, again increased as a result of the continued inflow of gold, and by the end of 1936 they stood at $2,250 million. Accordingly the Board of Governors decided, in the beginning of 1937, to make a further increase in reserve requirements in two stages up to the limit allowed by legislation. On 1st May, 1937, when the final increase was brought into effect, the excess reserves were reduced to $875 million; and on that occasion the Board of Governors[2] issued the following statement which afforded a concise explanation of the motives and forces behind this new method:

> 'So long as member banks had a volume of reserves far in excess of legal requirements, the customary instruments of credit policy, open-market operations and discount rates, were wholly ineffective ... Through the elimination of about $3,000 million of excess reserves, the Federal Reserve System was brought into closer contact with the market and was placed in a position where sales or purchases in the open market could tighten or ease credit conditions in accordance with the public interest.'

In April, 1938, however, 'as a part of the Government's programme for encouragement of business recovery',[3] the minimum reserves were reduced by 12½ per cent from their new high level, thereby releasing approximately $750 million reserves.* As a result of a further considerable inflow of gold, the excess reserves of member banks again increased to $3,600 million by January, 1939, and to $5,000 million by October, 1941, despite the growth in the amount of currency in circulation and the increase in the required reserves resulting from the expansion of bank deposits. This large increase in excess reserves finally led to the restoration, as from November, 1941, of the uppermost limit of reserve requirements allowed by legislation. It was

* Moreover, in its Annual Report for 1938 the Board of Governors referred to 'the so-called policy of monetary ease, which has been directed at keeping banks supplied with an abundant volume of reserves, so as to encourage them to expand their loans and investments'.

declared to be 'a further step in the Government's programme for combating inflation'.

After the entry of the United States into the war, there was a more rapid increase in the currency circulation and a further increase in bank deposits on account of bank purchases of Government securities, both of which had the effect of reducing the excess reserves of member banks. On 1st July, 1942, the excess reserves stood only at $2,259 million, while the prospective borrowing programme of the United States Government called for a much greater participation by the banking system in the financing of the war effort, and the contemplated expansion of war activities called for a continuous increase in the currency circulation.

To cope with the new situation, the Board of Governors was empowered to change the reserve requirements of member banks in central reserve cities (New York and Chicago) without changing requirements for those in other reserve cities or for country banks. In August, 1942, the Board reduced the reserve requirements against demand deposits for central reserve city banks where the decline in reserves was concentrated, from 26 to 24 per cent; and this was further reduced to 22 per cent in September and to 20 per cent in October, 1942. As a further contribution towards meeting the need of the banks for additional reserves, the Federal Reserve System expanded its open-market operations and increased its holdings of Government securities from $2,728 million on 1st July, 1942, to $6,189 million at the end of 1942 and $19,000 million at the end of 1944.

The next change was not made until February, 1948, when the reserve requirement against demand deposits for central reserve city banks was raised again from 20 to 22 per cent, followed by further increases to 24 per cent in June and 26 per cent in September, 1948. In the meantime, as a result of a strong plea by the Board of Governors for wider powers in order to be able to deal more effectively with the prevailing inflationary potential, the maximum limits of the reserve requirements were temporarily raised by Congress in August, 1948, by 4 per cent in the case of demand deposits, and 1½ per cent in the case of time deposits. Thus, in September, 1948, the reserve to be maintained by reserve city and country banks against their demand deposits was also increased, namely, from 20 and 14 to 22 and 16 per cent respectively, while that against time deposits was increased from 6 to 7½ per cent.

During the period May–September, 1949, however, the Board was induced by a recession in business activity to lower the reserve ratios, in stages, by 4 and 2½ per cent in the case of demand and time deposits respectively. But, in January, 1951, due to the renewed inflationary trend consequent upon the Korean war, the reserve requirements were raised once more to 24, 20 and 14 per cent against the demand deposits of central reserve city, reserve city and country banks respectively, and to 6 per cent against time deposits.

Then, in July, 1953, when a relatively severe monetary stringency existed, the Federal Reserve Board, 'in pursuance of a Federal Reserve policy designed to make available the reserve funds necessary to meet the essential needs of the economy and to help maintain stability of the dollar', lowered the reserve requirements to 22, 19 and 13 per cent against the demand deposits of central reserve city, reserve city and country banks respectively, and continued with the downward movement until the end of 1960* when the respective ratios stood at 16½, 16½ and 12 per cent, while that for time deposits was reduced to 5 per cent in 1954 and 4 per cent in 1962.

The reserve requirements in respect of demand deposits remained unchanged from the end of 1960 to the beginning of 1968 when the ratios for amounts over $5 million were raised to 17 per cent for reserve city banks† and 12½ per cent for country banks. These ratios were further increased by ½ per cent in April, 1969, when the same increase was also applied to demand deposits up to $5 million, i.e. to 17½ and 17 per cent respectively for reserve city banks and 13 and 12½ per cent respectively for country banks. The higher ratios were maintained until November, 1972, when a new system of cash reserve requirements in

* In 1960 it was provided that member banks could also count all their holdings of note currency and coin as reserves for the purpose of legal minimum reserve requirements, instead of only their credit balances with the Federal Reserve Banks.

† Central reserve city banks were removed from the classification of member banks in 1962, leaving only reserve city banks and country banks.

respect of demand deposits was brought into effect, which was uniformly applicable to all member banks irrespective of their location. It was based on the size of a bank's net demand deposits, in accordance with a graduated scale of reserve ratios which were to be applied *cumulatively*. The initial scale laid down ranged from 8 per cent on amounts up to $2 million and 10 per cent on amounts between $2 million and $10 million to 17½ per cent on amounts in excess of $400 million. While the average reserve ratio on this scale was substantially lower than on the previous basis, this was largely counter-balanced by the reduction of the banks' cash reserves resulting from the simultaneous new requirement that 'all banks served by the Federal Reserve check collection system (are) to pay for checks in immediately available funds the same day the checks are presented for payment by the Federal Reserve'.[4]

With regard to time deposits, a distinction had been made in the meantime not only between amounts over $5 million and up to $5 million, but a separate category had also been introduced for savings deposits in the case of all member banks, at the same rate initially as the lower rate for other time deposits up to $5 million. In November, 1972, the respective ratios stood at 5, 3 and 3 per cent and were not changed when the new system for demand deposits was brought into effect.

Furthermore, in October, 1969, member banks were also required to maintain minimum cash reserves of 10 per cent against balances due to their foreign branches or borrowings from foreign banks, above a specified base in both cases. This requirement was increased by the Board of Governors to 20 per cent in January, 1971, and this was intended to give member banks an added inducement to preserve their reserve-free bases against a time of future need instead of allowing their bases to be lowered automatically by repaying their Euro-dollar borrowings. The reason given by the Board[5] for its action 'to strengthen the inducement for US banks to retain their Euro-dollar liabilities', was 'the deleterious effect on the US balance of payments of the repayment by US banks of their Euro-dollar borrowings' which 'had already assumed heavy proportions'.

The foregoing survey showed, firstly, that an elaborate system of variable cash-reserve requirements for member banks was developed by the Federal Reserve authorities; that it was employed, like open-market operations and in conjunction therewith, as an instrument of monetary policy aimed at countering or mitigating cyclical fluctuations in business activity and inflationary or deflationary trends, but with a distinct expansionist bias in general; that it was also used at times as a means of absorbing or reducing excessive liquidity in the banking sector due to large surpluses in the balance of payments; and that since the end of 1960 there has been a marked decline in the frequency of changes in the minimum reserve ratios.

The general impression in banking and economic circles would appear to be that the system of variable reserve requirements developed in the United States has, on the whole, not proved to be sufficiently effective under modern financial conditions. The experience of various countries which have adopted this instrument of monetary policy has caused them to extend its coverage beyond the limits laid down in the United States, in respect of not only the classes of banking institutions but also the types of bank assets other than cash reserves subject to minimum reserve requirements. Thus, whereas in the United States reserve requirements have throughout been applied only to member banks and to their cash reserves, other countries have at least included all commercial banks, and in some cases also certain other banking and credit institutions, and an increasing number of countries have also imposed minimum liquid-asset and/or secondary-reserve requirements on the institutions concerned, as will be shown later.

It should be mentioned, however, that the Federal Reserve authorities had frequently made representations to Congress for the extension of the system of reserve requirements in the United States. In its Annual Report for 1945, the Board of Governors asked for 'new powers that would serve as a partial substitute for those traditional powers which had become largely unusable in view of the huge public debt'. In short, the Board considered it necessary in the prevailing circumstances to have the power to call upon member banks to maintain not only minimum reserve balances with their respective Federal Reserve Banks, but also minimum holdings of short-term Government securities and other liquid assets in order to limit their opportunities for disposing of such assets in order to increase their loans for general business purposes. The need for this additional power was repeated on various occasions. For example, in a statement before the Joint Congressional Committee on the Economic Report, in April, 1948, the Board specifically pleaded for the authority to impose such secondary reserve requirements on *all* banks, up to 25 per cent of their demand deposits and 10 per cent of their time deposits, if they continued to expand credit for the private sector by selling Government securities. Despite these repeated representations, Congress failed to respond.

Furthermore, in its Annual Report for 1970 the Board expressed its belief that at least the existing reserve requirements 'should apply to demand deposits in *all* institutions that accept deposits subject to withdrawal by check', and that 'because demand deposits held by any institution are part of the country's money supply just as are those in member banks, applying the same demand-deposit reserve requirements to *all* such institutions would facilitate the effective implementation of monetary policy'. Even on this narrower front, however, there was no response by the end of 1972.

New Zealand

In 1936, when the Federal Reserve System first exercised its power to change the reserve requirements for member banks in the United States, two other countries authorized their central banks to employ variable reserve requirements as an instrument of credit control, namely, New Zealand and Mexico.

New Zealand followed the method adopted by the United States and empowered the Reserve Bank, with the authority of the Minister of Finance, to vary the requirements in respect of reserve balances to be maintained with it by the 'trading banks', subject to such balances not being at any time less than those provided for in the original statute, namely, 7 per cent of demand liabilities and 3 per cent of time liabilities. These ratios, for which no maximum was laid down, were raised for the first time to 10 and 5 per cent respectively in August, 1952, then to 20 and 10 per cent in April, 1953, and to 25 and 12½ per cent in 1954, with fluctuations in between.

This method, which was employed by the Reserve Bank not only as a means of neutralizing the pronounced seasonal swings in bank cash but also to counter excessive liquidity due to surpluses in the balance of payments and to reinforce changes in the official discount rate, was used extensively until the mid-sixties. In the last quarter of 1964, for example, there were no less than nine changes in the reserve requirement against demand liabilities, namely between 22 and 31 per cent, while that against time liabilities was kept at 3 per cent. Subsequently, however, changes in the reserve requirement against demand liabilities came to be made less frequently and on a lower level. Moreover, as from October, 1969, the reserve ratios remained unchanged at 8 per cent of demand liabilities and 3 per cent of time liabilities and were still in effect at the end of 1972. In fact, according to the Governor of the Reserve Bank, 'these ratios are not intended to be changed in normal circumstances'.[6]

The new policy of relatively fixed reserve ratios was followed despite the fact that, in 1964, the Reserve Bank had been granted wider and more flexible powers in respect of variable reserve requirements. In the first place, the provision for minimum requirements of 7 and 3 per cent against demand and time liabilities respectively was omitted from the new Act, so that there was neither a minimum nor a maximum limit. Secondly, the Bank was authorized, with the approval of the Minister of Finance, to require the trading banks from time to time to hold either minimum balances at the Reserve Bank or minimum assets of a specified kind or kinds, including balances at the Reserve Bank, equivalent to a percentage of all or any specified part or parts of their assets, or both at the same time, or an amount determined in any other manner. Thirdly, the Government and the Reserve Bank were provided 'with flexible authority to take such monetary action within, and to some extent outside, the conventional banking system as may be appropriate to the times'.[7]

At the end of 1972, however, the cash-reserve requirement was still applied only to trading banks, and no minimum liquid-asset requirement was yet prescribed, although it was under consideration. The only change which had been made was that 'finance companies' were required, in 1969, to maintain a minimum holding of Government stock equivalent to 10 per cent of borrowings (deposits, debentures or notes) invested by them in certain types of financial assets, which was increased to 12½ per cent in 1970 and 15 per cent in 1971, and which was intended to 'divert to the public sector funds which would otherwise be lent to the private sector'.[8]

The main reason for the limited use by the New Zealand monetary authorities of the wider and more flexible powers in respect of reserve requirements, would appear to be that, in the prevailing circumstances and for the time being at any rate, greater reliance was placed on the use of credit ceilings and other methods of direct control of bank credit, for which wider powers were also granted in the Act of 1964.

Mexico

In 1936 Mexico adopted a formula similar to the one which had previously been proposed by the 'Committee on Bank Reserves of the Federal Reserve System' but not carried into effect in the United States, namely, that the minimum reserves to be maintained with the central bank should be based on the activity as well as the volume of the deposits held by a member bank. Thus, all banking institutions in Mexico accepting deposits for less than thirty days were required to keep with the Bank of Mexico minimum balances amounting to 7 per cent of their deposit liabilities, plus 50 per cent of the average daily payments on their deposit accounts. In addition, the Bank was empowered to raise the proportion of deposit liabilities from 7 to 15 per cent or reduce it to 3 per cent, and also to apply any such increase or decrease to one single category of deposits (sight, time or savings-account deposits) or to a definite banking zone. In 1941, however, the provision for the inclusion of 50 per cent of the average daily withdrawals was abolished, and the upper limit for the proportion of deposit liabilities, which the Bank could fix as a minimum reserve balance to be maintained by any bank on any of its deposits, was raised from 15 to 20 per cent, while the lower limit was increased from 3 to 5 per cent. Furthermore in 1942 the Bank was authorized, subject to the consent of the Treasury, to raise the maximum limit as high as 50 per cent if the economic conditions warranted it.

On account of the exceptionally liquid position of the banking sector, due to a persistent surplus in the balance of payments, the ratio in respect of sight liabilities for banks in Mexico City was raised in stages to the maximum limit of 50 per cent by January, 1944, and to 35 per cent for banks in cities with branches of the Bank of Mexico and 33 per cent in other towns. By May, 1945, the respective ratios stood at 50, 50 and 45 per cent, but the latter two were lowered to 45 and 40 per cent respectively by January, 1947. Owing to the financial needs of the Government, it was also decided in 1947, while retaining the existing reserve ratios, to allow the banks to include additional investments in Government bonds as part of the required reserves up to 15 per cent. Moreover, banks outside Mexico City were permitted a deficiency of up to 25 per cent without the usual penalty if offset by new loans for agricultural and cattle-raising purposes. In 1948 banks in or outside Mexico City were also allowed to include private instead of Government securities within certain prescribed limits as part of their required reserves. Furthermore, as a result of the continued expansion of bank credit and the need to direct financial resources to high priority activities, all banks were required to maintain additional cash reserves equivalent to 100 per cent of any increase in their sight liabilities after 30th September, 1949, but it was provided that any deficiency in such reserves up to 70 per cent would not be subject to penalty if it was offset by new loans for equipment or other productive purposes. In 1950 this provision was recast in more positive terms, prescribing the minimum percentages of the additional required reserves to be held in the form of cash balances at the Bank of Mexico, Government or private securities and investments in productive activities. As Margaret Myers[9] said at the time, 'the principle of flexible reserve requirements was therefore adapted to the effort to direct bank credit into production loans'.

The Bank of Mexico continued to make extensive use of variable reserve requirements both as a means of controlling the credit-creating capacity of the banking sector and as an instrument for facilitating and reinforcing its measures of selective credit control. The system of 100 per cent reserve-asset requirements was developed and extended to provide not only for varying minimum proportions of their sight and time deposits to be maintained as cash balances with the Bank of Mexico by the 'deposit banks', on part of which interest was paid, but also for the allocation of their remaining deposit resources for the specific purposes determined by the monetary authorities from time to time. Furthermore, the system was gradually extended to include other financial intermediaries which had developed rapidly after World War II. Beginning in January, 1951, the savings banks were required to maintain a reserve deposit with the Bank of Mexico, and in 1955 they were also required to hold Government and other securities and to place new credits as directed by the monetary authorities. In 1958 the investment banks were likewise brought into the dual system of reserve-deposit requirements and selective credit control, while in 1963 the latter was also applied to the mortgage banks.

Thus, detailed schedules of ratios were set up, from time to time, for four types of financial intermediaries, namely, deposit banks (commercial banks), savings banks, investment banks and mortgage banks. Different average and marginal reserve and credit requirements were applied to foreign and domestic currency liabilities as well as to time deposits, savings deposits and sight liabilities, and, in the case of deposit banks, a distinction was also made as to whether the bank was located in Mexico City, in the border zones or in the interior of the country.

In June, 1973, for example, deposit banks in Mexico City were required to maintain a minimum reserve deposit of 49 per cent of their domestic currency liabilities, except time deposits, and, in addition, to apply 28 per cent of such liabilities to credits for specified purposes, as compared with 25 and 47 per cent respectively in the case of banks in the interior. As far as their foreign currency liabilities were concerned, there were three different sets of ratios depending on certain conditions, but the ratio for reserve balances with the central bank in respect of additional deposits since 1955 was the same for all banks, namely, 25 per cent. With regard to other assets, the ratios prescribed under the selective credit control differed substantially. In the case of

Government securities, for example, the ratios ranged from 35 per cent for border-zone banks to 55 per cent for banks in the interior.

As regards savings banks, there were various sets of ratios depending upon the date of the deposit. The reserve-deposit requirement stood at 10 per cent in June, 1973, while the ratio for government and private securities averaged approximately 20 per cent of their total liabilities subject to the reserve requirement. The remainder of the 100 per cent legal cover in each case was distributed among credits for specified purposes and investments in production and commerce. The system of specified legal cover was also applied to the investment banks and the mortgage banks, except that the former were required to maintain a reserve deposit with the central bank only in respect of their issues of twelve-month promissory notes and other short-term liabilities and that, while mortgage banks were not obliged to maintain a reserve deposit, they were required to channel 30 per cent of their resources through the central bank into government bond issues and for low-income housing.

Thus, the allocation of bank credit, in general, as an instrument of monetary policy was conducted as part of the system of reserve-asset requirements in Mexico and will again be referred to in the next chapter.

Sweden

Between 1936 and 1941 several other countries authorized their central banks to employ variable reserve requirements, namely, Sweden, Ecuador and Costa Rica in 1937, Venezuela in 1940 and Australia in 1941. In Ecuador and Costa Rica, the legal reserve requirement took the form only of minimum balances which were to be kept with the central bank by the commercial banks and which could be varied by the central bank, at first between 5 and 15 per cent and later between 10 and 50 per cent of their demand and time deposits, while in Venezuela the banks were merely required to hold with the central bank a minimum of one-third of their legal cash reserves which were to consist of at least 15 per cent of their demand deposits and 8 per cent of their time deposits, but which could be increased by the central bank subject to the consent of the Federal Executive.

In Sweden, where the commercial banks were required by law to maintain a minimum reserve of certain liquid assets equivalent to 25 per cent of their sight liabilities, legislation was introduced in 1937 giving the Government the power to authorize the Riksbank, at the latter's request, to prescribe at will the minimum proportion of their legal reserves which the commercial banks should keep in the form of balances with the Riksbank. In 1950, when more stringent reserve regulations were adopted as an instrument of credit control, in view of the prevailing inflationary tendencies, it was laid down that at least one-quarter of the legal reserves was to be kept with the Riksbank; and the monetary authorities were empowered to increase the total reserve requirements for the commercial banks as well as to vary the proportion thereof which was to be held as a minimum balance with the Riksbank. Thus, the requirements in respect of liquid assets (more broadly defined and including certain housing bonds) were not only related to the banks' total liabilities instead of only their sight liabilities, but also different ratios were prescribed for the five largest banks, the medium-sized banks and the small banks. In January, 1960, for example, the ratios were as high as 45, 35 and 25 per cent respectively, but were reduced to 30, 25 and 25 per cent respectively by the end of 1961. In 1962 the Riksbank was also authorized to prescribe minimum liquidity ratios for savings banks, agricultural credit associations and the Post Office Bank.[10]

This method of flexible liquid-asset requirements, including flexible minimum balances with the central bank, was maintained in Sweden, although it was exercised at times during the fifties and sixties by voluntary agreement with the commercial banks or recommendation to them rather than by legal directive. It may be added, however, that the Riksbank also found it necessary at times to make extensive use of credit ceilings and quotas as well as open-market operations.

Australia

In Australia, under the National Security (Wartime Banking Control) Regulations issued in 1941, every 'trading bank' was required to 'lodge in a Special Account with the Commonwealth Bank such part of its surplus investible funds (i.e. the amount by which its assets in Australia at any time exceed the average of its assets in Australia in August, 1939) as is directed by the Commonwealth Bank in accordance with a plan approved by the Treasurer'. This legal requirement, which was introduced as one of the wartime anti-inflationary measures, was also designed to limit the profits of the trading banks and to place their lending and investment activities under the control of the central bank and the Treasury. It was incorporated in the Banking Act of 1945 and was, therefore, continued as a peacetime measure. According to the explanatory memorandum issued by the Treasury at the time, 'it has proved a simple, elastic and effective instrument of credit control and the Government considers that it should be used in the post-war years'; and 'if the central bank is to regulate the volume of credit it must . . . be able to ensure that the banks will have adequate liquid assets available in times of depression, but not too plentiful a supply in times of boom'.

In 1953 the system of special accounts was amended to change the basis for the calculation of the maximum amount which any trading bank could be required to hold with the Commonwealth Bank, namely, to the sum in its special account in October, 1952, plus 75 per cent of any increase in its deposits thereafter, and to provide that the maximum amount which could be called, must also be reduced by 75 per cent of any decrease in its deposits.

With the establishment of the Reserve Bank in 1959, however, provision was made for variable cash-reserve ratios instead of special accounts. Thus, the Reserve Bank was authorized to determine from time to time the minimum percentage of their deposit liabilities in Australia which the trading banks must keep as 'statutory reserve deposits' with the Reserve Bank, subject to a maximum of 25 per cent of their deposit liabilities, but which could be increased above 25 per cent in certain conditions and with forty-five days notice, although any ratio above 25 per cent could not remain in force for longer than an initial period of six months, and for succeeding periods of three months, unless the Reserve Bank gave notice of an extension at least forty-five days before the end of each period. The method of variable reserve ratios was adopted in line with the development in other countries because of objections to the special accounts system, which were mentioned by the Treasurer in Parliament, namely, that 'it is unnecessarily complex and is capable of being used in an arbitrary and discriminating manner'.

The Reserve Bank made substantial use of the flexible cash-reserve requirements.* Thus between January, 1960, and June, 1968, the ratio for the major trading banks was changed twenty-six times, the highest ratio being 17·5 per cent and the lowest 8 per cent, while lower ratios were prescribed for the smaller banks. In this connection, however, it was pointed out that 'not all adjustments made by the Reserve Bank in the Statutory Reserve ratio . . . indicate changes in general credit policy', and that 'on some occasions, particularly when changes in bank liquidity have been occurring as a result of other factors (e.g. international transactions), the ratio may be changed merely to maintain an existing policy position'.[11]

Furthermore, it must be mentioned that, although no legal provision was made in Australia for either fixed or variable liquid-asset requirements, an agreement was reached in 1956 between the central bank and the major trading banks under which the latter undertook not to let their ratio of certain liquid assets† to deposit liabilities fall below the agreed minimum. This ratio was first fixed at 14 per cent, but was increased, by agreement with the banks, to 16 per cent in 1959 and to 18 per cent in 1962. The importance of this additional requirement was reflected in the statement of the Reserve Bank that 'with the existence of a liquidity convention . . . a call to Statutory Reserve Deposit accounts is likely to have a greater and more immediate effect on bank lending to the private sector and, be-

* As in the case of the special accounts, interest was to be paid on the Reserve Deposits at a rate determined from time to time by the Reserve Bank with the approval of the Treasurer.

† Including notes and coin, cash with the central bank, and Commonwealth Treasury bills and Government securities, but excluding Statutory Reserve Deposits and loans to the short-term money market.

cause the impact on private borrowing is more direct, the effects on private spending of the Reserve Bank's action are likely to be more rapid and more certain'.[12]

Widespread Extension of Variable Reserve Requirements since the Forties

Most of the many new central banks which were created during the forties, fifties and sixties, were empowered in their original statutes, as in the case of the central banks of Venezuela and Costa Rica, to employ variable reserve requirements in one form or another, while the statutes of most of the central banks already in existence were amended to grant them such power, as had previously been done for the central banks of the United States, Mexico, New Zealand, Sweden, Ecuador and Australia. In short, the action and experience of these central banks set in motion such a strong trend in favour of the new instrument of credit control that it came to be adopted almost throughout the world. As in the case of the aforementioned countries, however, there were substantial differences not only in respect of the minimum or maximum limits (if any) of the legal reserve ratios and as to whether they were related to the total deposit liabilities of the institutions concerned or separately to their demand or time or savings deposits, and in conjunction with increases in deposit liabilities or not, but also whether the reserve requirements were applied merely to commercial banks or certain other banking and credit institutions as well and whether they consisted only of variable cash-reserve requirements or variable liquid-asset* or reserve-asset requirements, or both combined.

With regard to the countries which, since the early forties, granted their new or existing central banks the legal authority to impose variable reserve requirements only in respect of cash reserves (whether balances with the central bank only or also including notes and coin), the following examples can be mentioned in chronological order, namely, Thailand, Paraguay, Guatemala, Peru, Pakistan, West Germany, Ceylon, Korea,

* There were also substantial differences in the definition of 'liquid assets'.

Egypt, Burma, Norway, Syria, Ghana, Argentina, Japan, Kenya and France.* On the other hand, a number of countries provided only for variable liquid-asset or reserve-asset requirements, for example, Chile, Uruguay, Dominican Republic, Italy, Philippines, Iraq, Cuba, India† and Indonesia. Moreover, some countries authorized their central banks to employ both variable cash-reserve and variable liquid-asset requirements, either simultaneously or separately, for example, Belgium, Colombia, Canada, Austria and South Africa. Furthermore, mention must be made of a few central banks which employed variable reserve requirements by voluntary agreement with the banking institutions concerned, for example, in the Netherlands since 1954, Switzerland since 1955, and Great Britain since 1960, and also Sweden at times, as mentioned previously. Finally, some of these countries, as in the case of Mexico and the United States, applied the reserve requirements not only to the domestic liabilities of their commercial banks but also to their foreign liabilities, or made a distinction between liabilities to residents and non-residents, and at times a higher ratio was imposed on the latter than on the former as a means of discouraging the inflow of foreign funds.

West Germany

Variable reserve requirements were introduced in West Germany in 1948 when the Bank Deutscher Länder (Bank of the German States) was established as the new central bank in the place of the Reichsbank. It was provided that the minimum cash reserves which the commercial banks had to maintain in the form of balances with the central bank, could be varied between 8 and 20 per cent of their demand deposits and between 4 and 10 per cent of their time and savings deposits. From the start substan-

* In France variable liquid-asset requirements were introduced in 1961, but were replaced in 1967 by a system of variable cash balances with the central bank, in conjunction with a fixed liquid-asset requirement.

† In India variable cash-reserve requirements were adopted in 1956 but were subsequently replaced by variable liquid-asset requirements, in addition to fixed minimum cash balances with the central bank.

tial use was made of this power by the Bank as a means of influencing the liquidity of the banks and reinforcing its discount-rate policy.

When the Bank Deutscher Länder was reconstituted as the Deutsche Bundesbank in 1957, the system of minimum reserve requirements in the form only of balances with the central bank was retained, but no lower limit was laid down while the maximum limits within which the Bundesbank could vary the minimum reserve balances to be maintained by 'credit institutions', were raised to 30 per cent of their sight liabilities, 20 per cent of their time liabilities and 10 per cent of their savings deposits. The Bank was also authorized, within these limits, to prescribe reserve ratios on a differential basis, and this was done in several ways, namely, depending upon the size (volume of deposits) of the credit institutions concerned or their location (whether in places where the Bundesbank had a branch or not) or between their liabilities to residents and non-residents or between total liabilities and increases in liabilities.

The Bundesbank made extensive use of flexible reserve requirements, as a result of its having intermittently to cope with excessive liquidity, due not only to surpluses in the country's current balance of payments but also to periodic inflows of foreign funds, followed at times by substantial outflows. For this reason the Bank resorted at times to higher reserve ratios for the banks' liabilities to non-residents than to residents, and sometimes also prescribed special requirements in respect of increases in their foreign liabilities which were not applied to their domestic liabilities.

In December, 1968, for example, the banks were required, apart from the reserve balances to be held against their total foreign liabilities, to deposit with the Bundesbank the whole of any increase in their foreign liabilities after the 15th November, and this was maintained until November, 1969, when the reserve requirements for foreign and domestic liabilities were placed on the same basis, as well as on a lower level. After a few months, however, the ratio for foreign liabilities was again raised above that for domestic liabilities, in order to discourage the inflow of funds, and soon thereafter the ratios for both were increased. Then, in September, 1970, reserve requirements were once more introduced in respect of increases in both domestic and foreign liabilities, namely, 40 per cent for sight and time deposits and 20 per cent for savings deposits, but three months later this was replaced by an increase in the requirements on total liabilities, plus a reserve of 30 per cent against any increase in foreign liabilities.

It is evident, therefore, that the Bundesbank employed flexible cash-reserve requirements not only frequently but also in various ways and for various purposes, and that, judging by the apparently experimental nature of some of the changes, this instrument was not always found to be promptly or sufficiently effective for the purpose concerned. There would, however, appear to be no doubt that it was an indispensable instrument of monetary policy in West Germany, in view of the severe fluctuations in its balance of payments due mainly to the inward and outward movements of foreign funds, and that, in conjunction with the Bundesbank's increased open-market operations and as a means of reinforcing changes in the official discount rate, it performed a vital function.

Korea

As in the case of several other new central banks prior to its establishment in 1950, the Bank of Korea was empowered in its original constitution to vary the minimum reserve requirements with which the commercial banks had to comply, namely, between 10 and 50 per cent of their deposit liabilities. The Bank was also authorized, in periods of pronounced inflation, to impose a supplementary requirement of up to 100 per cent in respect of any increase in deposits after a specified date, and to prescribe different reserve ratios for different classes of bank deposits.

The reserve requirement was applied only to cash reserves, but apart from their balances with the central bank the banks were allowed to count their holdings of currency as part of the legal reserves up to 20 per cent of the total amount required, which was subsequently increased to 25 per cent. Moreover, the Bank availed itself of the right to prescribe different reserve ratios for different classes of bank deposits and specified three classes in its early years, namely, special deposits (of public institutions and Government agencies), time and savings deposits, and other deposits (demand deposits). During this period a higher reserve ratio than in the case of time and other deposits was 'required for the deposits of the government's financial funds of specific categories in order to limit the extent of deposit creation by banks on the basis of such funds'.[13] From 1957, however, a distinction was made only between demand deposits and time and savings deposits.

The Bank soon decided to use its power to vary the reserve requirements, particularly in respect of demand deposits, the ratio for which was as high as 25 per cent in October, 1955, and as low as 10 per cent in June, 1962, while the ratio for time and savings deposits during this period was maintained at the minimum of 10 per cent. The Bank also decided at an early stage, 'in the face of mounting inflationary pressure', to impose a supplementary requirement against an increase in the deposit liabilities of the banks, namely, 50 per cent of any increase after September, 1952, which was reduced to 45 per cent in January, 1953, and then withdrawn in view of the currency reform at the time.[14]

According to Kim, 'the effectiveness of this instrument of credit control was neutralized on account of the ready access by the commercial banks to the Bank of Korea credits', in the sense that 'the restrictive effect of increased reserve requirements was frequently evaded by the commercial banks through their borrowing the needed additional reserves from the Bank of Korea'.[15] This observation was relevant to various other central banks which were accustomed or authorized only to prescribe minimum cash-reserve requirements and yet felt obliged, as a matter of general principle, to accommodate the commercial banks under all circumstances and without severe penalties, through rediscounts of bills or collateral loans against Government or other public securities.

South Africa

In South Africa the principle of variable reserve requirements was first adopted in 1956 when the Reserve Bank was empowered to require the commercial banks to maintain supplementary reserves, i.e. over and above the minimum credit balances which they had to keep with the Reserve Bank and which had since 1923 remained fixed at 10 per cent of their demand liabilities and 3 per cent of their time liabilities. Two different bases for such supplementary reserves were laid down, namely, up to 10 per cent of their total liabilities to the public or up to 90 per cent of any increase in such liabilities after a specified date. The banks were, however, not required to hold the whole of the supplementary reserves in the form of balances with the Reserve Bank, since they were allowed to deduct therefrom an amount equivalent to any net increase in the aggregate of their holdings of Treasury bills, Government stock with a maturity not exceeding three years, Land Bank bills or advances to the Land Bank and such other assets as might be approved of by the Reserve Bank for this purpose. This was intended not only to compensate the banks to some extent for having to maintain supplementary reserves, as the Reserve Bank was prohibited from paying interest on deposits, but also to induce them, at such times, to employ their surplus cash in short-term Government securities and/or credit facilities extended to the State-owned Land Bank, with a view to avoiding or reducing the creation of central bank credit for meeting any special needs of the public sector.

In 1965, however, a new system of reserve requirements was introduced which covered all banking institutions* (except discount houses), instead of commercial banks only, and which provided for variable liquid-asset ratios in respect of their short† and medium-term‡ liabilities, as well as a fixed ratio of short-term liabilities to be kept as minimum balances with the Reserve Bank. The latter requirement applied only to banking institutions whose short-term liabilities exceeded R500,000, and was fixed at 8 per cent of such liabilities, while the ratios for liquid assets (including balances with the Reserve Bank) could be varied, for

* Those specifically named were merchant banks, hire-purchase banks, savings banks and general banks.

† Deposits or other liabilities payable within thirty days or subject to less than thirty days' notice.

‡ Payable after thirty days or subject to not less than thirty days' but less than six months' notice, and including savings deposits.

any and all classes of banking institutions, between a minimum of 20 per cent and a maximum of 40 per cent in respect of their short-term liabilities and between 10 and 30 per cent in the case of their medium-term liabilities, i.e. 10 per cent on either side of the normal ratios of 30 and 20 per cent respectively. Alternatively, the Reserve Bank could require institutions in any category to maintain supplementary liquid assets up to 70 and 80 per cent of any increase, after a specified date, in their short and medium-term liabilities respectively. Provision was also made for a fixed minimum liquid-asset ratio of 5 per cent of their long-term liabilities. Moreover, the legal definition of 'liquid assets' was tightened, as compared with the one used for the former liquidity ratio of 30 per cent of the commercial banks' total liabilities, with a view to reinforcing the use of variable liquidity ratios as an instrument of monetary policy.

In the special circumstances which prevailed in South Africa during the years 1965–68, however, the scope for increasing the supplementary liquid-asset requirements proved to be inadequate for the purpose of countering the exceptional liquidity of the banking sector. This liquidity was due not only to a net surplus in the balance of payments, but also to substantial net borrowing by the Government from the banking sector, during the first half of the period, as well as an increase in bank credit to the Land Bank by means of bills and advances, both of which ranked as liquid assets for the banks. Under these abnormal conditions the Reserve Bank first tried, as usual, to restrict bank credit to the private sector through moral suasion, but later resorted to the use of special powers granted to it under a Government proclamation in September, 1967, enabling it to impose credit ceilings on any class of banking institution as an additional method of credit control, and also to prescribe supplementary cash-reserve requirements in the form of reserve balances with the Reserve Bank or call deposits with the National Finance Corporation. These powers were employed until 1972 when, in accordance with the recommendations of a Technical Committee, the Banks Act was amended and the Reserve Bank's powers in respect of variable reserve requirements were extended, as follows.

In the first place, the supplementary liquid-asset requirements in respect of the short- and medium-term liabilities of any class of banking institutions may be raised up to 30 per cent and 20 per cent above the normal ratios of 30 and 20 per cent respectively, i.e. to total maximum ratios of 60 per cent and 40 per cent respectively, instead of 40 and 30 per cent as was previously the case. Secondly, the liquidity ratio for long-term liabilities, which was previously fixed at 5 per cent, may be increased up to 10 per cent. Thirdly, the former provision for supplementary liquid assets up to 70 and 80 per cent of any increase, after a specified date, in the short and medium-term liabilities respectively, was retained at 70 and 50 per cent respectively and also made applicable to long-term liabilities up to 20 per cent of any increase, but instead of serving only as an alternative to the requirement in respect of the total amount concerned, the Bank was authorized to apply both methods simultaneously, subject to certain adjustments. Fourthly, the imposition of supplementary liquid-asset requirements in respect of total short- and medium-term liabilities, which was previously limited to a maximum rate of 4 per cent per month, may be made at a rate of up to 10 per cent per month, and up to 5 per cent in the case of long-term liabilities. Fifthly, the definition of 'liquid assets' was further narrowed, and it was also laid down that a bank's holdings of bankers' acceptances, trade bills, agricultural bills and promissory notes eligible for rediscount with the Reserve Bank, shall rank as liquid assets only up to 20 per cent of its normal or supplementary liquid-asset requirements. Sixthly, all banking institutions (other than discount houses) are required to maintain with the Reserve Bank a minimum balance of 8 per cent of their short-term liabilities, irrespective of the size of such liabilities. Finally, the Reserve Bank may prescribe, as a part or the whole of any supplementary liquid-asset requirements, additional cash reserves to be maintained as reserve balances with the Reserve Bank or call deposits with the National Finance Corporation.

The amended Banks Act came into operation on the 1st November, 1972, and as from that date the existing ceilings on bank credit were removed, while all banking institutions were required to maintain liquid assets (including cash reserves) amounting to not less than the aggregate of 45 per cent of their short-term liabilities, 28 per cent of their medium-term and 5 per cent of their long-term liabilities. With regard to the cash reserves, they were required, apart from the minimum reserve balance of 8 per cent of their short-term liabilities to be held with the Reserve Bank, to maintain a supplementary reserve balance with the National Finance Corporation amounting to 10 per cent of such liabilities.

The present position, therefore, is that legal provision has been made for both variable liquid-asset and variable cash-reserve requirements 'whenever the Reserve Bank deems it desirable in the national economic interest' and 'with the consent of the Treasury'. The main emphasis is still placed on variable liquid-asset ratios as the more effective method in the long run, but experience has shown that variable cash-reserve ratios are also necessary at times to assist in neutralizing the effects, in particular, of an excessive inflow of foreign funds.

Great Britain

In Great Britain, where the commercial banks maintained conventional reserve ratios by agreement with the Bank of England, namely, 8 per cent of their deposit liabilities in cash (including notes and coin) and 28 per cent in liquid assets (including cash), a new arrangement with the banks was announced in 1958, under which 'the Bank of England will, if need be, restrict the liquidity of the banking system by calling for special deposits', i.e. in addition to the conventional reserve ratios. As explained by the authorities at the time, the 'special deposit scheme' was intended to reinforce existing monetary instruments, and it was hoped 'to dispense with official requests to restrict total advances'.

The first call for special deposits was made by the Bank of England in June, 1960, namely, 1 per cent of gross deposits from the London clearing banks and ½ per cent in the case of the Scottish banks. These special deposits, however, were not to be counted as liquid assets for the purpose of the minimum liquidity ratio on the ground that they were not at the free disposal of the banks, and interest based on the current Treasury bill rate was to be paid by the Bank of England on such deposits.* The special-deposit ratios, which were raised in stages to 3 per cent for the London banks and 1½ per cent for the Scottish banks by 1962 and subsequently reduced to nil, stood at 2 and 1 per cent respectively in July, 1966, and remained at that level until May, 1970, when the ratios were increased to 2½ and 1¼ per cent respectively, and in November, 1970, to 3½ and 1¾ per cent respectively. The former increase (in May) was made 'to emphasize the need for continuing restraint', and the latter because 'lending by the London and Scottish clearing banks grew rapidly' and 'a further increase in Special Deposits . . . was therefore called for'.[16]

In September, 1971, however, the existing special deposits of the London and Scottish clearing banks were released and all current ceiling limits on lending were removed, while new arrangements with the banking sector were brought into effect, under which all banks in Great Britain were required to maintain minimum holdings of 'eligible reserve assets' equivalent to 12½ per cent of their 'eligible liabilities'.† Moreover, the Bank retained the right to call for special deposits from all banks on a uniform basis whenever the conditions warranted it. As explained by the Bank of England, 'the essence of the new scheme is to allow banks more scope for competition and innovation by moving away from a system based on quantitative restrictions to a generalized method of control where the allocation of credit is determined primarily by its cost'.[17]

In connection with the release of the existing special deposits in September, 1971, it should be added that the authorities arranged with the London clearing banks to subscribe to £750

* This meant, in effect, that not only the minimum cash ratio but also the minimum liquidity ratio was raised whenever special deposits had to be made with the Bank of England.

† '*Eligible liabilities*' were defined as sterling deposit liabilities, excluding deposits having an original maturity of over two years, plus any sterling resources obtained by switching foreign currencies into sterling, while '*eligible assets*' comprised balances with the Bank of England (other than special deposits), money at call with the London money market, British Treasury bills and Government stocks with one year or less to final maturity, local authority bills and commercial bills eligible for rediscount at the Bank of England.

million of new Government stocks, in order to avoid their holding a disproportionate amount of reserve assets from the start of the scheme. Nevertheless, the minimum reserve ratio of 12½ per cent which was to be uniform for all banks, appeared to be relatively low on average, considering the definition of reserve assets and the removal of credit ceilings, but the authorities, no doubt, relied on their wide scope for open-market operations as well as their right to call for such special deposits* as were found to be necessary for the control of credit.

Similar credit control arrangements to those with the banks were agreed by the Bank with those members of the Finance Houses Association, and certain other instalment credit institutions outside the Association, whose sterling liabilities exceed £5 million. Under the new scheme, these participating houses were required to maintain a minimum reserve ratio of 10 per cent and were also to be subject to calls for special deposits with the Bank of England, as in the case of the banks. It was also agreed with the discount houses that they would maintain a minimum of 50 per cent of their borrowed funds in public sector debt.

Thus, in Great Britain the instrument of variable cash-reserve requirements, which was at first confined to the London and Scottish clearing banks, was extended to cover not only all other banks but also the principal finance houses, and it was employed in such a manner that it was, in effect, also a variable liquid-asset requirement.

Conclusion

The foregoing survey showed that the principle of employing variable reserve requirements as an instrument of monetary policy, which was first introduced in the United States through appropriate amendments of the Federal Reserve Act in 1933 and 1935, was subsequently adopted, in one form or another, over a very large part of the world; that, in general, the central banks were granted specific legal powers for the performance of this

* A call for special deposits of 1 per cent of total eligible liabilities was made by the Bank of England in November, 1972, and a further call of 2 per cent was made in December, 1972.

function, but that some of the older central banks evidently preferred to do so by voluntary agreement with the commercial banks and other banking institutions concerned, as in the case of the Bank of England, the Netherlands Bank and the National Bank of Switzerland, and also the Riksbank of Sweden at times; that the extensive adoption of this new instrument of monetary policy was, no doubt, attributable to the fact that it was capable of being implemented for the control of bank credit in all kinds of countries, whether there were organized money markets or not and whether their economies were well developed, semi-developed or underdeveloped, and that it particularly lent itself to modifications and adaptations to suit the different circumstances of different countries at different times; and that it was not only used in various ways but also for various purposes.

The employment of variable reserve requirements was adopted generally as an alternative or additional means of exercising control over the money supply by controlling the available amount of bank cash and thus the volume of bank credit. In many countries this instrument was employed only in the form of changes in cash-reserve requirements, and in some only in respect of commercial banks, and both these factors tended to limit its effectiveness as a restrictive measure. In the case of the former, an increase in the cash-reserve requirement, particularly where there was not even a fixed minimum liquid-asset requirement, could be partly or wholly neutralized by the commercial banks realizing some of their liquid assets through rediscounts or collateral loans from the central bank or sales of Government securities to the central bank in the open market, while in the latter case the restrictive effect on the commercial banks could be partly or wholly nullified by an increase in the activities of other banking or credit institutions. For these reasons various countries decided to prescribe either a fixed liquid-asset requirement in addition to a variable cash-reserve requirement, or a variable liquid-asset requirement with a fixed minimum cash-reserve requirement, and some countries even came to adopt both variable cash-reserve and liquid-asset requirements, although not necessarily to be used simultaneously, in the effort to find a more effective method of coping with abnormal circumstances. Some countries also decided to extend the reserve requirements to certain other institutions as well as the commercial banks.

While many countries employed the one or other form of variable reserve requirements only as an instrument of quantitative credit control, it was also used in some countries as a means of selective credit control, namely, to promote the financing of agriculture or cattle-raising or productive equipment, as in Mexico, or of housing, as in Sweden, or exports of capital goods, as in various countries, by allowing the bills or loans concerned to be counted by the banks as 'reserve assets'. This likewise applied to the inclusion of certain types and maturities of Government securities as a means of ensuring a minimum contribution from the banking sector for the financing of the Government, and in some countries a secondary reserve requirement was also imposed on the banks to hold a minimum amount of Government bonds, not only to assist in the financing of Government capital outlays but also to limit the opportunities of the banks for disposing of Government bonds in order to increase their loans for general business purposes.

In this connection it deserves to be mentioned that, in the relevant legislation as well as in actual practice, too much emphasis would appear to have been placed in most countries on the need to control bank credit to the private sector, as compared with the public sector. In fact, experience has shown that the tendency of Governments to have excessive recourse at times to both central bank and commercial bank credit has been one of the principal factors limiting the effectiveness of variable reserve requirements.

In conclusion, while it is evident that a comprehensive system of variable reserve requirements, such as one comprising both variable cash-reserve and liquid-asset requirements (with an appropriate definition of 'liquid assets') and covering all the necessary banking institutions, should normally be able to exercise its direct and full impact on the available amount of bank cash, and consequently on the volume of bank credit and the supply of money and near-money in the desired direction, it should be borne in mind, as pointed out in Chapter 10, that the simultaneous operation of certain counterforces can at times neutralize partly or wholly the effects of changes in reserve requirements on the money supply, as in the case of open-market operations. Despite such limitations, however, there is no doubt that variable reserve requirements have an important role to play in the execution of monetary policy to the extent that it can be made effective at any particular time, either as the principal or a subsidiary instrument. In the latter capacity, it can at least help the central bank to make its discount-rate policy or open-market operations or direct control of bank credit more effective than would otherwise be the case, or to render it less necessary to take drastic or frequent action with the other methods of credit control. In the final instance, its effectiveness as an instrument of monetary policy, as in the case of the others, depends not only on the co-operation of the banking sector, but also on the support of the Treasury in the form of an appropriate fiscal policy and sound management of Government debt.

References

1 *Federal Reserve Bulletin.* August, 1936.
2 *Ibid.* May, 1937.
3 *Ibid.* May, 1938.
4 *Federal Reserve Bulletin.* November, 1972. p. 994.
5 *Annual Report of the Board of Governors of the Federal Reserve System for 1970.* p. 81.
6 *Reserve Bank of New Zealand Bulletin.* May, 1971. p. 98.
7 *Ibid.* January–February, 1965. p. 4.
8 *Ibid.* May, 1971. p. 98.
9 Myers, M., in *Banking Systems.* Ed. Beckhart. Columbia U.P., 1954. pp. 584–6.
10 *Eight European Central Banks.* Ed. Bank for International Settlements. Allen & Unwin, 1963. pp. 327–30.
11 *Reserve Bank of Australia.* Reserve Bank, 1969. pp. 8–9.
12 *Ibid.* pp. 9–11.
13 Kim, B. K. *Central Banking Experiment in a Developing Economy.* Korean Research Centre, 1965. p. 163.
14 *Ibid.* pp. 164–6.
15 *Ibid.* pp. 167 and 177.
16 *Bank of England Annual* Report *for 1970–71.* pp. 13–14.
17 *Bank of England Annual* Report *for 1971–72.* p. 11.

CHAPTER TWELVE

Other Methods of Credit Control

Rationing of Central Bank Credit

Towards the end of the eighteenth century, rationing of credit was found to be employed as an instrument of credit control by the Bank of England, which placed a limit upon its discounts for any one house or rejected a proportion of each discount application whenever total demands exceeded the sum which it was prepared to discount on any one day.[1]

As long as the Bank was prohibited by the usury law from raising its discount rate beyond the maximum of 5 per cent, it was obliged to resort to other methods of restricting the demands for accommodation made upon it during times of stringency and declining gold reserves; and the methods which it chose to use under the circumstances were not only the rationing of credit by limiting the amount available to each applicant, but also the shortening of the currency of bills eligible for rediscount. Both these methods invariably elicited severe protests, since they tended at times to operate very harshly and unjustly against certain houses and certain trades, and also to engender fears of a panic or crisis whenever a credit stringency developed.

The usury law was relaxed in 1833, when bills of exchange of up to three months were exempted from the legal restriction, followed a few years later by the extension of the exemption to bills of any currency. Bank rate was, however, not used as an instrument of control till 1839, and it was not until after the Bank Act of 1844 was brought into operation that the Bank came to rely upon Bank rate as its primary weapon. It was then decided to discontinue rationing credit either as an alternative or as a supplement to a rise in Bank rate, since the Bank was gradually developing in the direction of accepting the position of being the lender of last resort, and since the allocation of credit quotas or other forms of arbitrary credit restriction in a crisis were considered difficult to reconcile with the duty and responsibility of the lender of last resort. This situation developed also in other countries where the discount rate came to be adopted as the principal weapon. It was only under war or other highly abnormal conditions that further instances of credit rationing by some European central banks emerged from time to time.

Thus, owing to the exceptionally difficult and critical conditions with which some countries had to contend as a result, directly or indirectly, of the aftermath of World War I, credit rationing in one form or another was adopted on several occasions by the central banks of such countries. Wagemann,[2] for example, noted that under the pressure of necessity credit rationing might be said to have been 'rediscovered' for the purpose of credit control, as reflected in credit rationing and credit restriction in Germany in 1924, 'when the currency which had been stabilized by the introduction of the Rentenmark was endangered'; in 1929, 'when the Paris negotiations in connection with the Young Plan led to the withdrawal of foreign money from Germany and to attacks on the German currency', and when 'the Reichsbank wanted by means of credit restriction to force the banks to do everything in their power to counteract this manoeuvre'; and in 1931, when 'the Reichsbank used credit quotas to prevent the collapse of the large banks'.*

In the meantime, Soviet Russia adopted an elaborate system of credit rationing by or through the central bank as an essential element in the financial structure of a communist, authoritarian economy. Katzenellenbaum,[3] for example, pointed out (in 1929) that the discount rate of the State Bank of the U.S.S.R. 'is neither an index of the supply and demand of loan funds nor a

* After 1931, Germany preferred to exercise general control over the capital market, which will be discussed in Chapter 14.

regulator of such supply', but that 'the State Bank is guided by another principle in regard to the investment of its inflowing funds, namely, the allocation of funds among financially sound credit aspirants in accordance with a definite plan', and that 'at times when the demands for credit exceed the State Bank's available resources . . . the State Bank is obliged to divide these funds in some definite way among the enterprises which have need of them'.

In Mexico the central bank also employed 'the rationing of credit as principal regulating weapon',[4] owing to such circumstances as the rigid economic structure of the country and the slight development of the local money market. In 1932 the Bank of Mexico was authorized to fix lines of credit for commercial banks and other associated institutions, and the first basis adopted for its credit limits was the amount of the 'social capital' of each associated bank, but this was changed in 1936 to the amount of each bank's total resources.

Prior to World War II there were few other examples of the rationing of central bank credit, apart from such 'direct action' by some central banks as refusing to rediscount for banks whose credit policy was regarded as being inconsistent with the maintenance of sound credit conditions, or to grant further rediscounts or collateral loans to banks whose borrowings from the central bank were considered to be excessive in relation to their capital and reserves or to their proportionate share (as compared with the other banks) of the resources of the central bank. In this connection, legislation was actually passed in the United States, in 1933 and 1935, to the effect that each Federal Reserve Bank was to keep itself informed of the general character and amount of the loans and investments of its member banks, with a view to ascertaining whether undue use was made of bank credit for speculation in securities, real estate or commodities, and that in determining whether to grant or refuse advances, rediscounts or other accommodations, the Federal Reserve Banks should give due consideration to such information. Such action, however, was regarded by most central banks at the time as detracting from their fundamental position as the lender of last resort, and they preferred, therefore, to raise their eligibility requirements for rediscounts or to charge the offending banks varying penalty rates over and above the official discount rate instead of actually refusing to grant them rediscount facilities.

Since the war, however, various central banks have resorted to the rationing of their credit to the banking sector, particularly at times when other methods of quantitative credit control proved to be inadequate to curb strong inflationary pressures. Thus, in France rediscount quotas as an instrument of general monetary policy, and as an anti-inflationary measure in particular, was introduced for the first time in 1948, when a directive was issued by the Bank of France which allocated to each bank a maximum limit for its rediscounts of commercial paper. These rediscount quotas had a substantial restrictive effect since in France rediscounts of commercial bills traditionally played an important part in the regulation of banking liquidity, but no ceilings were imposed on rediscounts of Treasury bills or bills issued by certain Government credit institutions. Moreover, the rediscount quotas for commercial bills were adjusted from time to time depending upon the prevailing circumstances.

In West Germany, where ceilings were imposed by the central bank on the total lendings of commercial banks to reinforce its policy of credit restriction in 1948, and again in 1950, it was found necessary on the latter occasion to resort also to the rationing of central bank credit by means of rediscount quotas, which was the method of credit restriction that had been used by the Reichsbank during the twenties.

As in France, each bank was allocated a specific quota for its rediscounts with the central bank, although the banks were permitted to obtain additional credit through collateral loans at a higher rate than the official discount rate, and subject to certain conditions. The allocation of rediscount quotas in West Germany, which was introduced by the Bank Deutscher Länder in 1950, was continued by the Bundesbank and employed as another variable instrument of credit control.

The rationing of central bank credit in one way or another was adopted by various other countries, not only in Western Europe but also in other parts of the world. It was, for example, used by the Bank of Japan during the post-war period until 1955, with penalty rates for its rediscounts and loans in excess of the limit for each bank, and also subsequently at certain times. It was also employed in Korea during the fifties, in conjunction with ceilings on commercial bank loans.

Furthermore, after the war the Soviet system of comprehensive credit rationing as a medium of detailed economic planning was transplanted to all the so-called satellite communist countries in Eastern Europe.

In general, it is evident that the rationing of central bank credit by means of fixed quotas, even if they are adjusted from time to time, is a method of control which, for its effective employment, requires either a fully planned and regimented economy, as in the authoritarian and totalitarian communist states, or at least a very large measure of general economic control, as in some other countries in Asia and Latin America. In fact, it can be regarded as a logical concomitant of the extensive and intensive economic planning practised in such countries. There is, however, also some justification or need for its use in countries where the conventional instruments of credit control cannot be used to any great extent, if at all. Wagemann,[5] for example, pointed out that, 'in more primitive economic conditions, the setting of credit quotas is the only decisive method which the central bank has in order to prevent excessive credit demands on the part of business'. Otherwise, credit rationing which cannot, in any case, be reconciled with the central bank's function as the lender of last resort, can be justified only as an abnormal measure dictated by special circumstances or as a temporary expedient until more suitable measures can be brought into effect.

Direct Quantitative Control of Bank Credit

As mentioned previously, some central banks have at times employed both the rationing of central bank credit and the imposition of ceilings on the total loans and discounts of commercial banks and other banking institutions concerned. In recent times, however, the latter has become the more general method of quantitative credit restriction and has, as in the case of variable reserve requirements, been adopted by all kinds of countries because of the intermittent inadequacy or undesirability of other available instruments of credit control. In fact, many central banks have resorted at times to ceilings on total bank lendings in conjunction with increases in cash-reserve and/or liquid-asset requirements, in order to reinforce their efforts to curb excessive expansion of bank credit or even to bring about a reduction thereof if considered necessary owing, for example, to a serious deficit in the balance of payments. Moreover, while central banks generally have been granted, directly or indirectly, the legal power to restrict bank credit by means of ceilings or other methods for purposes of monetary policy, some central banks have, as in the case of variable reserve requirements, preferred to do so by consultation and voluntary agreement with the banks concerned.

In general, credit ceilings were usually based on each bank's lendings to the private sector at a particular date, and were originally imposed mainly with a view to preventing a further expansion thereof and maintaining the volume of such bank credit at or close to the prescribed level for as long as it was considered necessary, although there were occasions when the central bank was pressed to raise the ceiling one or more times before it was finally removed. In recent times, however, various central banks have employed a more systematic and flexible method of credit restriction in accordance with a predetermined policy of permitting the expansion of bank lendings within a prescribed maximum percentage per annum, which could nevertheless be varied if conditions changed. The Netherlands Bank, for example, allowed an annual growth rate of 10 per cent in respect of short-term bank lending to the private sector for 1969, which was reduced to 9½ per cent in 1970 and 9 per cent in 1971, before the ceiling was suspended* in March, 1972, while the Swiss National Bank permitted an annual growth rate ranging from 9 to 11½ per cent for 1969/70, depending upon the individual bank's previous lending activity, and this was reduced to an average of 8¼ per cent for 1970/72.

Moreover, many central banks which have employed ceilings

* According to the *Annual Report of the Netherlands Bank for 1971*, 'the suspension implies that the Bank reserves the right to reimpose the restrictive measures if the banks' lendings and investments should expand too strongly' (p. 130).

on total bank lendings for purposes of quantitative credit restriction, either as a long or short-term measure, have also resorted to control over the purposes for which bank credit could be used, and in some cases also the maximum amounts which could be allocated for such purposes. While the two methods have been employed simultaneously at times, namely, the latter within the total limits of the former, the general trend in the countries concerned would appear to have been in the direction of the more frequent and extensive use of Selective Credit Control, which will be discussed separately.

With regard to quantitative credit ceilings, the experience of some central banks has evidently not been satisfactory, since they have either abandoned this method or relegated it to the background. For example, the Bank of England, which had formally used it for the first time in 1957 and also resorted thereto on various occasions during the sixties as well as in 1970/1,* decided to abolish the existing credit ceilings in September, 1971, and the reasons given for this decision were 'to strike off the shackles that had been frustrating initiative and innovation in the provision of financial services',[6] and 'to allow banks more scope for competition and innovation by moving away from a system based on quantitative restrictions to a generalized method of control where the allocation of credit is determined principally by its cost'.[7]

Furthermore, the South African Reserve Bank, which had resorted to credit ceilings for the first time in 1965, under conditions of excessive banking liquidity and credit expansion, and employed this method of credit restriction continuously, with occasional upward adjustments of the original ceilings, decided finally to abandon it on 1st November, 1972, when the amended Banks Act came into operation and a new stricter system of both variable liquid-asset and cash-reserve requirements for banking institutions generally was introduced. As the background for this decision, the following excerpts from two official reports deserve to be mentioned:

* The last occasion was when the banks and finance houses were requested to restrict increases in their lendings to the private sector and overseas borrowers to 2½ per cent above the limits which had been set for June, 1971, as compared with the previous restriction to 5 per cent above the limits set for March, 1971.

(i) 'A consequence of the application of direct control measures is that in certain important respects healthy competition among the controlled banking institutions is restricted. In addition, the Reserve Bank as the administrator of the credit ceilings is burdened with the comparatively extensive additional task of the collection of data, inspection and supervision. Furthermore, the Reserve Bank is more or less constantly subjected to pressure either to raise the ceilings as such or to grant concessions for special purposes not to be included in the ceilings.'[8]

(ii) 'The direct quantitative control by means of ceilings on discounts, advances and investments was rejected by banking institutions ... as ineffective and harmful, because these restrictions restrain competition in the banking sector and, moreover, stimulate the grey market.'[9]

In conclusion, it would appear that the imposition of ceilings on total bank lending to the private sector has not proved to be a method of credit restriction suitable for general adoption. It is a blunt and cumbersome weapon that can obviously be justified only in highly abnormal conditions when other available means have been found to be inadequate, and only as a temporary expedient until more appropriate arrangements can be made. It is inherently inequitable not only between one bank or group of banks and another, particularly in a rapidly developing economy, but also because the restrictions on bank credit have usually been applied only to the private sector, whereas it has frequently been the excessive spending and borrowing of the public sector that has been the main cause of the over-expansion and other maladjustments of the economy. In other words, credit ceilings should be regarded only as an instrument of last resort.

Selective Credit Control

As mentioned previously, the general trend in many countries, including some of those which have employed quantitative credit ceilings, would appear to have been in the direction of the more frequent and extensive use of qualitative or selective credit control.

Selective credit control was practised by various central banks prior to World War II, but usually by means of moral suasion and/or such technical measures as differential discount and interest rates and restriction of credit instruments eligible for rediscounts or collateral loans. The main exceptions were Soviet Russia, Nazi Germany and Fascist Italy, where not only the banking sector but the economy as a whole was controlled. Since the war, however, many central banks have been specifically empowered by law to exercise direct control over the credit operations of the commercial banks and, in some cases, also other banking institutions.

Some central banks were authorized to continue using their wartime powers of credit control under normal legislation. In Australia, for example, the Banking Act of 1945 provided that 'the Commonwealth Bank may determine the policy in relation to advances to be followed by banks . . . and may give directions as to the classes of purposes for which advances may or may not be made by banks'.* The Commonwealth Bank was also enabled to control interest rates on bank advances and deposits, and this was used to fix maximum rates from time to time. In 1956, however, the Bank adopted the principle of selective interest rates, which had already been followed by some of the Latin-American central banks, although in a different form. The method adopted by the Commonwealth Bank was that of permitting the trading banks to aim at an average return of 5½ per cent, with the right to vary their rates for advances within a maximum limit of 6 per cent, but on the understanding that advances for such 'nationally desirable' purposes as promoting exports or the production of import-saving goods would qualify for rates below the average, while those for financing business in consumer goods purchased abroad would be charged at rates above the average.

The power to control the purposes of bank advances and the interest rates paid or received by banks was also granted to the

* According to the explanatory memorandum issued by the Australian Treasury at the time, these powers were granted to the Commonwealth Bank 'to ensure that at all times the credit resources of the nation are put to the best use, and that the making of advances by banks does not lead to an unbalanced expansion of credit in any particular field'.

Reserve Bank when it was established in 1959, but its general practice has been to 'exercise a qualitative influence over trading bank lending' only 'at times, especially when policy is restrictive', and then 'it may request the banks in the allocation of their loans to have special regard to the needs of particular classes of borrowers, such as primary producers or exporters, or to avoid lending for certain purposes such as speculative stock-building'.[10] With regard to interest rates on bank advances and deposits, the Reserve Bank's practice has been to fix only maximum rates after discussion with the banks and with the approval of the Treasurer.[11]

The Reserve Bank of New Zealand was another example of a central bank which was authorized to continue using its wartime powers of credit control, and which was granted similar normal legal powers as in Australia. But contrary to the subsequent development in Australia, the general trend in New Zealand has been to make an extensive use of a combination of both quantitative and selective credit controls. Thus, the new Act of 1964 empowered the Reserve Bank to give directions to the trading banks not only as to the aggregate amounts and limits of advances, discounts and investments for the time being deemed appropriate, but also the classes of advances and discounts that should be encouraged or restricted or refused, and the classes of investments that may or may not be made or held. Ceilings were set for total bank advances in two tiers, the top tier covering all forms of export activity for which 'priority treatment is justified in principle by the importance of exports to New Zealand's balance of payments and economic growth', and the bottom tier consisting of all other advances to which 'a specific and carefully calculated ceiling is applied'. In a recent address, the Governor of the Bank admitted that 'unfortunately the system is becoming more and more complicated and the arbitrariness of it is becoming more obvious', but concluded that 'we have now a fairly long history of detailed control of bank advances and it is hard to break away' and 'it is desirable to maintain some kind of priority system in the provision of credit'.[12]

In Mexico, where credit was already rationed and controlled during the thirties, variable reserve requirements came to be employed by the Bank of Mexico not only as a means of controlling the credit-creating capacity of the banking sector, but also as an instrument for facilitating and reinforcing its measures of selective credit control. Thus, apart from the minimum cash balances which were to be maintained with the central bank by the 'deposit banks', savings banks and investment banks against their deposit and other short-term liabilities, provision was made for the allocation of their remaining deposit resources for the specific purposes determined by the monetary authorities from time to time. With reference to 1971, for example, it was reported that 'in accordance with the targets set by the Administration, monetary and credit policies were also directed towards channelling an even greater volume of resources to top-priority sectors in the economy such as agriculture, the promotion of exports, tourism, and housing for low-income families', and that 'policies also endeavoured to step up the flow of funds to the public sector and to diminish its needs for external financing'.[13] The top-priority sectors were likewise supported through the various trust funds created by the Federal Government and administered by the Bank of Mexico. Similar measures of selective credit control were also adopted by Argentina and several other Latin-American countries.

In India the Reserve Bank was authorized, in 1949, to determine the general advance policy to be followed by the commercial banks and to lay down the purposes for which bank advances may or may not be made, the margins to be maintained and the rate of interest to be charged on advances. All of these powers have been used at times, but the principal form of selective credit control would appear to have been the regulation of total bank advances against specified commodities, i.e. by tightening or relaxing or removing or re-imposing restrictions on such advances, depending upon the prevailing circumstances of supply and demand. Thus, the Annual Report of the Reserve Bank for 1971/72 noted (p. 43) that 'in the field of selective credit controls, while those in regard to advances against raw cotton and kapas, foodgrains, oilseeds, vegetable oils (including vanaspati) were relaxed during the year, controls on advances against sugar, gur and khandsari were re-imposed'. As far as the purpose of the restrictions was concerned, Simha[14] pointed out that the selective credit regulations 'discouraged speculation and hoarding, and price rises' and 'they made bankers cautious in aiding speculation'.

The selective control of bank credit, in one form or another, was also entrusted to various other central banks, some of whom used it to a substantial extent and fairly regularly to restrict or prohibit credit for certain purposes and promote the granting of credit for other specified purposes, or just the former or the latter. In some countries special measures were adopted for the restriction or regulation of consumer instalment credit and credit for speculation in securities and real estate, which will be treated separately.

While in theory there can be no doubt about the advantages of selective credit control in all kinds of countries, both on its own account and in conjunction with purely quantitative credit controls, in practice the scope for its effective employment has been restricted by inherent administrative difficulties and other limitations. Its success or failure has depended not only upon the prevailing economic, political and social conditions and policies in the countries concerned, but also upon the extent to which it has been pursued and practised as a method of control.

Thus, the opportunity for errors of judgment is smaller if selective credit control is applied in a general way, as in some countries where broad guidelines for bank advances have been indicated or prescribed from time to time, than in a highly specialized manner as in those countries where detailed directions have been given for the allocation of bank credit for certain specified purposes only, subject to adjustment from time to time. It is also easier to employ selective credit control in an underdeveloped country, where there is usually greater need as well as scope for such control, than in a highly developed industrial country with its complicated and diversified economic and financial structure; or in a country that has become accustomed to a large measure of general economic control, than in a country whose economy is based mainly on private initiative and enterprise; or in a country with a relatively small number of commercial banks with nation-wide branches than in a country with thousands of independent unit banks, as in the United States.

In conclusion, therefore, it would appear that, while selective credit control has certain obvious advantages, it should be employed only where and to the extent that it is considered to be both necessary and practicable.

Regulation of Consumer Credit

Under an Executive Order issued by the President of the United States on 9th August, 1941, and authorizing the Board of Governors to regulate the terms and conditions under which credit repayable in instalments may be extended for purchasing or carrying consumers' durable goods (other than a residential building in its entirety), the Federal Reserve System was given an additional instrument of credit control. As the Chairman of the Board said at the time: 'The purpose of instalment credit regulation is to help dampen the demand for goods the civilian supply of which has already been reduced and must be further reduced because of defence needs ... Demand for these goods tends to cause inflationary price rises as well as to absorb materials increasingly needed for defence. The regulation ... is a supplemental instrument to be used in conjunction with the broader, more basic fiscal and other Governmental powers in combating inflation.'

The initial regulation issued by the Board became effective on 1st September, 1941, and applied to automobiles, motor-cycles, aircraft, boats, refrigerators, washing machines, stoves, cleaners, sewing machines, radio sets and musical instruments. The original list of articles did not include some types of goods that are commonly bought on instalment credit, nor were restrictions imposed on all types of consumer credit.

In May, 1942, the list of articles covered by the regulation was substantially broadened, and provision was made for stricter credit terms. Semi-durable goods for civilian consumption were included as well as durable goods, and the Board of Governors stated at the time that 'the revised regulation contemplates that the volume of outstanding consumer credit, already substantially reduced, will be further contracted in keeping with the Government's purpose to prevent the rapid bidding up of prices'.[15] The maximum permissible maturity of instalment sales was reduced to twelve months, and the required downpayment for all listed articles was increased to $33\frac{1}{3}$ per cent with some exceptions such as automobiles for which the previous maximum maturity of fifteen months was retained, and furniture and pianos for which the required downpayment was placed at 20 per cent.

Although this instrument of credit control was introduced in the United States as a defence measure, and later extended as a war measure, it was continued after the war and regarded by the Board of Governors as a necessary means of selective control. Thus, in its Annual Report to Congress in June, 1946, the Board took the opportunity to express the opinion that 'from time to time . . . the expansion and subsequent contraction of consumer credit have gone so far as to accentuate the upswings and downswings of the business cycle', and that 'there is no way of preventing such excessive expansion and contraction except governmental regulation of the terms on which consumer credit shall be made available, such as the downpayment required on instalment sales or financing and the length of time permissible for instalment contracts'.

In November, 1947, however, the Board's power to control consumer instalment credit was allowed by Congress to lapse. As a result of strong representations by the Board, this power was restored to it in August, 1948, but only for a short period, namely, to 30th June, 1949. In September, 1950, owing to the fear of inflation following the outbreak of hostilities in Korea, the Board again assumed control over consumer credit under the authority granted to it by the Defence Production Act, which also empowered it to impose restrictions on credit for residential building. Subsequently the Board was likewise authorized to regulate certain other types of real estate credit. It decided, moreover, to make full use of these powers with the avowed object of lessening inflationary pressures and making labour and material available for the needs of the defence programme. With the adoption of a tighter monetary policy and the lessening of inflationary pressures, the control over consumer credit was suspended in May, 1952, and that over real estate credit in September, 1952.

In May, 1957, when the regulation of consumer instalment credit was again discussed in the United States, it was announced that the President would not ask Congress for stand-by authority for this purpose, and this decision was based on a report by the Federal Reserve Board that, while it recognized the importance of instalment credit as a factor of instability, it felt that past fluctuations had been 'within limits which could be tolerated in a rapidly growing and dynamic economy'; that 'a special peacetime authority to regulate consumer credit is not now advisable'; and that 'the broad public interest is better served if potentially unstabilizing credit developments are restrained by the use of general monetary measures and the application of sound public and private fiscal policies'.

The control of consumer instalment credit, on more or less the same basis as that followed in the United States, also came to be adopted by various other countries, where extensive, and sometimes excessive, use was made of such credit, for example, Great Britain, France, Netherlands, Belgium, Spain, Canada, Australia, New Zealand and South Africa. Contrary to the position in the United States, however, most of these countries continued to employ variable restrictions* on consumer instalment credit, from time to time, as one of their instruments of credit control to counter strong inflationary tendencies and an adverse trend in the balance of payments.

In France, for example, the minimum downpayment on instalment purchases of certain consumer goods was raised in March, 1969, from 20–25 to 30 per cent and the maximum repayment period reduced from 21 to 18 months, and in September of that year the former was further increased to 40–50 per cent and the latter reduced to fifteen months, before being eased again twice during the first half of 1970. Moreover, in South Africa the restrictions on hire-purchase credit were severely tightened in October, 1970, and also extended to consumer credit on open account in respect of the same goods. The minimum downpayment on motor cars, for example, was raised from 33⅓ to 40 per cent and the maximum repayment period reduced from 24 to 18 months, but the former was lowered to 33⅓ per cent in April, 1972, and to 25 per cent in June, 1972, while the latter was increased to twenty-four months in February, 1971, and to thirty months in June, 1972. With regard to other durable consumer

* The restrictions, moreover, were imposed and administered by a Government Department instead of by the central bank.

goods, the minimum downpayments prescribed in October, 1970, which varied from 15 per cent in the case of household furniture to 45 per cent in the case of jewellery, cameras, radiograms, sporting and pleasure vessels, were reduced to a range of from 10 per cent to 25–40 per cent respectively in February, 1971, and to 10 per cent generally in October, 1972. Furthermore, the restrictions on open-account credit which were introduced in October, 1970, were withdrawn in October, 1972, except in the case of motor cars.

It is evident that the tendency towards an excessive use of instalment credit in certain countries has made it necessary at times to regulate the availability of such credit for durable and semi-durable consumer goods. While it is a method which covers a relatively narrow field and cannot, therefore, achieve much by itself, it has apparently proved to be a useful supplement to other methods of credit control in times of inflationary pressures.

Variable Margin Requirements on Security Loans

Under the Securities Exchange Act of 1934, the Federal Reserve System was given an instrument of selective credit control, designed specifically to assist it in controlling the volume of credit used for speculation in securities. The Board of Governors was empowered to prescribe rules and regulations with respect to the amount of credit that can be extended by banks against securities* registered on national securities exchanges for the purpose of carrying on trading in such securities, and with respect to margins for loans by brokers to their customers.

In 1936, the Board fixed a margin requirement of 55 per cent for loans by banks or brokers to their customers for the purchase of Stock Exchange securities; and in November, 1937, this margin was reduced to 40 per cent† of the current market value

* Provision was made for the exemption of certain securities, such as Government securities.

† In the case of loans by banks to brokers and dealers in securities for the purpose of financing customers' commitments, and loans by brokers to other members, brokers and dealers, the margin requirement was reduced from the previous 40 per cent to 25 per cent.

of the securities held as collateral, as a result of the slump in the market prices of securities. For the same reason it was decided to fix a margin requirement of 50 per cent for short sales with a view to restraining the activities of bears.

After 1937, no change was made in margin requirements until February, 1945, when the requirement for purchases of stocks was raised to 50 per cent. This action was probably intended as a warning against a panicky market, in view of the distinctly favourable turn in the war situation. In July, 1945, after the end of hostilities in Europe, the margin for purchases as well as for short sales was raised to 75 per cent; and six months later it was further increased to 100 per cent. In February, 1947, the margin was again lowered to 75 per cent, and in March, 1949, it was further reduced to 50 per cent. With a recurrence of inflationary and speculative activity, however, it was increased to 75 per cent in January, 1951, but was again reduced to 50 per cent in February, 1953.

During the next twenty years the margin for purchases as well as short sales of stocks was changed twelve times, with peaks of 90 per cent from October, 1958, to July, 1960, and 80 per cent from June, 1968, to May, 1970, and a lowpoint of 50 per cent. Since 1968 the Federal Reserve Board has also laid down margin requirements for bonds convertible into stocks, at somewhat lower rates than for stocks.

This method of variable margin requirements on security loans was also adopted by Japan, where the Minister of Finance was granted 'the authority to (1) fix margin rates and (2) approve and order changes in the methods and conditions of loans to be extended by securities finance corporations', while the Bank of Japan was authorized 'to regulate the methods and conditions of loans from financial institutions (including banks) to securities dealers'.[16]

It is obviously an instrument of credit control which can only be justified in countries where a strong tendency prevails towards periodic excessive speculation in securities, with undue disturbing effects on general economic activity. As Burgess[17] said at an early stage of its adoption in the United States, 'it is a form of control which is in some degree paternalistic and restrictive', and it 'has placed upon the Reserve System a responsibility which is likely to prove onerous, for the System will find itself at times required by circumstances to take action which will directly and immediately influence the profits and even solvency of considerable groups of people', but speculation in securities had proved itself 'so destructive of economic stability in this country that some vigorous form of control of this sort appeared to be necessary'.

Advance-Deposit Requirements for Imports

Since World War II, another new method of selective control was developed in the form of a requirement that advance deposits be made by importers with the central bank, which served both as a prerequisite to obtaining import or exchange licences and as an additional medium of restricting imports during periods of deficit in the country's balance of payments. This method not only had the effect of increasing the difficulties and costs of financing imports, but also that of reducing the cash reserves and lending capacity of the commercial banks, to the extent that they had to finance the importers for the purpose of such advance deposits. To this extent, therefore, it had the same impact on the banks as an increase in their reserve requirements.

The instrument of advance-deposit requirements was first adopted by some Latin-American and Asian countries which had to cope with serious balance of payments deficits after the war, and it was also used in West Germany for the same purpose in 1950/1. During the fifties and sixties this method spread over a large part of the world, as in the case of variable reserve requirements and credit ceilings and quotas. It came to be employed at times in several countries in Europe as well as many countries in Latin America and Asia and some countries in Africa. It was introduced, for example, in France in 1957, and it was also adopted in Great Britain towards the end of 1968, at the rate of 50 per cent of the value of certain categories of imports (mainly manufactured goods), which was reduced to 40 per cent at the end of 1969, 30 per cent in May, 1970, and 20 per cent in September, 1970, before the requirements were finally withdrawn at the end of that year and the last repayments of import deposits made in the middle of 1971. Moreover, in Spain the import-deposit requirements which were imposed in 1969, were relaxed in the beginning of 1971 and terminated later in the year.

While in some countries the advance deposits were required only in respect of certain specified imported goods and on the basis of a uniform percentage of import value at any particular time, which sometimes amounted to 100 per cent, in other countries the imported goods were divided into categories with differential deposit ratios. In Japan, for example, when advance deposits were imposed for the third time in October, 1961, there were five categories of imports subject to deposit ratios varying from 0·1 per cent to 35 per cent.

The use of advance import-deposit requirements as an instrument of credit control has shown a declining tendency in many countries in recent years. It is a method which, in any case, can only have a temporary and limited effect, and must, therefore, be regarded as a measure of last resort to reinforce other methods of countering overimportation of goods generally or non-essential goods in particular.

Moral Suasion

Moral suasion was regularly employed by the older central banks as one of their main instruments of monetary policy, in conjunction with discount-rate policy and such open-market operations as could be undertaken at the time; and it was also accepted by the Federal Reserve Banks, when they commenced operations in 1914, and by the other new central banks which were established during the twenties that they could not rely only on their statutory privileges and powers but would also need to exercise moral suasion, as far as possible, in the course of carrying out their duties and responsibilities.

Since the thirties, however, the tendency for central banks, in general, has been to depend less on moral suasion and more on their legal powers of credit control which were increased from time to time. The movement started in the United States where the regulative powers of the Federal Reserve Banks were considerably increased during the thirties, and this was followed in due course, in a greater or lesser degree, by the other existing central banks, while the new central banks which were subsequently created, were granted wider powers from the start than was customary previously. The process of extending the legal powers of central banks continued to prevail in recent times.

The trend towards greater reliance on statutory powers can be attributed to various factors which have been mentioned previously, such as the lack of tradition and voluntary co-operation and the absence of active money markets in the case of many of the new central banks; the proliferation of all kinds of banking and other credit institutions in most countries; the development of more difficult and complicated economic and financial conditions and problems generally; and, in the case of the United States in particular, thousands of independent unit banks. Another factor which can be mentioned is the evident preference of some banks for the use by the central bank of compulsion rather than persuasion, so as to ensure that their competitors would also have to carry out the restrictive policies of the central bank.

Nevertheless, despite their increased powers, some of the older central banks, such as the Bank of England,* the Netherlands Bank, National Bank of Switzerland and the Riksbank of Sweden, have continued to carry out their duties and responsibilities by moral suasion and voluntary agreement with the banks, and, where detailed directions were issued, by doing so in the form of requests and guidelines rather than as legal directives. Some of the newer central banks have also adopted this practice at times, for example, the Bank of Canada, the Reserve Bank of Australia and the South African Reserve Bank. The reasons for this attitude on the part of some central banks would appear to be, firstly, that moral suasion has at least the advantage of creating a less unfavourable psychological reaction than in the case of obvious compulsion associated with legal directives, and that this has been found more conducive to securing the willing

* In a memorandum to the Radcliffe Committee, the Governor of the Bank of England, referring to the willingness and ability of the British banking system to co-operate with the authorities, emphasized that 'much would be lost if this co-operation had to be replaced by coercion'. See *Memoranda of Evidence*, Committee on Working of Monetary System, 1960, Vol. I, p. 3.

and active co-operation of the banking institutions directly concerned, in the spirit as well as the letter; and, secondly, that moral suasion can also be used over a wider area than the banking sector, i.e. beyond the area usually covered by the central bank's legal powers.

It is evident, however, that all central banks should be equipped with adequate statutory powers of credit control, for use if and when considered necessary, since the mere possession of such powers has served to strengthen the position of the central bank and to increase its ability to exercise moral suasion. Moreover, as pointed out in Chapter 8, experience has shown that the central bank needs the wholehearted and continuous co-operation of the commercial banks as well as other banking institutions for the effective execution of its credit policy; that it should, therefore, endeavour to maintain or establish the requisite relations and means of communication with the banking sector as a whole; and that it should also strive to extend its moral influence over other financial institutions and the business community, with the aid of publicity in the form of periodical reviews and reports. Finally, while the monetary policy to be carried out by the central bank must take due account of the Government's fiscal policy as well as its other economic policies, the central bank must also try to exercise the appropriate moral suasion on the Government if it has good reason for concern about the financial or other economic consequences of any Government policy.

References

1 *See* King, W. T. C. *History of the London Discount Market*. Routledge, 1936. pp. 13 and 71.

2 Wagemann, E. *Wirthschaftspolitische Strategie*. Hanseatische Verlagsanstalt, 1937. pp. 321–5.

3 Katzenellenbaum, S. S., in *Foreign Banking Systems*. Ed. Willis & Beckhart. Henry Holt, 1929. pp. 953–4.

4 Ostos, Martinez, in Appendix I to *Banca Central*. Fondo de Cultura Economica (Mexico), 1941. p.456. (Spanish language edition of the author's *Central Banking*.)

5 Wagemann, *op. cit.* p. 321.
6 *Bank of England Quarterly Bulletin.* December, 1972. p. 514.
7 *Bank of England Annual Report for 1971–72.* p. 11.
8 *Report on Fiscal and Monetary Policy in South Africa.* 1970. p. 147.
9 *Report by the Technical Committee on Banking Legislation.* South Africa, 1972. p. 1.
10 *Reserve Bank of Australia.* Reserve Bank, 1969. p. 13.
11 *Ibid.* p. 15.
12 *Reserve Bank of New Zealand Bulletin.* May, 1971. pp. 98–9.
13 *Annual Report of the Bank of Mexico for 1971* (English version). pp. 30 and 40.
14 Simha, S. L. N. *Central Banking in South and East Asia.* Ed. Davies. Hongkong: Oxford, 1960. p. 41.
15 *Federal Reserve Bulletin.* May, 1942. pp. 399–400.
16 *The Bank of Japan, Its Function and Organization.* Bank of Japan, 1962. p. 50.
17 Burgess, W. R. *Reserve Banks and the Money Market.* Harper, 1936. pp. 263–4.

CHAPTER THIRTEEN

Exchange Control – International Monetary Co-operation

Introduction

The technical limitations of credit control and its restricted scope and range under modern economic and financial conditions, which were discussed in Chapter 8, made it increasingly necessary, in pursuing the aim of economic growth with a reasonable degree of internal and external stability, to employ other methods as supplements or alternatives to whatever instruments of credit control the central bank had at its command.

One of these additional methods was the control of exchange rates and exchange transactions. It was not sufficient, however, to look at internal monetary policy and possible alternatives or supplements in the field of foreign exchange merely from the national viewpoint. The foundation stone of the world monetary edifice which was erected after World War II was international co-operation in the sphere of trade and payments. Having regard to this fact, the effects of control measures, designed to promote the internal and external stability of particular nations, upon international trade and world currency stability could no longer be ignored without serious consequences. This chapter will, therefore, deal with both exchange control and international monetary co-operation.

Other alternatives or supplements to monetary policy, such as fiscal policy and compensatory Government action and the general control of investment, will be discussed in the following chapter.

Exchange Control in the Interwar Period

Since World War I, as mentioned in Chapter 5, the central banks of most countries came, either as a natural development in monetary control or as an emergency measure, to play an increasingly important part in foreign exchange operations, whatever monetary standards were in force at the time. Their foreign assets performed the functions of a 'buffer' or 'shock-absorber' and served as an instrument for the regulation of exchange rates, while their dealings in foreign exchange were also used as one of the means of regulating money-market conditions.

Thus, such direct participation in foreign exchange operations was increasingly adopted by central banks during the twenties in connection with the reinstatement of the gold or gold-exchange standard, particularly in those countries where money-market conditions were relatively unresponsive to the ordinary methods of credit control. As a result of the great depression of the early thirties and the general abandonment of the gold standard, however, it was employed on a much larger scale. Many central banks were granted wide powers for the purpose of acquiring foreign exchange and controlling the exchange markets of their countries. In other cases, State exchange equalization or stabilization funds were brought into being, or a system of general exchange control was introduced. In general, under the individual or regional managed currencies of the thirties, the regulation of exchange rates came to be a more conscious and comprehensive instrument of economic or financial policy.

(a) Adjustment of Spot-Exchange Rates

An interesting example of direct action in the spot foreign-exchange market coupled with credit control was provided by Sweden from the time of its abandonment of the gold standard in September, 1931, to the outbreak of World War II. The object was to promote varying monetary policies deemed necessary from time to time in the national economic interest.

Initially, monetary policy was aimed at the maintenance of the domestic purchasing power of the krona. It was feared that costs and prices in Great Britain would rise after that country left the gold standard, and accordingly the Riksbank decided, by means of active intervention in the exchange market and a substantial increase in the discount rate, not to let the krona depreciate to the same extent as sterling in terms of gold. When, however, prices did not increase in Great Britain but tended to decline further, the krona was allowed to depreciate and the discount rate was lowered. The continuing decline in world prices caused Sweden to adopt a policy aimed not only at preventing a further decline in domestic prices but at raising them to a level more appropriate for the purposes of economic equilibrium. In consequence, the Riksbank depreciated the krona even relative to sterling and bought foreign exchange freely which, in conjunction with a further lowering of the discount rate, created easy money conditions. Subsequently, when prices rose in the United States and Great Britain as a result of reflationary policies in those countries, Sweden abandoned the policy of fluctuating exchange rates on London and stabilized the sterling-krona rate for as long as economic conditions and policies in Great Britain were deemed suitable for Sweden.

During the thirties, many other countries deliberately made adjustments in their exchange rates or gold parities as a means of contributing towards equilibrium in the balance of payments or general equilibrium. Nevertheless, although varying degrees of success attended these adjustments, depending *inter alia* upon the circumstances and the countries involved, they did not by any means achieve all that was expected of them. The experience, however, at least revealed the limitations of the belief that exchange-rate adjustments could be made to suit domestic economic and social policies and to offset a rise in production costs resulting, for example, from economic and social reforms.

(b) Adjustment of Forward-Exchange Rates

Forward-exchange rates have always played a useful role in enabling exporters and importers (including short-term borrowers or lenders abroad) to cover their exchange risks. Additionally, and when the monetary system permitted of such transactions, they were used to cover interest-arbitrage transactions. In general, central banks normally intervened in such forward transactions only to extend or improve the available facilities or to replace facilities which disappeared as a result of exchange restrictions.

Even under the gold standard, however, some central banks made adjustments in forward rates as a *supplement* to discount-rate policy with the aim of influencing the movement of short-term balances in the desired direction and maintaining the spot-exchange rates within the gold points. There were instances also of the deliberate adjustment of forward rates as an *alternative* to the use of monetary policy measures which were deemed to be undesirable from the domestic viewpoint. For example, the Austro-Hungarian Bank between 1907 and 1912 adjusted the forward rates to prevent either an excessive inflow or an excessive outflow of short-term funds and the accompanying unduly large changes in its reserves, thereby avoiding alterations in Bank rate which were considered to be inappropriate for the internal economy. The Bank of France also undertook forward-rate operations in 1927–8 for the purpose, in particular, of encouraging an outflow of funds so as to reduce the volume of money and credit and prevent inflation.[1]

During the disturbed international monetary conditions of the thirties, speculative attacks on certain currencies were by no means uncommon, and Einzig[2] gave various examples of official intervention in France, Italy, Great Britain and the Netherlands for the purpose of defending their currencies against these attacks. Forward rates were supported either at or above their interest parities, or depreciated well below their interest parities, with the aim of discouraging speculative inflows or outflows of short-term funds. Such preventive action also took the form of prohibiting speculative operations in forward exchanges by law or by moral suasion.

Both Keynes and Einzig were strong advocates of adjustments in forward rates as a means of countering undesirable tendencies in the international movement of funds. As far back as 1923, Keynes[3] pointed out that, by varying the forward rates, central banks 'would be able, in effect, to vary the interest offered for *foreign* balances, as a policy distinct from whatever might be their bank-rate policy for the purpose of governing the interest obtainable on *home* balances'. This idea was further developed in a later work[4] when he advocated forward-rate adjustments as an alternative to raising Bank rate, in order to restrain an outflow or attract an inflow of capital whenever the domestic economic situation would be detrimentally affected by higher money rates. He admitted, however, that such a device was not meant to combat either a fundamental disequilibrium or a general flight of capital which would naturally reflect an inherent weakness of the currency.

Einzig went rather further in strongly advocating a forward-rate policy, not merely as a supplement to discount-rate policy, but mainly as an independent instrument for regulating the international flow of short-term capital. He maintained that 'while a forward-rate policy can no more influence the movement of uncovered funds than a bank-rate policy can, it can give rise to transfers of covered balances in a direction opposite to the trend of uncovered balances'.[5] He did acknowledge, however, that the great volume of 'hot' money which had periodically to be contended with during the interwar period was as indifferent to forward exchange rates as to interest rates.

(c) The Use of Stabilization Funds

After a period of considerable fluctuations in the sterling exchange rates consequent upon the abandonment of the gold standard, Great Britain decided in April, 1932, to establish the Exchange Equalization Account. This was a stabilization fund designed both to even out the effect of speculative exchange transactions and capital flows on the exchange rates, and to neutralize the influence of capital and gold movements on the internal credit situation. In pursuing the first objective, the

Account bought gold and foreign exchange when the balance of payments took a temporarily or artificially favourable turn, and sold gold and foreign exchange when the balance of payments became temporarily unfavourable. Its operations in this field were not intended to maintain sterling at a fixed parity with gold or any other currency.

The second objective, namely, insulation of the internal credit structure from gold and capital movements, was achieved through the sale of Treasury bills by the Bank of England (obtained from the British Treasury for this purpose) in the London money market or the purchase of Treasury bills from the market. These bills were sold to buy up any surplus gold and foreign exchange, thus withdrawing from the market the equivalent of the funds accruing from a favourable balance of payments; and Treasury bills were purchased when the Account sold gold and foreign exchange to meet an unfavourable balance of payments, thus restoring to the market the funds which it lost as a result thereof.

Various other countries such as the United States, France, the Netherlands, Belgium and Switzerland, introduced stabilization funds after they left the gold standard, but these funds differed from the British Equalization Account in several ways, and were not used to any significant extent for insulating the internal credit structure. Even the United States, which, as a reflationary measure, had devalued the dollar by 40·9 per cent early in 1934 and had adopted the policy of maintaining the dollar at a fixed gold parity and of buying all gold offered to it at a fixed price of $35 per fine ounce, made little use of the Stabilization Fund for the stabilization of the dollar rates of exchange. Despite its huge favourable balance of payments on both current and capital accounts, the devaluation of the dollar was maintained by means of the unlimited purchase of gold at the fixed price. These purchases were financed by funds obtained from the Federal Reserve System in exchange for gold certificates.

(d) Other Measures Aiming at Currency Stabilization

In general, the various stabilization funds were not measures restrictive of world trade and payments or significant weapons of the economic nationalism which was such an unfortunate feature of the interwar period. The same cannot be said of some of the other measures which were adopted during these years with the aim of achieving various forms and degrees of currency stabilization.

The measures in question included the development of various currency areas or blocs with relatively stable exchange rates between the members of each such group; the tripartite monetary agreement of 1936 between the United States, Great Britain and France, and later applied in limited degree to the Netherlands, Belgium and Switzerland; the adoption of clearing and payments agreements to facilitate settlements between certain countries; the granting of stabilization loans internationally; the adoption of differential rates of exchange or multiple currency devices; and the promulgation of exchange and import restrictions over a large part of Central and Eastern Europe, Latin America and Asia.

An illustration of the use of several of these methods was provided by Germany. Following upon a large outflow of foreign short-term funds in 1931, and with a view to maintaining the gold parity of the Reichsmark, steps were taken to prohibit the export of domestic capital and to ensure that all export proceeds were transferred to the Reichsbank. So-called Standstill Agreements were made with certain foreign banking creditors, and regulations were issued which eventually subjected all foreign payments to official control. Restrictions were later imposed upon the export of notes, coin and securities and on the transfer of interest, dividends and other current liabilities to foreigners.

The substantial decline in German exports and the reduction in the country's reserves led to a whole series of bilateral payments and clearing agreements and to the control of exchange transactions generally. Control over foreign trade as a whole followed, imports being limited more or less according to exports. Furthermore, to stimulate exports and other sources of foreign exchange and to reduce foreign liabilities, special depreciated rates of exchange were quoted for such purposes while the official rate was still maintained at parity. Thus, by the outbreak of war in September, 1939, Germany had established an elaborate and comprehensive system of exchange and other controls and restrictions.

During the war, general controls over foreign exchange and foreign trade were necessarily adopted by the belligerent countries, in particular for the purpose of checking the flight of capital, mobilizing national exchange reserves to ensure their application to the best national advantage and preventing trade and financial transactions of possible benefit to the enemy. The disruption of war also necessitated the adoption of controls in neutral countries. Broadly speaking, the controls resembled those evolved in Germany before the war.

It was evident that the majority of the measures which were adopted during the interwar years for purposes of currency stabilization, were designed to serve the interests of particular countries or groups of countries. Little or no regard was paid to their effects upon other countries and, in consequence, they encouraged the adoption of retaliatory measures. Whatever the immediate apparent benefits to the countries applying them, these measures involved, in varying degrees, elements restrictive of world trade and payments and, moreover, encouraged an artificial orientation thereof. World War II itself affected individual countries in varying degrees. Not only did certain countries, such as Switzerland and Sweden, remain neutral, but among the belligerent countries themselves the degree of destruction and disruption differed widely.

Exchange Control after World War II

It was quite apparent before the end of the war, in fact, that world trade and payments would face virtual strangulation without close and effective international co-operation, and that such co-operation could only be achieved through the establishment of appropriate and active international organizations and arrangements for the various purposes concerned.

There was already an international banking organization in existence, namely, the Bank for International Settlements, which had been established in 1930 by the central banks of Europe, and which had served as a valuable medium for improving and facilitating co-operation among the member central banks. It was, however, restricted in its scope both as to the number of countries involved and the field of activity covered. Moreover, it was confined to central banks, whereas the collaboration of Governments as well as central banks had become essential since Governments everywhere assumed more directly the responsibility for the determination of monetary policy. There was also fairly general agreement at the time concerning the great need for international monetary co-operation in the world as a whole.

The final result was the establishment of two sister organizations, namely, the International Monetary Fund and the International Bank for Reconstruction and Development, which commenced operations early in 1947. Furthermore, the General Agreements on Tariffs and Trade (GATT) was signed in October, 1947. The Fund, which was concerned primarily with the international currency and payments system, and the GATT, whose main purpose was the promotion of multilateral international trade, were naturally to work in close co-operation.

The International Monetary Fund

Of primary importance in the context of this chapter were the arrangements in the Fund's statutes relating to exchange rates and exchange restrictions. In fact, these arrangements represented the corner-stone of the postwar international currency and exchange system. Briefly, member countries* of the Fund were required to fix exchange parities in terms of gold, and the permitted range of fluctuation in the spot-exchange rates was 1 per cent on either side of the parity. The initial par values were based on the exchange rates prevailing in 1946 and changes in parities, beyond an initial 10 per cent, could only be made with the consent of the Fund and in the case of a fundamental disequilibrium in the balance of payments.

As far as exchange restrictions were concerned, the Fund arrangements did not preclude restrictions on capital movements provided they did not delay or restrict current payments

* The Fund started with about 40 member countries, and this number increased to over 80 in 1962 and 120 in 1972.

unduly. Even as regards restrictions on current payments, it was recognized that the elimination of those which were in existence after the war would take many years. A transitional period, of which most member countries availed themselves, was thus provided for before members were required to accept the obligation of convertibility of their currencies. No limit in time was specified for the transitional period but, after the lapse of five years, the Fund was obliged to consult annually with members still availing themselves of the facility.

To assist members in avoiding new restrictions on current transactions, or in reducing or removing them, and for maintaining stability in their exchange rates, the Fund was empowered to make its resources (obtained from members' subscriptions) available for temporary periods within certain limits and subject to certain repayment provisions. The Fund could also limit or refuse assistance if members did not meet their obligations under the Fund's rules.

It is important to note in this context that the Fund system of stable exchange rates based on fixed parities, in conjunction with its aims of promoting multilateral trade and payments, demanded adequate resources at all times to meet temporary disequilibria in its members' balances of payments. As world trade and financial transactions increased, so would the resources necessary to meet the inevitably greater swings in countries' balances of payments. In the Fund system, as envisaged originally, these resources consisted of members' own gold reserves, their holdings of dollars (the only currency freely convertible at the time into all other currencies and gold) and the Fund's own lending facilities. It followed, as was recently pointed out,[6] that 'the effective functioning of the system depended on two conditions: that there be a regular increase in total reserves and IMF facilities adequate to ensure that countries with realistic exchange rates could finance the greater swings apt to rise in their balances of payments; and that the increase in the total reserves of the system be shared between gold and dollars in such proportion that, given appropriate policies in the United States, the convertibility of the dollar into gold remained assured'. These conditions did, in fact, prevail until the late fifties.

It can be said that during this period, and having regard to the surrounding circumstances, the Fund system functioned satisfactorily on the whole. In the field of exchange-rate stability, some of the initial par values proved to be unrealistic as a result of the considerable distortion in world trade and payments immediately after the war. The strain became so severe that in September, 1949, twenty-nine countries almost simultaneously devalued their currencies in terms of gold and the US dollar. Great Britain, which took the lead, devalued by 30·5 per cent and was followed, to the same extent, by the majority of the countries concerned, while in Canada, France, West Germany, Italy and Portugal, the devaluation varied from 10 to 20 per cent. Thereafter, and until the end of the fifties, only France among the leading nations made a further devaluation, namely, in August, 1957.

For all practical purposes, the competitive devaluation of currencies ceased among the Fund's members. Moreover, the extent of *temporary* adjustments in spot-exchange rates, purely as a supplement or alternative to internal monetary policies in overcoming disequilibria – as distinct from such adjustments as a trade competitive device – was reduced in view, *inter alia*, of the narrow margin of permitted fluctuation in the spot rates. Within the narrower range, nevertheless, this measure was used extensively in later years to assist in the control of unwanted capital movements as, for example, in West Germany. The Fund rules covering stability in the exchanges necessarily placed greater emphasis upon internal measures as a corrective.

Also of importance was the trend towards a narrowing of the spread between the official rates for a number of the principal currencies, and those quoted in the external free markets. The latter markets developed largely because of exchange controls and the distinction made in these between so-called 'hard' and 'soft' currencies. The transactions in these markets were related largely to capital transfers and bank notes, although in some cases current transactions with hard-currency countries were involved. The Fund's aim was to bring about the unification of free-market rates with the official rates, and an important step in this field was the permission granted to the British Exchange Equalization Account in February, 1955, to operate in the external-sterling free markets so as to assist in correcting disturbing patterns of trade. These free-market rates must be distinguished from multiple rates of exchange which were rates quoted in the domestic market and were official or officially tolerated rates, such as auction rates. Multiple rates were, in fact, regarded by the Fund as also being exchange restrictions.

Progress was also made during the fifties in the forward-exchange markets. The Fund was permitted to prescribe a margin for forward rates but, in view of the many difficulties, did not do so. Countries increasingly came to entrust the provision of forward cover for their traders to the forward markets whereas, earlier, such cover was not available or was provided by the authorities. Besides being influenced by interest differentials, the forward rates in the market also came to reflect the fear or anticipation of parity changes as, for example, in 1957 when forward discounts on the French franc widened to as much as 26 per cent, and forward rates for other currencies showed extensive discounts against the West German mark. It should, however, be mentioned that, although central banks normally regarded intervention in the forward-exchange markets as outside their province, a number of them did, in practice, intervene at times mainly to assist in controlling unwanted flows of short-term capital.

While the Fund enjoyed a substantial measure of success in reducing or removing the numerous restrictions on current trade and payments, progress towards the convertibility of currencies was slower than desired. Initially, only the United States and four Latin-American countries were able to accept the obligations of convertibility as laid down in Article VIII of the Fund Agreement, and by the end of March, 1958, only nine members out of a total of sixty-eight, had done so. In other words, fifty-nine members continued to avail themselves of the transitional arrangements. It must be borne in mind, however, that many other members had progressed a long way towards accepting these obligations by that time.

The trend towards the liberalization of trade and payments continued throughout the fifties, but there were setbacks from time to time. In the years 1950 to 1953, for example, the Korean war led to serious deliberalization in a number of countries owing to the associated balance of payments difficulties. Severe import restrictions were imposed in Great Britain, France and in some sterling-area and Latin-American countries. Moreover, in 1957/8, liberalization suffered another setback by reason of balance of payments disequilibria in France and West Germany which gave rise to speculation on the devaluation of the franc (which actually occurred) and the revaluation of the mark.

As regards multiple currency practices which, as mentioned earlier, the Fund deemed to be exchange restrictions, progress towards their removal was rather disappointing. This type of restriction took many forms. Exchange taxes were applied to all or to various categories of exchange transactions, as in Paraguay and Cuba in 1957. Excessive spreads between buying and selling rates was another device, as in Costa Rica and Nicaragua at that time. Other forms with varying degrees of complexity included special rates for particular currencies; sales of proportions of export proceeds at varying rates; differential rates for various export and import commodities, as used for example, in Indonesia, Uruguay and Brazil. The Fund consistently sought to induce progress towards a unitary rate structure and convertibility, generally proceeding by way of a gradual reduction in the number of rates and the adoption of appropriate internal policies. It also provided financial assistance to various countries, either directly or in collaboration with other entities, such as the US Treasury Stabilization Fund and American commercial banks, to stabilize their currencies, to prevent the imposition of controls or to assist in their removal. Cases in point were the stabilization funds established in February, 1954, to assist Peru, and in April, 1956, to stabilize the Chilean currency.

A particularly valuable feature of the Fund's activities which had a considerable bearing upon exchange and trade controls, was the annual consultations with its members. These covered the entire state of a member's economy and its economic and financial policies. Possible measures to improve the situation and to bring it more into conformity with the Fund's aims were discussed and included in a report to the Fund and the member. Considerable leverage towards strengthening the recommendations in these reports and in securing adherence to the Fund's rules, was provided by the Fund's power to reduce or withhold financial assistance if members failed to co-operate. In fact, the so-called 'stand-by' arrangements introduced by the Fund which were intended to give members advance assurance that financial assistance would be forthcoming without further consultation with the Fund, contained a series of undertakings which the member was expected to fulfil.

The European Payments Union; the European Monetary Agreement; the Free Trade Association; and the European Economic Community

Following upon the unsuccessful efforts to restore the convertibility of sterling by means of a large loan in the summer of 1947, several European countries entered into an agreement whereby the trade deficit of one country could be offset against its surplus with any of the others. This was followed by the establishment of the European Payments Union, which came into operation in July, 1950. In brief, this organization, with the assistance of capital provided by the United States, sought to promote multilateral trade and payments among its 15 members by providing 'a simple mechanism for the complete settlement every month, partly in gold and dollars and partly by the extension of credit, of each member's position vis-à-vis all the other members'.[7]

Apart from the International Monetary Fund, the creation of the European Payments Union (EPU) was also of great importance in the field of exchange control. The liberalization of trade and payments in Europe after the war was obviously of significance for the world as a whole. The EPU, moreover, encouraged the adoption of sound internal policies among its members, thereby promoting balance in their international accounts. Most of the members were also members of the Fund and thus, in a very important area of Fund membership, the EPU furthered the Fund's basic aims. In fact, close co-operation with the Fund was mentioned in its statutes.

In general, the EPU can justifiably be said to have achieved a considerable measure of success.* Thus, the inter-transferability

* In comparing the overall success of the Fund and the EPU, it should be borne in mind that the former had a much wider membership involving much greater differences in basic economic situation and development among its members and in their institutional and administrative organization.

of members' currencies in the monthly settlements encouraged the growth of a similar transferability at all other times through the normal exchange markets. Exchange arbitrage between member currencies on these markets was introduced, and was later extended to most of the outside non-dollar currencies. Official and free-market exchange quotations narrowed, and conversion into dollars through the free markets became possible at a small discount. As members' positions improved, the use of gold and dollars in the monthly settlements was raised in stages from 40 per cent initially to 75 per cent in 1955. Trade liberalization between members also increased with the assistance of the credit facilities made available by the EPU. The original aim in this field was the freeing of 75 per cent of imports from quota restrictions. This figure was later increased to 90 per cent and, additionally, restrictions on imports from the dollar area were considerably reduced.

The strengthened condition of members, in conjunction with an improvement in their terms of trade and services during 1958, enabled all of them, apart from Greece, Iceland and Turkey, at the end of that year, to take the important step of simultaneously introducing current-account convertibility for non-residents.[8] Some restrictions on capital movements still remained and were reflected in the free markets, but even here the rates did not, in most cases, differ widely from the official quotations.

The move to current-account convertibility made the automatic credit facilities unnecessary for settlements among members and resulted in the dissolution of the EPU and its simultaneous replacement by the European Monetary Agreement at the end of 1958. This Agreement involved two elements, namely, a European Fund and a Multilateral System of Payments. The purpose of the Fund, which had a capital of $600 million, was to provide short-term credit facilities to members for meeting temporary imbalances in their international accounts. The Multilateral System of Payments provided a means whereby members could settle monthly certain *specified* claims and debts with other members on arranged terms. All settlements were effected in US dollars, not member currencies, through the Fund, and the automatic element in settlements disappeared. In practice, the bulk of transactions between members were settled through the foreign-exchange markets at current rates.

At the end of 1958, thus, and thanks largely to the activities of the International Monetary Fund, the General Agreement on Tariffs and Trade, the European Payments Union and the generous assistance of the United States, all the important currencies of the world had achieved a large measure of convertibility for their currencies and had made significant progress in the field of multilateral trade. Progress in the leading countries of Western Europe had been particularly marked. In fact, by this time, intra-European trade had been liberalized to the extent of 90 per cent.

The liberalization of international trade and payments, and the progress towards convertibility of currencies, continued in the period after 1958. There was, for example, the coming into operation of the European Economic Community in terms of the Rome Treaty of 1957. Six of the Western European countries, namely, France, West Germany, Italy, the Netherlands, Belgium and Luxemburg, were signatories to this treaty, the aim of which was the gradual freeing from almost all restrictions of the trade in goods and services, and of movements of capital, between these countries. This was followed by the convention establishing the European Free Trade Association, signed by Austria, Denmark, Norway, Portugal, Sweden, Switzerland and Great Britain in January, 1960. The aim was to establish a free market in industrial products among these countries over a period of ten years. Agricultural problems were the major factor which prevented these countries from joining the European Economic Community. The International Monetary Fund also made progress, although at a slower rate, among its wider membership. By the end of 1970, for example, thirty-five members out of a total of 120, including the world's leading countries, had accepted the convertibility obligations of the Fund Agreement.

It is important to stress that the progress towards full convertibility of major currencies was naturally accompanied by a much greater mobility of capital. In the case of short-term capital particularly, the movement of funds in response to interest-rate differentials increased very considerably. Of major importance in this respect was the development of the so-called

Euro-Currency Market. European and British banks had, on an increasing scale, been taking deposits and making loans in currencies other than their own, and so there developed an efficient inter-bank market for moving short-term funds internationally from lender to borrower in response to interest-rate differences in various countries. While other currencies, such as the D. Mark and the Swiss Franc, were also involved in this market, the major element was the U.S. dollar.

The Development of International Balance of Payments Disequilibrium and the Main Causal Factors

The disturbing feature of the sixties and early seventies was the emergence of serious, and sometimes persistent, balance of payments disequilibria among the principal countries. This problem was attributable mainly to the large size and persistent nature of the deficit in the balance of payments of the United States from 1958 to 1971, which, on an official reserve-transactions basis, amounted to approximately $56 billion. Corresponding surpluses, of course, appeared in the international accounts of other countries. In fact, most of the other leading countries of the world showed fairly consistent surpluses during this period, but of relatively small dimensions in each case, apart from West Germany and later Japan. In the case of Great Britain, the surpluses were not unduly large and were interspersed with big deficits in some years, but temporary assistance from other countries as, for example, in 1963, 1964 and 1966, tended to conceal the real problem.

There were various factors which contributed to these developments, some of them more basic in character and of wider application than others. Mention has already been made, for example, of the much greater mobility of short-term capital resulting from the progress made in the principal countries towards full convertibility. That this mobility became a highly disequilibrating element in the situation, particularly in the later sixties and early seventies,* was in large measure due to

* In September, 1968, for example, the Bundesbank of West Germany had to purchase about $3·8 billion in short-term funds. In early 1969, US

currency fears and interest-rate differentials arising out of inadequate, or inadequately considered, measures designed to secure or maintain reasonable internal and external balance. In some cases, there was too much concentration upon domestic issues, while an absence of any international co-ordination in the type of measure applied to restore balance to the internal economy, was evident on several occasions.

With regard to the more basic reasons behind the development of widespread balance of payments disequilibria, mention may first be made of the increasing competitiveness, after the middle fifties, of the Western European nations and Japan vis-à-vis the United States. The last-named country had emerged from the war in a dominant position in respect of both monetary reserves and productive capacity. There was little competition from other leading countries, most of which had suffered extensive disruption during the war. Price considerations were unimportant in these circumstances as supplies of the goods required for reconstruction and development were, for the most part, only available in the United States. By 1955/6, however, reconstruction in Western Europe had been practically completed. Moreover, wage rates were considerably lower in Europe than in the United States and, although wage rates subsequently increased rapidly in Europe, the increases on average did not exceed those in the United States and started from a lower level. Furthermore, American manufacturers established subsidiaries in Europe (especially in the EEC countries) to take advantage of the lower labour costs. Mention must also be made of the adverse effects, on the foreign trade of the United States, of the devaluation of the French franc in August, 1957, and again in August, 1969, and of sterling in November, 1967.

The outcome was that the European countries came to supply, to an increasing extent, their own needs as well as those of other countries and of the United States itself, and this trend, together with the rapid growth of Japan's production and foreign trade, obviously contributed largely towards the erosion of the United States' trade surplus which had been the major source of strength in its balance of payments. The trade surplus, in fact, turned into

banks drew approximately $9 billion from the Euro-dollar market, and from November, 1969 to May, 1971, replaced $13 billion in this market.

a deficit in 1971. Other unfavourable factors for the United States' balance of payments were the heavy costs involved in the Vietnam war as well as foreign military aid generally and foreign economic aid.

Another important factor in the development of internal imbalances was the marked reluctance of the major countries to adjust the parities of their currencies, even though a fundamental disequilibrium existed either in the form of persistent deficits or surpluses. Such adjustments were a vital element in the International Monetary Fund system, and the failure to make them timeously tended to undermine that system. Admittedly, it was not always easy to establish whether a disequilibrium in the balance of payments was fundamental or not. The concept included the assumption that all the necessary internal monetary and fiscal measures had been taken but that the disequilibrium still persisted. As noted earlier, the Fund system tended to emphasize the use of such internal measures rather than the superficially easier, and frequently less unpopular, course of effecting parity changes. Moreover, the extent to which the parity or parities should be adjusted was generally difficult to ascertain and, in many cases, the only practicable, but not necessarily exact, method was to let the currency float for a time. The Fund could not approve such action, but it nevertheless proved flexible in the matter. Examples may be found in the case of a number of Latin-American countries and, in 1971, a number of Western European countries including West Germany and the Benelux countries. Thus, there was ample room for serious differences of opinion in this field. Furthermore, changing a parity from one fixed point to another nearly always gave rise to considerable speculation and, in the case of leading countries, this factor evidently added to the difficulty of the operation.

The third major factor contributing towards international imbalances during the years after 1958 was the nature of the measures actually applied in trying to correct the disequilibrium in various countries. In general, it would appear that, although at times perhaps unavoidable, the measures were largely of an ad hoc nature and did little if anything to bring about the necessary basic adjustments in the external accounts of the leading countries. The problem was indeed aggravated particularly after

1967, by the huge flows of speculative short-term funds, but these capital movements really reflected the failure of the adjustment mechanism provided for in the Fund arrangements and, in turn, resulted in growing currency uncertainties. Many countries apparently could not, or would not, face up to the disciplines required to make the mechanism work effectively. In some cases, the measures adopted were aimed largely at preventing or offsetting the capital movements so as to insulate the internal economy from their effects, while insufficient attention was given to the existence, and the need for correction, of internal disequilibrium.

With regard to the United States, which occupied the key position in the international monetary sphere, an important fact to be borne in mind was that, in view of the sheer strength of its gold reserve for many years after the war as well as the relatively small part traditionally played by foreign trade in its economy, monetary and general economic policies in that country tended to be orientated far more towards the attainment of internal economic aims than towards external equilibrium. Thus, it was not until the early sixties, after a persistent drain on the gold reserve due to the large net outflow of capital in one form or another, that steps were taken towards countering the serious deficit in the balance of payments.

The first important measure, which was taken in 1961/2, was the conclusion, on American initiative, of a series of Reciprocal Currency Arrangements between the Federal Reserve System, the Bank for International Settlements and the central banks of various countries, under which any member of the group could draw on the others for temporary assistance in meeting balance of payments disequilibria. This was a flexible and useful facility but it was not meant to finance fundamental disequilibria and evidently served to delay necessary adjustments. The US Treasury also issued special certificates and bonds, sometimes denominated in the foreign creditors' currencies and with maturities ranging from one to five years, to assist in mopping up surplus dollars in the hands of foreign official holders, which might otherwise be converted into gold. This was followed by the imposition of the Interest Equalization Tax to discourage the raising of foreign loans in the New York market, and by the so-called 'voluntary restraint programme'. Other countermeasures were also introduced from time to time, but the deficit in the US balance of payments continued to prevail, on a relatively large scale, throughout the sixties, and so also the decline in its gold reserve, on the one hand, and the increase in its short-term foreign liabilities, on the other.

Problem of International Liquidity

In the meantime, it had become apparent that, owing to the increasing industrial and hoarding demand for gold, the additions to the gold reserves of monetary authorities were insufficient to provide the necessary international liquidity for meeting even the normal swings to be expected in view of the growing volume of world trade and payments.

One of the manifestations of this problem was the tendency of the free-market price of gold to show a premium at times, rising, for example, to $40 per fine ounce in October, 1960. With the assistance of American supplies of gold, the price was gradually reduced to the parity price plus shipping costs, but the trouble flared up again in 1961. The result was that arrangements were concluded between the central banks of the United States, Great Britain, France, West Germany, Italy, Netherlands, Belgium and Switzerland, to form a gold pool for the purpose of keeping the market price for gold at about the official level.

Moreover, as a means of increasing international liquidity the resources of the International Monetary Fund (IMF) were increased by about 25 per cent in 1965. This was done because it was felt that the necessary increase in liquidity should not be derived from payments deficits in some of the leading countries, particularly the United States, as had in fact been the case for some time, nor from an increase in the official price of gold and the revaluation of gold reserves.

Nevertheless, an uneasy situation, with a background of currency fears, continued to prevail, and after sterling was again devalued in November, 1967, the speculative demand for gold in the free market increased to such an extent that the 'gold pool' suffered large losses and finally ceased operations in March, 1968.

The pool countries met to consider the situation and the outcome was the so-called Washington Agreement. This Agreement provided that the United States would continue to buy gold from, and sell gold to, monetary authorities at $35 per fine ounce; that official gold holdings would be used only for transfers among monetary authorities, and that the central banks involved would not buy gold from, or sell gold to, any free market or to any monetary authority which sold gold in the free market. Other central banks were expected to co-operate in support of these measures. The Agreement thus established a 'two-tier' system of gold prices, namely, the fixed official price for dealings between monetary authorities and the fluctuating free-market price where all other gold needs had to be met.

It was also stated in the Washington Agreement that existing official gold reserves were deemed adequate, in view of the proposed creation of Special Drawing Rights with the IMF. Eventually, in the middle of 1969, the Fund Agreement was amended to make provision for such Special Drawing Rights (SDR's). This step represented a deliberate creation of an international reserve asset, the amount of which, it was contended, could be regulated according to the world's real need for liquidity. To meet the views of those who believed that failure of the adjustment process was the basic cause of the trouble, the issue of SDR's to the participants in the scheme (in effect the Fund's members) was to be made dependent upon their working towards a better balance in their international accounts and towards a better functioning of the adjustment process. At the annual meeting of the IMF in October, 1969, it was decided to proceed with an allocation of SDR's to the total amount of $9·5 billion spread over the three years 1970–2.

International Monetary Crisis

Neither the Washington Agreement nor the issue of SDR's made any positive contribution towards removing the underlying factors making for balance of payments disequilibria and persistent currency fears. The movement towards a better balance in the international accounts and a better functioning of the adjustment process, which had inspired the issue of SDR's, did not in the event occur, and the strength of the US dollar which was the world's major reserve currency, remained in doubt. In fact, it only required one or two particularly adverse developments to set-off a run on the dollar, and this took place in 1970 and 1971. First there was the distinct adverse trend in the United States' trade balance in 1970 accompanied by a considerable net outflow of capital to Western Europe, which, together, caused an enormous deficit in the United States' balance of payments amounting to almost $10 billion. Moreover, a worse deficit was foreseen in 1971, and as the year progressed the truth of this view became apparent.

The real crisis started early in May, 1971, when the large inflow of dollars forced West Germany to close its exchange market. Austria, Belgium, the Netherlands and Switzerland followed suit within a few days. After discussion, West Germany decided to float the mark and the Netherlands followed. Austria and Switzerland revalued their currencies by 5 and 7 per cent respectively, and Belgium reopened its strictly controlled exchange market. These events steadied the situation, but failed to restore confidence in the dollar in view of the continued weakening in its balance of payments.

During the first half of August, 1971, a further large capital outflow from the United States began to take place owing to rumours that the dollar's convertibility into gold might be suspended. In the event, such convertibility as still existed, namely, for central banks and Treasuries where necessary, was officially suspended on 15th August. In addition, a surcharge of 10 per cent was imposed on dutiable imports into the United States. The result was that by the end of August, all the major world currencies had been floated and had risen to varying premiums against the dollar. The exception was the French franc which maintained the previous parity, but only for commercial and official transactions.

Eventually, when the floating rates began to impair business confidence and fears arose that there would be a widespread return to exchange and trade restrictions, further discussions among the principal countries were held in Rome and Washington, the outcome of which was the so-called Smithsonian Agreement of December, 1971. In terms of this Agreement, the US dollar was devalued by 7·9 per cent in terms of gold, and the Italian lira and the Swedish krona by 1 per cent, while the pound sterling and the French franc remained on their existing gold parities. On the other hand, the West German mark, the Japanese yen, the Dutch guilder and the Belgian franc were revalued in terms of gold by from 7·7 to 2·8 per cent, while the Swiss franc and the Austrian schilling maintained their earlier revaluation. Moreover, the margin of fluctuation on either side of the gold parities, or so-called central exchange rates in some countries, was widened from 1 per cent to 2¼ per cent, thus providing more flexibility. Finally, the import surcharge was removed.

After this Agreement, there was renewed speculation against the dollar, but the exchange markets settled down when it was realized that the central banks were fully prepared to support the agreed realignments of currencies until the adjustment process could show results. In June, 1972, however, the British authorities found it necessary to let sterling float at a lower level than its previous parity. This did not in itself cause any serious repercussions, but in the beginning of 1973 speculative capital movements again assumed large proportions and another monetary crisis developed.

The first manifestation of this crisis was the floating of the Swiss franc and the Italian lira, followed on 12th February by the decision to devalue the US dollar by 10 per cent in terms of gold, and to let the Japanese yen float upward. This, however, proved insufficient to calm the speculation and restore confidence, and under pressure of renewed speculative capital movements the foreign-exchange markets of many countries were closed from 2nd March, 1973, while the EEC countries were considering their line of action in the prevailing circumstances. On 16th March it was announced that, after an initial revaluation of the West German mark by 3 per cent, the EEC countries with the exception of Great Britain, Italy and Ireland, would continue to keep their currencies interlinked within narrow margins, but floating jointly against the US dollar, while sterling and the lira would continue to float independently in the meantime.

Committee of Twenty and International Monetary Reform

In the meantime, in October, 1972, a Committee of Twenty Governors of the International Monetary Fund had been appointed to investigate and report on the reform of the international monetary system; and a First Outline of Reform was submitted by the Chairman of the Committee to the Fund's Board of Governors at their annual meeting in September, 1973.

According to this Outline, there appeared to be considerable support in the Committee for moving in the direction of making a modified form of Special Drawing Rights the numeraire and principal reserve asset of the reformed international monetary system and reducing the role of reserve currencies, and eventually also of gold. But there was as yet no agreement on the nature and valuation of the proposed new SDR's, the means of restoring dollar convertibility or the steps necessary to improve the working of the balance of payments adjustment process.

The Outline also revealed a lack of agreement on the arrangements to be made for gold in the reformed system. While it could foresee a continuing monetary role for gold, it could merely mention three possible 'solutions' of the gold problem. The third 'solution', for example, would be to abolish the official gold price and permit monetary authorities not only to deal in gold with one another at a market-related price but also to sell and buy gold on the private market.

Furthermore, while the Outline proposed an exchange rate system of 'stable but adjustable par values' with provision for floating rates in particular situations, it could not yet give any indication of the nature of the code of conduct or rules which would be prescribed for such floating.

It is clear, therefore, that by September, 1973, the Committee had not yet made much progress in carrying out its task and that virtually all the basic reform issues were still unresolved. The need for a new orderly international monetary system, however, would appear to be so urgent that, unless a workable compromise agreement could be reached by the Committee in the near future, events might overtake it and bring about the requisite reform largely by market forces.

References

1 *See* Einzig, P. *Theory of Forward Exchange*. Macmillan, 1937. pp. 329–49.
2 *Ibid.* pp. 368–78.
3 Keynes, J. M. *Tract on Monetary Reform*. Harcourt, Brace, 1924. p. 135.
4 —— *Treatise on Money*. Macmillan, 1930. Vol. II, p. 326.
5 Einzig, P. *Foreign Balances*. Macmillan, 1938. pp. 108–17.
6 *See Annual* Report *of the Bank for International Settlements for* 1971–72.
7 *See Annual* Report *of the Bank for International Settlements for* 1958–59.
8 *Ibid.*

CHAPTER FOURTEEN

Fiscal Policy and Compensatory Government Action – Control of Investment

Compensatory Government Action

As far back as 1909, Bowley had suggested to the Poor Law Commission of Great Britain that public works should be postponed during periods of active trade and industry with a view to their being put in hand as soon as a recession appeared; and in 1919, at the first International Labour Conference in Washington, a recommendation was adopted that each Member State should 'co-ordinate the execution of all work undertaken under public authority with a view to reserving such work as far as practicable for periods of unemployment'. Not much public attention, however, was given to this matter until the thirties, when several countries adopted it as part of their general financial policy and Keynes and other economists focused particular attention on public-works planning as a necessary supplement to monetary policy.

As stated in Chapter 8, Keynes had, in his *Treatise on Money* (1930), stressed the factor of disequilibrium between saving and actual investment being the primary cause of cyclical fluctuations in business activity. Under the influence of the Great Depression and its aftermath during the thirties, this method of analysis led him to suggest that, in the absence of general control of investment, the business cycle should be controlled by adjusting the capital outlays of the State and public bodies generally according to the exigencies of the business situation. By retarding investments in times of active trade and speeding up investments in times of declining trade, public bodies could help to restore equilibrium between savings and investment; and it was naturally easier to confine this duty to the official bodies than to try to extend it over the entire sphere of production. As Keynes said, in 1937, 'the best we can hope to achieve is to use those kinds of investment which it is relatively easy to plan as a make-weight, bringing them in so as to preserve as much stability of aggregate investment as we can arrange at the right and appropriate level'.[1]

The public-works plan of combating business cycles was widely discussed during the years 1933–8. In 1935, Gayer's comprehensive treatise on *Public Works in Prosperity and Depression*, which was a revised version of his report submitted to the National Planning Board of the United States in the previous year and which dealt with the utilization of public works as an agency of economic stabilization, was published by the National Bureau of Economic Research. In 1937, Marriner Eccles[2] (Chairman of the Board of Governors of the Federal Reserve System) stated that 'the Government must be looked upon as a compensatory agency in this economy to do just the opposite to what private business and individuals do', since 'the latter are necessarily motivated by the desire for profit', while 'the former must be motivated by social obligation'; and that the Government should always 'be ready to incur a budgetary deficit' if spending the total revenue is not sufficient to meet the unemployment situation and stop credit contraction. In the same year, a group of economists of Oxford, including MacGregor, Salter, Cole and Henderson,[3] argued that public authorities as well as industry ought to have plans ready for important capital works in preparation for the following slump or recession; and Robbins[4] was also in favour of some planning of public works to smooth out the business cycle, as far as public works can be conveniently held up.

Moreover, the idea of a deliberate programme of public works and deficit financing as a means of counteracting unemployment and a decline in business activity was actually translated into practice in Sweden during the period 1930–35 and was held out in prospect for future recessions,* and, conversely, a policy of retarding public works and budgeting for a surplus in times of prosperity was enunciated. In the United States, a Public Works Administration and a National Planning Board were created in 1933; and, according to a statement made by the Secretary of the Treasury in November, 1937, the Government had, during the period 1933–37, 'deliberately used the unbalanced budget to meet a great emergency'. In Finland, a Budget Equalization Fund was established in 1934 for the declared purpose of counteracting cyclical fluctuations in business activity. Budget surpluses were paid into this Fund and the proceeds invested in gold, foreign exchange and deposits with the central bank. In the beginning of 1938 Sweden also decided to set up a Budget Regulation Fund, to which the Minister of Finance proposed to transfer the estimated surplus of £1,000,000 for the year.

In Norway, public-works planning likewise attracted the attention of the authorities, for in the Annual Report of the Bank of Norway for 1936 the following statement occurred: 'It is to be wished that the works and the orders of the State and the Municipalities should not follow the fluctuations up and down of industry and trade, because in that case new difficulties will be added to those already existing. What is needed is, in other words, planning at long sight, so as to keep in reserve works that can be commenced when private business slackens.'

With regard to Great Britain, a circular was addressed by the

* In June, 1938, owing to fear of a business recession developing in Sweden, an Enabling Act was rushed through the Riksdag, providing for an Emergency Budget of 250 million kronor for public works to be carried out in the event of depression. The Swedish Government also tried to extend this policy to the sphere of private industry by having a law passed which would tend to encourage industrial investment during periods of depression, by exempting companies from the income tax on such part of their net profits as could be shown to have been funded for depression investment purposes, subject to a limit of 10 per cent of annual profits or 2 per cent of share capital for building investments and 20 per cent of profits or 4 per cent of capital for investment in accessories and inventory. The funded money was to be used only in years fixed by the Government with a view to levelling out the trade cycle, and only for writing off buildings, machinery, etc., constructed during such years. See *The Times*, London, 25th May, 1938.

Ministry of Health to Local Authorities in the beginning of 1938, emphasizing not only that 'by an ordered planning of their prospective capital works on a basis which will admit of adjustment should circumstances make it desirable, Local Authorities can make a valuable contribution to the stabilization of the conditions in industry over a considerable period', but also that 'the adoption of such a policy will enable them to take the fullest advantage, in the interests of their ratepayers, of periods when industrial resources are not unduly strained and conditions are therefore most favourable for the execution of necessary works'.

Furthermore, in its Report for 1937–8, the Board of Directors of the Commonwealth Bank of Australia expressed the opinion 'that expenditure on public works should be relatively low in times of prosperity and that plans should be ready for expansion in times of depression', because 'preparation of plans of useful public works, expenditure on which can be increased or decreased as circumstances require, would help in the timing and regulation of capital expenditure and contribute towards stability of employment'.

Fiscal Policy

Since 1938 circumstances have led to even closer and wider attention being devoted to the theoretical aspects and practical application of expenditures on public works and deficit financing, and also of taxation, as instruments for supplementing monetary policy in the minimization of cyclical fluctuations in business activity.

For example, after stating that 'in the majority of highly industrialized communities it is expenditure on private investment which is the most usual and most potent cause of instability in total expenditure, and consequently in employment', the British White Paper on Employment Policy (published in May, 1944), laid down *inter alia* the following as the guiding principles of the Government's policy in maintaining total expenditure: 'Everything possible must be done to limit dangerous swings in expenditure on private investment'; and 'public investment, both in timing and in volume, must be carefully planned to offset unavoidable fluctuations in private investment'. With this end in view, Government policy would also be directed to securing the co-operation of local authorities and public utility undertakings and 'to encouraging privately-owned enterprises to plan their own capital expenditure in conformity with a general stabilization policy'. As regards public expenditure, 'the Government believe that in the past the power of public expenditure, skilfully applied, to check the onset of a depression has been underestimated'. With regard to the maintenance of the community's expenditure on consumption, the Government favoured the adoption 'of a scheme for varying, in sympathy with the state of employment, the weekly contribution to be paid by employers and employed under the proposed new system of social insurance'; and it had also examined 'a number of other devices for influencing the volume of consumption, such as the variation of rates of taxation and the incorporation of some system of deferred credits as a permanent feature of national taxation'. Reference was also made to the advantage of adopting, if found practicable, of a device similar to that of deferred tax credits and calculated to stimulate private capital expenditure at the onset of a depression.

According to the Canadian White Paper on Employment and Income (published in April, 1945), it was the 'firm intention of the Government to institute a system of managing its capital expenditures so that they may contribute to the maximum to the improvement and stabilization of employment and income'. The Government would aim at 'advance planning of all necessary and desirable Dominion projects so that there may be available a "shelf" of soundly planned projects, ready for execution when prospective employment conditions make it desirable to increase public investment expenditures', and also at encouraging advance planning on the part of the provincial and municipal governments and seeking their co-operation on the timing of such expenditures'. Moreover, the Government would be 'prepared in periods when unemployment threatens, to incur the deficits and increases in the national debt resulting from its employment and income policy, whether that policy in the circumstances is best applied through increased expenditures or reduced taxation'.

The Australian White Paper on Full Employment (published in May, 1945), also emphasized 'the part which public capital expenditure must play in maintaining full employment' and 'in stabilizing the level of total expenditure'. It stated that, should a decline in spending threaten to leave resources idle, the Commonwealth and State Governments and the local and semi-governmental authorities 'must be prepared to take advantage of the opportunity to employ those resources in accelerating and expanding their own programmes for national works, housing, improvement of capital equipment and provision of facilities for social and cultural activities'; and 'similarly, when private spending is tending to expand, some reduction may be made in public capital spending'.

In South Africa the Social and Economic Planning Council, in a report on Taxation and Fiscal Policy submitted in 1945, recommended *inter alia* that 'governmental expenditure be increased during depression, as far as possible in such a way that it generates further increases in total expenditure'; that 'a system of anti-cyclical budgeting be adopted, whereby deficits are incurred during depression and surpluses collected during prosperity'; and that 'the income-tax be used, on expert advice, as an anti-cyclical instrument, the rates being if necessary lowered during depression and raised during an inflationary boom'.

In Sweden, the Ministry of Finance had an inventory drawn up by the local authorities throughout the country and by the State-owned economic undertakings, listing the various useful public works schemes that might be resorted to in order to provide employment in a crisis. In selecting the public works schemes, particular attention was to be paid to the ability of each project to contribute rapidly towards increasing the national income.

In the United States, an Employment Act was passed in 1946, which declared it to be 'the continuing policy and responsibility of the Federal Government to use all practical means consistent with its needs and obligations and other essential considerations of national policy . . . to co-ordinate and utilize all its plans, functions and resources for the purpose of creating and maintaining . . . conditions under which there will be afforded useful employment opportunities, including self-employment, for those able, willing, and seeking to work, and to promote maximum employment, production and purchasing power'. The Act also required the President to transmit to Congress every year at the opening of the session, an economic report covering in substance all important phases of the nation's economic life, together with a programme of action; and it created a Council of Economic Advisers to assist the President in the formulation of his economic reports, as well as a Joint Committee of Congress to receive these reports and to make studies of its own.

After the war, moreover, several countries, such as Great Britain, the United States and Canada, generally aimed at budget surpluses, through relatively high taxes on personal and corporate incomes and on consumption, with the deliberate object of checking inflation. In 1951 Holland and Australia also adopted drastic fiscal measures for the same purpose. In Holland, for example, a fiscal programme was launched which aimed at an overall reduction in demand through a 5 per cent cut in consumption, a 25 per cent reduction in private investment and a substantial decrease in non-defence Government expenditure.

In Canada, moreover, the Government decided, in 1951, as a means of deterring non-essential business capital expenditures, to postpone for a period of four years the right to claim depreciation as a reduction of taxable income for certain types of new capital expenditure. In Great Britain the existing high initial tax allowances for depreciation of newly-acquired fixed assets of business undertakings were also withdrawn in 1952. Sweden even resorted to an investment tax on all new expenditure by business undertakings on buildings and machinery in order to prevent excessive capital outlays. With the lessening of inflationary pressures, however, Canada and Great Britain restored the previous system of tax allowances for depreciation at the end of 1952 and in April, 1953, respectively; and in April, 1954, Great Britain also introduced an 'investment allowance' of 20 per cent, in addition to the ordinary depreciation allowance, in respect of new industrial plant with a view to encouraging the modernization of industry.

In one way or another, therefore, taxation came to be adopted in various countries as an anti-cyclical instrument. As the

British Chancellor of the Exchequer said in his Budget Speech of March, 1952, about the role of taxation: 'Its job is not merely to balance the Government's expenditure. It has a part to play in so regulating the purchasing power available to the community as a whole that this purchasing power does not outrun the amount of goods and services available.'

In fact, fiscal policy had already attracted so much attention by 1941 that Williams[5] was induced to say that, 'while it grew out of monetary policy and was designed to supplement and strengthen it, fiscal policy has ended up by threatening to supplant monetary policy altogether'. He held that, properly managed, deficit financing and central bank policy 'could be mutually re-enforcing', and that 'in recovery from depression the deficits might play the larger role, both by creating new income directly and by helping to implement an easy money policy', while 'in a boom monetary policy could play an important and perhaps even the predominant role'. He stressed, however, the unfavourable implications of fiscal policy for monetary policy and the banking system if budgetary deficits were financed largely by the banks, and particularly if such deficit financing was continued for a long time. For example, the supply of money might be unduly increased by the banks' purchases of Government securities, and an excessive increase in their holdings of longer-term securities would make their financial position unstable, owing to possible changes in the prices of such securities, or would compel the central bank to support the Government-bond market. The need for such support would, in conjunction with the increase in the money supply, render monetary control difficult if not impossible. Thus, in order to keep the door open for the successful application of monetary control, where necessary, 'the real solution, and the only logical one, would be to finance deficit spending outside the banking system'.

Hansen[6] also emphasized that monetary policy must be supplemented by fiscal policy, and discussed cyclical fiscal policy under two headings, namely, a cyclically adjusted public-spending programme and a cyclically administered tax policy. With regard to public spending, he distinguished between 'pump-priming' and compensatory spending as an offset to fluctuations in private investment. The former 'carries with it the implication that a certain volume of public spending, varying under different conditions, will have the effect of setting the economy going on the way toward full utilization of resources on its own power without further aid from governmental spending'; while the latter 'connotes no implications with respect to setting the system going on its own momentum', but 'implies merely that public expenditures may be used to compensate for the decline in private investment'. Pump-priming expenditures, therefore, merely served the purpose of an anti-cyclical instrument, whereas compensatory spending also covered long-run compensatory action which he considered essential to stability in a slowly expanding, mature economy. He pointed out that the amount of pump-priming or compensatory governmental expenditures required to achieve their respective objects depended upon the degree ('leverage co-efficient') in which particular types of expenditure increased national income and employment, i.e. through their secondary effects upon consumption expenditures (on the 'multiplier' principle) and the induced effects upon private investment (on the 'acceleration' principle).

With regard to taxation as a cyclical compensatory measure, Hansen considered that 'for a dynamic, expanding economy enjoying vigorous booms a fluctuating consumption tax may be the appropriate tax policy'. He showed that 'taxes on pay-rolls and sales taxes can . . . very effectively be manipulated and timed according to the requirements of the cycle', in order 'to check an undue expansion of consumption in the boom and, through their removal together with the return of previously collected taxes, to stimulate consumption in the depression'. 'On the one side, this policy would tend to hold in check an abnormal rise in consumption and thus dampen the induced stimulus (via the Acceleration principle) to investment. On the other side, such a policy would provide funds for investment more largely from voluntary savings and thereby minimize the excesses of bank credit expansion.' As regards a less rapidly expanding, mature economy, 'a fixed but steeply progressive income-tax structure is indicated', since in such an economy the continuous stimulation of consumption expenditures was important and the cyclical fluctuations of private investment could best be offset not by a tax programme, but by compensatory fluctuations in governmental expenditures.

During the thirties and forties the emergence of a chronic tendency towards over-saving and under-investment in the less dynamic and more mature economies was widely discussed and raised the question of more or less permanent deficit financing, although in varying degrees depending upon the particular stage of the business cycle. Williams, however, forcibly pointed out the banking difficulties and the reduced scope for monetary control involved in deficit financing, with the aid of bank credit, as a long-run compensatory measure, and considered that such difficulties constituted an added reason for seeking correctives for secular defects in a mature economy in other directions, including taxation, and for using deficit spending primarily for business cycle changes.[7]

Hahn[8] also held that governmental deficit spending, in conjunction with the lowering of interest rates, was 'defensible, even advisable' as a means of shortening the transition period from a cyclical depression to recovery, but that it could not be used effectively for the purpose of compensating structural maladjustments. Thus, if measures were not taken to correct (i.e. 'to adjust rather than compensate') structural maladjustments, government spending would have to go on indefinitely; and 'if government spending goes on indefinitely and therefore represents an ever-increasing burden on the community, the day must eventually come when it outlasts and outgrows the illusion effect, which is, by its very nature, transitory and limited'. In short, compensating reactions by the public would, in due course, neutralize the effects of compensatory spending by the Government.

Since the fifties, however, the position has changed dramatically in the mature economies, and their preoccupation, as well as that of the semi- or underdeveloped countries, has become the problem of coping with persistent inflationary pressures, much of which can be attributed to deficit financing by their Governments with the aid of both central bank credit and commercial bank credit, as pointed out previously. The result has been that less attention has been devoted by economists and Governments to the merits of deficit financing as a means of long-run compensatory action, and more to the deliberate adoption of fiscal policy as an anti-cyclical instrument, by means of adjustments in the level of public investment and current expenditures as well as in the incidence of taxation on private investment and consumption.

Thus, in many countries the Government has come to make regular use of the annual budget as an integral part of general economic policy and to adapt its programme of both capital and current expenditures and taxation to the current and prospective trends in the internal economy, such as increasing taxation generally to curb excessive expansion and inflation or only certain taxes designed to restrain consumption, or curtailing certain expenditures for the same purpose, or, on the other hand, increasing certain expenditures and/or reducing certain taxes aimed at encouraging expansion of production and/or consumption, depending on the prevailing circumstances. Extensive use has been made, for example, of investment allowances in the income tax on companies in order to promote or retard new capital investment in industrial plant and equipment, and sometimes also buildings. Moreover, in some countries the Government has acquired the legal authority to increase or decrease certain taxes, such as sales or purchase taxes, at any time between the annual budgets, with a view to discouraging or encouraging consumption.

The experience of Governments with fiscal policy has, however, shown certain limitations in practice. As regards expenditure on public works and enterprises, for example, many of the activities of the Government and other public authorities are intimately connected with business movements and the increase or decrease in effective demand. While in a time of prosperity some of the construction projects may be held up, in anticipation of the following slump, without unduly hampering business activity, there are others which cannot be postponed for fear of congestion or inability to meet the legitimate requirements of business or other consumers. On the other hand, while some projects may be taken in hand during a depression in anticipation of an increased demand when business swings upwards again, there are others which it might be inadvisable to undertake in advance owing to new inventions being experimented with or to rapid improvements in methods and technique or to likely changes in the character and direction of demand. The imperfect mobility of labour is also a factor to be reckoned with. Moreover, in a democratic state it is not easy for the Government and other public authorities to maintain a policy of deliberate budgeting for surpluses and building up reserves or paying off debts in times of prosperity. At such times, the general public is infected with optimism and does not see the necessity for high taxation and redemption of public debt in anticipation of a slump.

While there are limits to the efficacy both of fiscal policy and of credit control as means of smoothing out the business cycle, it does not relieve public authorities and central banks of the duty and responsibility of exerting themselves to the utmost to achieve whatever they can in those directions, collectively and individually. Even allowing for the limitations referred to, the combination of these two methods could be made to operate with great advantage to national and international economic welfare.

The importance of fiscal policy as a supplement to credit control by central banks is derived, in particular, from the fact that a business recession is accompanied by psychological factors which reduce the velocity of the monetary circulation and the willingness of entrepreneurs and investors to take risks. Experience has shown that under such circumstances central banks cannot 'pump out' much credit into active use merely by creating conditions of easy money. The credit base may at such times be increased by central banking operations without an increase in the effective demand for credit and for goods and services. It is then that spending by public authorities out of hoarded funds or borrowed money, provided the objects of expenditure have a reasonably sound basis and have been carefully planned beforehand to avoid wasteful expenditure, can be of great benefit in increasing the effective quantity of money flowing into active use.

Control of Investment

During the thirties, control of capital issues in one form or another was adopted by several countries as an emergency measure or an instrument of financial control; and, as in the case of exchange control, it was developed to the greatest extent in those countries where there was acute disequilibrium in the balance of payments and where totalitarian regimes had been established.*

In Germany, as stated in Chapter 12, the rationing of credit as a method of control was abandoned after 1932, and direct control of the capital market was introduced. Wagemann[9] pointed out that Germany's capital-market policy was directed, in the first instance, towards the consolidation of the large amount of public short-term debt issued during the depression, i.e. the conversion of the short-term debt into medium and long-term bonds so that they would be viewed mainly as capital investments. This consolidation, as well as the raising of additional money for Government purposes, was made possible by the radical restriction of private issues; and even such private issues as were permitted 'were connected with the financing of projects directly related to the development of national military needs and the Four Years Plan'. The restriction of issues thus became 'one of the most important methods of distributing capital in accordance with capital investment requirements'. In order to make the new loans attractive in comparison with already existing issues, the Law for the Investment of Surplus Dividends was passed, which practically restricted dividends paid out to 6 per cent. The decisive importance of this law, according to Wagemann, was that it prevented a large flow of money from the bond market to the stock market in the expectation of steadily increasing dividends, and that it promoted the issue of the large Government loans both through investment of surplus dividends and through making general stocks and shares relatively unattractive. Moreover, to prevent the flow of funds not only to the stock market but also to other bonds bearing higher interest, the great German bond conversion was carried out which reduced the nominal interest of all bonds to 4½ per cent. This conversion was applied also to private loans 'with the definite purpose of bringing about in a direct way a general reduction of

* Soviet Russia had, of course, already implemented complete financial and physical controls during the twenties, as part and parcel of the authoritarian communist regime.

the interest level', and, in particular, with a view to reducing the interest burden on business.

As Wagemann said at the time (1937), 'the planned control of the capital market has naturally attained its greatest extent where the Government has taken over the economic leadership, thus especially in Germany and Italy'. In Great Britain, on the other hand, the control of capital issues during the thirties was mainly of a general regulatory nature and designed to obviate overlapping and congestion in the London capital market. It was only in connection with the conversion of the £2,000,000,000 War Loan from a 5 to a 3½ per cent basis, in 1932, that a complete ban was imposed on new domestic and foreign issues. Thereafter, restrictions were maintained on foreign issues, with the assistance of a foreign investment advisory committee. As regards domestic issues, a queue system for loans by local authorities was introduced. On the whole, the regimentation of borrowing by British local authorities, and by the British Dominions and Colonies generally, became largely a matter of timing the respective issues. At first, the main purpose of control of foreign loans was to protect sterling against pressure on account of an undue outflow of capital, but later the protection of domestic against foreign requirements of capital came to be an equally important factor. While the regulation of capital issues facilitated the general lowering of interest rates and the conversion of Government loans, the primary stimulus for easy money was derived from the discount-rate policy and open-market operations of the Bank of England.

In Japan, when the so-called 'China Incident' was embarked upon, a capital adjustment law was introduced in September, 1937, the purpose of which was, according to the Vice-Governor of the Bank of Japan,[10] 'to facilitate the execution of the national policies by rendering smooth the supply of funds required for the equipment of industries which are essential and urgent in the present situation, and, at the same time, by preventing the locking up of capital in enterprises which are not urgent or essential'. Autonomous adjustment bodies were formed in accordance with the provisions of the law, and subject to the supervision of the Bank of Japan in order to prevent any flow of capital to speculative use.

During World War II, control of the capital market was obviously extended in belligerent countries as one of the means of mobilizing resources for war purposes and applying them to the best national advantage. In Great Britain, for example, war requirements constituted the sole criterion permitting new capital issues; and a Capital Issues Advisory Committee, including representatives of the Treasury and the Bank of England, was set up to ensure that this policy was carried out in the most effective manner. Control of capital issues was applied also to new bank advances and all mortgage loans in excess of £10,000 in any period of twelve months, as in the case of other issues. In addition to such measures of financial control, physical controls were established to secure the efficient mobilization and co-ordination of real resources for the maximum war effort.

With the cessation of hostilities in Europe, control of capital issues in Great Britain was relaxed 'to meet the changed situation'. A Memorandum of Guidance was issued to the Capital Issues Committee (at the end of May, 1945), 'in order to set out the principles which will until further notice govern the grant of Treasury consent to new issues of capital'. In terms of this memorandum, which did not apply to the control of issues to be made by local authorities or of overseas issues, the primary object of the control was to ensure that, subject to the possibilities of the capital market and the circumstances, the order of priority of capital issues would be determined according to their relative importance in the general national interest, having regard, particularly, to current Government policy in respect of physical investment. It was provided that the Committee would give specially sympathetic consideration to (*a*) undertakings producing or selling for export; (*b*) issues required to establish, re-start, convert or expand undertakings in the areas designed as 'Development Areas' in furtherance of the policy of balanced distribution of industry; (*c*) undertakings which had been concentrated or requisitioned; and (*d*) undertakings which had suffered war damage. Subject to circumstances requiring at any time a stricter control, consent would usually be given to issues of securities for the purposes of public utility undertakings and housing associations; the development of agricultural land and of the fishery industry; the production and exploitation of raw materials; transport and storage; and for such other productive and constructional purposes as might be notified to the Committee from time to time by the Treasury after consultation with the appropriate other Government Departments. In the case of public or private issues of £100,000 or more, however, it would still be necessary to arrange with the Bank of England (acting on behalf of and in consultation with the Treasury) as to *the time of making the issue*.

In 1946 legislation was passed in Great Britain in order to extend indefinitely the Government's wartime powers to regulate demands upon the supply of new capital. For the purpose of exercising these powers, the Capital Issues Committee was retained, and instructions were issued from time to time by the Treasury for the guidance of the Committee. In April, 1949, for example, the Committee was asked to consider four basic principles in deciding whether or not to give their approval to new capital issues, namely, the improvement of supplies of basic materials; the increase of exports to hard-currency markets; the saving of hard currencies; and the development of new techniques and of research contributing to industrial progress and the immediate reduction of manufacturing costs. In April, 1951, moreover, the Committee was instructed to give priority also to projects essential to the defence programme.

In all the other countries directly involved in World War II, general control of investment was, in one form or another, necessarily adopted as a war measure. The degree in which it was carried out during the war depended mainly on the magnitude of the war effort and the capital resources of the country concerned, as well as the general repercussions of the war on its economy. After the termination of hostilities,* some of these countries saw their way clear to considerably relaxing physical and financial controls and retaining only certain general principles concerning control of capital issues.

A tendency towards some control or direction of investment was also manifested in several neutral countries. Under their totalitarian regimes and the pressure of circumstances, Spain and

* In the United States, for example, most of the controls were abolished almost immediately after the surrender of Japan, while the remaining control measures were to be withdrawn as soon as circumstances permitted.

Portugal established economic councils and investment planning bodies. Among the democratic states, Sweden, for example, set up an Investment Council, consisting of representatives of the Government and industry, to study the trend of business activity and make recommendations to industry with a view to levelling out industrial investment activities as far as possible. Thus, while Sweden was, as explained in the preceding discussion of fiscal policy and compensatory Government action, committed to a policy of adjusting public investment to fluctuations in private investment, the Investment Council was to aim at minimizing such fluctuations. Apart from the voluntary co-ordination of private capital expenditures, it was also to investigate other methods of evening out the flow of private investment, such as direct control of investment and flexible tax and interest policies.

In fact, the control of capital issues has been retained in many countries, in one form or another, as an instrument of general economic control and in conjunction with credit control. The limitations of monetary policy under increased economic rigidity and complexity, and the prevailing conditions of economic disequilibrium over a large part of the world, have enhanced the need for some sort of investment planning or control to exercise a direct influence on financial activities which can only inadequately be covered by means of credit control. In some countries, circumstances may not actually warrant anything more than broad planning of direction of general investment by a representative advisory body, with such tangible support in the form of compensatory public expenditure and taxation as may be found necessary at times to counteract substantial fluctuations in private investment.

There has, however, been considerable difference of opinion concerning the degree in which financial controls can be effective without physical controls, or the extent to which investment planning can be employed as an instrument of control without general economic planning and the restriction of individual freedom and private initiative.

Many have held the view that, if physical controls are absent or inadequate, financial controls will not achieve equity and efficiency. As the *Economist*[11] said:

> 'If the job (of planned investment) is to be done at all, it must be done by controls of real resources. If these are effective, financial control of the new issues type will have no priority function to perform . . . If, on the other hand, physical controls cannot be made effective in peacetime – either because the administrative machine cannot cope with them or the public will not stand for them – a financial priority control will be a very indifferent substitute. It would stop some non-priority borrowers at the main entrance, but non-priority industries with cash in their pockets would be scrambling through the gaping hole in the hedge at the back.'

Comprehensive physical controls, on the other hand, imply intensive economic planning and regimentation, which constitute a logical concomitant of the situation in an authoritarian regime but cannot be reconciled with basic conditions in a democratic economy. Some hold that a democratic framework nevertheless affords sufficient scope for broad planning and direction by the State in combination with private enterprise, while others claim that the two are incompatible. Aldrich,[12] for example, emphasized that there was a limit to the adaptability of democracy, and maintained that 'a democratically planned economy is an impossibility' and that 'free enterprise and democracy must fall together, as they arose together'.

Under the prevailing conditions in many countries, however, there would appear to be no clear choice between a 'planned economy' and 'free enterprise'. The problem of modern democracy has inevitably become that of combining a minimum of central planning and investment control with private initiative and enterprise in order to obtain the advantages of both and, in conjunction with monetary and fiscal policy, to maintain as high and stable a level of economic activity and employment as possible. The real difficulty is that too much State direction and intervention will hamper private enterprise, while too little will leave a gap.

References

1 Keynes, J. M., in *The Times*, London. January, 1937.
2 Eccles, Marriner, in *American Banker's Association Journal*. February, 1937.
3 Macgregor, D. H., Salter, Sir Arthur, Cole, G. D. H., Henderson, H. D., *et al.* Letter to *The Times*. June 1937.
4 Robbins, L. C. (now Lord Robbins), in *Lloyds Bank Monthly Review*. May, 1937.
5 Williams, J. H. 'The Implications of Fiscal Policy for Monetary Policy and the Banking System'. *American Economic Review*, December, 1941. (Reprint from *Proceedings of the American Economic Association.*)
6 Hansen, A. H. *Fiscal Policy and Business Cycles*. Allen & Unwin, 1941. pp. 261–300.
7 Williams, *op. cit.* p. 20.
8 Hahn, A. 'Compensating Reactions to Compensatory Spending.' *American Economic Review*, March, 1945. pp. 28–39.
9 Wagemann, E. *Wirthschaftspolitische Strategie*. Hanseatische Verlagsanstalt, 1937. pp. 323–6.
10 *See* Special Japan Supplement to *Statist*. 24th August, 1940.
11 *The Economist*. 25th August, 1945.
12 Aldrich, W. W. *The Incompatibility of Democracy and a 'Planned' Economy*. Reprint of a lecture, 1939. pp. 5 and 19.

CHAPTER FIFTEEN

Constitution and Administration of Central Banks

Introduction

In view of the fact that the central bank was entrusted with a complete or residuary monopoly of the note issue and with the general control of credit in the national economic interest, and that the major responsibility for the determination of monetary policy came to be vested in the State, the latter almost everywhere claimed the right to increasing participation in the affairs of the central bank. Such participation by the State took the form of sole or part ownership of the capital of the central bank and/or the appointment of all or some of its directors and chief executive officers and/or a share in its profits.

Ownership of Capital

Prior to 1936 there had been only a small number of entirely State-owned central banks, namely, those of Sweden, Finland, Russia, Bulgaria, Uruguay, Iceland, Australia, China and Iran. Between 1936 and 1945, however, the central banks of Denmark, Canada, New Zealand, Bolivia and Guatemala were nationalized, while virtually all the new central banks which were established during that period were founded as State institutions, namely, those of Ireland, Poland, Thailand, Ethiopia, Costa Rica, Paraguay, Nicaragua and Afghanistan.

After World War II the process of nationalization of existing central banks was considerably extended. Thus, the central banks of England, France, Germany,* Netherlands, Norway, Czechoslovakia, Yugoslavia, Hungary, Roumania, Argentina, India, Indonesia, Egypt, Spain, El Salvador and Peru were also converted into State-owned institutions. With regard to the many new central banks which have been created since the war, it would appear, with a few exceptions, to have been accepted as a formality that they should be owned entirely by the State.

Despite this strong trend, there are still some countries whose central banks have not been nationalized, or at least not to the full extent. Of these there are a few where the Government holds at least half of the capital stock of the central bank, namely, 55 per cent in Japan, 51 per cent in Mexico and Pakistan, and 50 per cent in Belgium† and Venezuela. There are also a few central banks in which the Government has a minority interest, namely, those of Portugal,‡ Chile, Colombia§ and Ecuador. With regard

* In West Germany, the new central banking system which was set up in 1948, in the place of the Reichsbank, consisted of a separate bank in each of the several constituent 'Länder' (States) of the Federal Republic, as well as a central supervising and co-ordinating institution called the 'Bank Deutscher Länder'. The capital for this institution was subscribed by the 'Land Central Banks' which were, in turn, owned by the respective 'Land Governments'. In 1957, however, when the central banking system was reconstituted as the 'Deutsche Bundesbank', the Federal Government itself subscribed the whole of the capital. As far as East Germany was concerned, the new central bank (Deutsche Notenbank) was established as a Government institution in 1950.

† The National Bank of Belgium, which had been established as a privately owned institution in 1850, was semi-nationalized in 1948 as a result of the doubling of its capital and the Government subscribing the whole of the additional capital.

‡ In 1972 the Government held only about 22·5 per cent of the capital stock of the Bank of Portugal, but the voting rights of private shareholders were limited to ten votes per person, regardless of the number of shares held by them individually.

§ As at the end of 1972, the Government directly owned only 29·5 per cent of the capital stock of the Bank of the Republic of Colombia and the commercial banks 41·1 per cent, but semi-official banks held 26·6 per cent and the Stabilization Fund 2·7 per cent, leaving only 0·1 per cent in the to those countries where the Government still does not have any direct share in the ownership of the central bank, the following can be named: the United States, Italy, Switzerland,* Greece,† and South Africa.

In some countries the commercial banks were required by law to subscribe the whole or a part of the capital of the central bank. The twelve Federal Reserve Banks of the United States are the only examples of central banks which are owned solely by commercial banks. When the Federal Reserve System was brought into being, all the national banks‡ were required to become members of the System, while the State banks§ which conformed to certain requirements and conditions could become members on application. All these member banks had to subscribe for stock of the Federal Reserve Bank in their particular area to the amount of 6 per cent of their capital and surplus, and of this amount one-half was to be paid up and the other half to be at call.

In Mexico, all banks receiving deposits for less than thirty days were required, in 1932, to take shares in the Bank of Mexico up to an amount of at least 6 per cent of their capital and reserves. This requirement was subsequently imposed also on branches of foreign banks; and in 1936 it was applied to all banks and credit institutions authorized to receive sight, fixed or savings deposits.

In South Africa, Chile, Colombia, Peru, Cuba, Ecuador and El Salvador, the banks were likewise required to subscribe a part of the original capital of the central bank, on the basis of a proportion of their paid-up capital and reserves. In South Africa, however, the banks were subsequently relieved of the obligation

hands of individuals. It was, however, intended to enact legislation in 1973 for the transfer of almost the whole of the capital stock to the Government.

* While the Federal Government of Switzerland does not own any part of the capital of the National Bank, the Cantons have a substantial shareholding in the Bank.

† The statutes of the Bank of Greece provide that the State and State undertakings shall not directly, or indirectly, hold shares of the Bank amounting, in the aggregate, to more than one-tenth of the nominal issued capital, but it is not known whether this limited right has been exercised.

‡ Banks operating under the National Bank Act of the Federal Legislature.

§ Banks operating under laws or charters of the individual States.

to hold a certain amount of Reserve Bank stock, as a result of which they sold most of their holdings to the public, while in the case of most of the other countries concerned the nationalization of the central bank naturally removed this requirement.

In Italy, where the capital of the central bank had formerly been held entirely by private persons, provision was made in 1936 for the repayment to those shareholders of the capital and part of the reserves and for the subscription of the new capital by 'public law' banks and credit institutions, savings banks, insurance companies and provident societies.

Distribution of Profits

In the case of almost every State-owned central bank, the whole of the annual profits, after providing for a maximum allocation to the reserve fund, was to be paid to the Government as the only shareholder or proprietor, either directly and entirely to the Treasury or partly to the Treasury and partly to a Government fund or agency. In the case of the Bank of England, for example, it was provided in 1968 that the profits of the Issue Department were henceforth to be paid to the National Loans Fund instead of to the Treasury, while in Spain the Minister of Finance was authorized in 1964 to allocate part of the profits of the Bank of Spain for writing off advances granted by the Bank to public agencies.

With regard to other central banks, provision was made for the Government sharing in their profits, whether it owned a part of the capital or not. Where the Government was a shareholder, it was entitled to a portion of the profits in accordance with a scale or procedure laid down by statute, in addition to receiving dividends in respect of its shareholding on the same basis as other shareholders.

Two principal methods were devised for ensuring an adequate share to the Government in the profits of such institutions. The one method was that of providing for a cumulative dividend of, for example, 6 per cent in the case of the Federal Reserve Banks, the National Bank of Belgium and the South African Reserve Bank, as a first charge on the net profits, and thereafter a division of profits between the reserve fund, the Government and the shareholders, or just between the reserve fund and the Government. Thus, the Federal Reserve Banks were to pay a cumulative dividend of 6 per cent, which was also the maximum, while the balance of the profit was to be allocated to the surplus fund until it amounted to the subscribed capital; and thereafter 10 per cent of the excess profit was to be paid into the surplus fund and the remainder to the Government.* The South African Reserve Bank, on the other hand, was to pay a cumulative dividend of 6 per cent, while the surplus was to be allocated to the reserve fund until the latter amounted to one-quarter of the capital; thereafter and until the reserve fund equalled the capital, one-half of the surplus was to be allocated to the reserve fund, one-quarter to the Government and one-quarter to shareholders up to a total maximum dividend of 10 per cent, and any balance remaining was to be paid to the Government; and when the reserve fund equalled the capital, the whole of the profit after a payment of a dividend of 10 per cent was to go to the Government.†

The second method was that of providing for the payment of a specified proportion of the net profits to the reserve fund as a first charge on the profits, and a minimum dividend to shareholders as a second charge, the remainder to be divided between the Government and the shareholders in accordance with a prescribed scale. Some countries have adopted variants of this method. In the case of the Bank of Mexico, for example, it is provided that, after the allocation of 10 per cent of the profits to the reserve fund and the payment of a dividend of 6 per cent to the shareholding banks and a contribution to the Auxiliary Fund

* In 1933 this provision was amended to the effect that the whole of the net earnings, after payment of a cumulative dividend of 6 per cent, was to be paid into the surplus fund of the Federal Reserve Bank concerned. In 1947, however, it was decided to levy an interest charge on Federal Reserve notes issued by the Federal Reserve Banks, with a view to restoring to the Treasury the payment by the Federal Reserve Banks of approximately 90 per cent of their net annual earnings.

† In 1944, however, when the reserve fund was already equal to the capital, it was provided that one-tenth of the surplus remaining after payment of the maximum dividend of 10 per cent was to be allocated to the reserve fund before the balance was paid to the Government.

for employees of the Bank, the whole of the remaining profits is to be paid to the Federal Government. In the case of the Bank of Portugal, however, the Government is entitled to 50 per cent of the profits after the transfer of 10 per cent to the reserve fund, followed by the allocation of 10 per cent for distribution to employees and the payment of a dividend of 6 per cent to shareholders, while of the remaining balance 75 per cent is to be paid to the Government and the rest retained by the Bank after deducting what may be required to raise the dividend to 7 per cent.

In general, it may be said that the Government claimed a share in the profits of the central bank because the latter was granted a monopoly of the note issue, which usually constituted a valuable privilege not only for purposes of control, but also as a source of profit. The Government's share was also intended in many cases to operate as a means of restraining the incentive to make large profits, and for this purpose statutory limits were likewise imposed in most instances on dividends to shareholders and on allocations to reserve funds.

Administration of Central Banks

As in the case of banking institutions generally, every central bank is administered by a Board of Directors or the equivalent of such a Board, whether called a Council of Administration (as in Mexico), or a Council of Regents (as in Belgium), or a General Council (as in Denmark, France, Spain and Switzerland), or a Supervisory Council (as in Norway), or a Board of Commissaries (as in Holland), or a Policy Board (as in Japan), or a Monetary Board (as in several Latin-American and Asian countries). In some countries, however, such as Belgium, Denmark, Holland, Japan, Norway, Sweden, Switzerland and West Germany, the central bank also has a Management Board to attend to the daily business of the bank, consisting of the Governor or President as Chairman, the Deputy-Governor or Vice-President and from two to four other members who are, in most instances, full-time members. In the Bank of England, on the other hand, while there is no formal Management Board, there are four full-time executive directors besides the Governor and Deputy-Governor.

With regard to the extent of participation by the State in the appointment of directors, a distinction must first be drawn between entirely State-owned central banks and others. In the case of the former, all the directors are, with few exceptions, appointed by the Government, whether through the medium of the Head of the State (King, President or Governor-General), as in England, Australia, New Zealand and some Latin-American countries, or by the Cabinet or Council of Ministers, or directly by the Minister of Finance with or without the statutory requirement of Cabinet approval, as in Canada and Ireland respectively. In Sweden and Norway, however, the directors are appointed by the Legislature,* with the exception of the Chairman who is appointed by the King; and in Denmark eight of the directors are elected by the Legislature from among its own members, two by the Minister of Trade, Industry and Shipping, and the remainder by the other directors.

As regards the central banks in which the State owns only a part of the capital or none at all, it has claimed varying degrees of participation in the appointment of the directors and of the Governor and Deputy Governor(s) or President and Vice-President(s) who are, with some exceptions, also members of the Board of Directors. Thus, for example, in Portugal three out of the eleven directors of the central bank are appointed by the Government; in Belgium five out of fifteen; in the United States † and Colombia three out of nine and ten respectively; in Chile four out of eleven; in Mexico and Venezuela five out of nine; in South Africa six out of twelve; in Pakistan eight out of eleven; and in Switzerland twenty-five out of forty. In Italy, however, all the directors are elected by the general meeting of

* In Sweden, although it is not provided in the statute of the Riksbank, the general practice is to appoint three members of the Legislature to the Board of Directors of the Bank. In Norway this also applies to the Management Board.

† In each of the twelve Federal Reserve Banks, the three directors concerned are not appointed directly by the Government but indirectly through the Board of Governors of the Federal Reserve System, all of whose members are appointed by the President of the United States.

shareholders, except the Governor who is nominated by the Board of Directors with the approval of the Government, while in Japan all the directors are appointed by the Government.

In some countries where commercial banks have been required by law to subscribe the whole or part of the capital of the central bank, they have been given the right to nominate some of their directors or employees as directors of the central bank. In the United States, for example, three out of the six directors of each Federal Reserve Bank elected by its member banks shall be representatives of such banks; and in Mexico the four and in Colombia and Chile the three directors elected by the shareholding banks may be directors or employees of such banks. In South Africa, the shareholding banks were also originally authorized to nominate three bank representatives as directors of the central bank, but this authority was subsequently withdrawn.

In several countries, moreover, provision has been made for Treasury representation on the Board of Directors of the central bank. In Australia and New Zealand, for example, the Secretary of the Treasury is a director with voting power, while in Canada the Deputy-Minister of Finance, and in Japan a representative of the Ministry of Finance, is also a director, but without the right to vote. In Argentina and several other Latin-American countries, as well as in Indonesia, Ceylon, Korea and the Philippines, the Minister of Finance, or the Secretary of the Treasury, is the Chairman or a member of the controlling board of the central bank. In Belgium and Netherlands, on the other hand, there is a Royal Bank Commissioner who supervises the operations of the central bank on behalf of the Government.

As far as the relationship between the Board of Directors and the chief executive officers is concerned, the latter are not only members of the Board in the majority of central banks, but provision is also made in the case of many central banks for the Governor or President (as full-time officer) to preside at Board meetings, and for the Deputy-Governor or Vice-President (or the senior one where there are two or more) to act as Chairman in the absence of the Governor or President. As exceptions the following banks, apart from those where, as stated above, the

Minister of Finance or the Secretary of the Treasury is the Chairman, can be mentioned: the Riksbank of Sweden and the Bank of Norway, where the Chairman is the director appointed by the King; the National Bank of Denmark, the Bank of Mexico and the Central Reserve Bank of Peru, where the Chairman is appointed by the Directors from among themselves or from outside; and the Federal Reserve Banks, where the Chairman of the Board of Directors of each Federal Reserve Bank is nominated by the Board of Governors of the Federal Reserve System from among the three directors whom it appoints to each Board of Directors.*

There are also various exceptions to the general rule of appointments of chief executive officers by the Government. The Presidents and Vice-Presidents of the Federal Reserve Banks, for example, are appointed by the Boards of Directors subject to the approval of the Board of Governors; the Governor of the Riksbank of Sweden is appointed by the Board of Directors from among themselves, and the Deputy-Governor either from among themselves or from outside; the Governor and Deputy-Governors of the Bank of Canada are nominated by the Board of Directors with the approval of the Government; and the Director-General of the Bank of Mexico and the President of the Central Bank of Chile are also nominated by their Boards of Directors.

State Control over Central Banks

The process of nationalization of central banks was accompanied by wider powers of State control over their policy and operations. The extent to which this factor was reflected in different countries, however, depended upon the domestic political conditions or the stage of constitutional or economic development which had been reached in the country concerned.

* In the Federal Reserve Banks, moreover, the President is not a member of the Board of Directors. This also applies, for example, to the Director-General of the Bank of Mexico, the President of the Central Bank of Chile and the General Managers who are the chief executive officers of some Latin-American central banks, except in the case of the Central Bank of Ecuador where the General Manager is a member of the Board.

In some countries the only practical change was to give statutory definition to the relationship which had already been satisfactorily established between the central bank and the Government prior to nationalization. The new statute of the Bank of England, for example, merely provided that 'the Treasury may from time to time give such directions to the Bank as, *after consultation with the Governor of the Bank*, they think necessary in the public interest'. When the Reserve Bank of India was nationalized in 1948, a similar provision was included in the new Act; and in the case of the Netherlands Bank, while the Minister of Finance was empowered to give directions to the Bank 'in order to co-ordinate the Government's monetary and financial policy and that of the Bank', the Bank was specifically authorized to appeal to the Crown in the event of disagreement with such directions.

Furthermore, in Canada, where the central bank apparently maintained a semi-independent status in spite of nationalization as far back as 1938, the Minister of Finance who introduced the relevant Bill was reported to have given as the reason for nationalizing the Bank of Canada the fact that there had been a good deal of political controversy throughout the country with respect to monetary policy generally and the constitution of the Bank, and that it was highly undesirable and very much against the national interest that there should be continued political bickering concerning the constitution of the Bank itself.[1] In Belgium, the explanation given by the Government on the introduction of the Bill for semi-nationalization of the National Bank in 1948 was to the effect that, 'while not desiring the nationalization of the Bank of Issue, and without making the Governor of the Bank a functionary dependent on the Minister of Finance, it was felt necessary still further to ensure both the complete independence of the National Bank vis-à-vis private interests and its collaboration in the general policy of the public authorities'. This explanation sounded very much like a half-hearted compromise against political pressure. The nationalization of the Bank of England and the Netherlands Bank would also appear to have been largely a concession to partisan political feeling.

Moreover, in West Germany it was laid down in the statutes

of the Bundesbank, in 1957, that the Bank was obliged, while carrying out its duty of safeguarding the currency, to support the general economic policy of the Government, but it was added that the Bank was independent of Government direction in the exercise of its legal powers. It was also provided that the Bank and the Government had to consult each other on important matters of monetary policy, and that members of the Government had the right to participate in the deliberations of the Central Bank Council and to submit proposals, but they did not have the right to vote and could only delay a decision of the Council for up to two weeks.

There are, however, various countries where the outcome of nationalization was either a more or less formal subordination of the central bank to the Government, or at least a substantial decline in the status of the central bank in monetary and banking matters relative to that of the Treasury. Thus, in all the new Communist States of Europe, as in Russia, the Government was empowered to direct monetary and banking policies and use the central bank as an instrument for carrying out such policies. Moreover, in several Asian and Latin-American countries, although the central bank retained its separate status, its monetary policy had by law to be submitted to the Minister of Finance for approval or prior review. In Korea, for example, the Minister of Finance, who was in any case Chairman of the Monetary Board of the Bank of Korea, was granted the power, under an amendment of the Bank's statute in 1962, to request reconsideration of resolutions adopted by the Board, and if the request for reconsideration was overruled by the Board with a majority of two-thirds of its members, the final decision was to be made by the Government. According to Kim,[2] 'the foremost significance of the amendment lies in the fact that it established unmistakably the domination of the Bank by the Government and the firm grip by the hands of the Government on the ultimate control of the monetary policy'. Moreover, in the case of the Bank of Mexico, despite the fact that the Government did not hold more than 51 per cent of the Bank's capital stock, the Secretary (Minister) of Finance and Public Credit was authorized to veto any resolutions of the Bank's Council of Administration concerning monetary or foreign-exchange policy.

Furthermore, when the Reserve Bank of New Zealand was nationalized in 1936, it was provided that 'it shall be the general function of the Reserve Bank, within the limits of its powers, to give effect as far as may be to the monetary policy of the Government, as communicated to it from time to time by the Minister of Finance', while in 1939 it was further laid down that 'the Governor and the Board of Directors shall have regard to any representations that may be made by the Minister of Finance in respect of any functions or business of the Reserve Bank, and shall give effect to any decision of the Government in relation thereto conveyed to the Governor in writing by the Minister of Finance'. In 1950, however, the latter provision was amended and the Bank was required to give effect to resolutions of Parliament in respect of any functions or business of the Bank, instead of to decisions of the Government in relation thereto, although the Bank was still to carry out the monetary policy of the Government which was, in turn, subject to the broad monetary policy defined in the Act. Further amendments were made in 1960 and 1964, the final result being that the Bank was to give effect not only to the monetary policy of the Government as communicated to it in writing, from time to time, by the Minister of Finance in accordance with the definition of broad monetary policy* contained in the Act, but also to any resolution of Parliament in relation to that monetary policy.

With regard to the Commonwealth Bank of Australia, it was laid down in 1945 that 'the Bank shall, from time to time, inform the Treasurer (Minister) of its monetary and banking policy'; that 'if the Treasurer and the Bank are unable to reach agreement, the Treasurer may inform the Bank that the Government accepts responsibility for the adoption by the Bank of a policy in accordance with the opinion of the Government'; and that 'the Bank shall then give effect to that policy'. In 1951, however, it was provided that while, in the event of disagreement between

* The objectives of monetary policy to be observed by the Government under the Reserve Bank Act of 1964 were similar to those laid down previously, namely, 'the maintenance and promotion of economic and social welfare in New Zealand having regard to the desirability of promoting the highest degree of production, trade and employment and of maintaining a stable internal price level'.

the Bank and the Treasurer on any matter of monetary and banking policy, the Government could still determine the policy to be followed by the Bank, the Treasurer was henceforth to lay before Parliament a copy of the order determining the policy as well as separate statements by the Government and the Bank concerning the matter in respect of which the difference of opinion arose. When the Commonwealth Bank was split up and the Reserve Bank was established as the central bank in 1959, similar provisions were made for dealing with a fundamental difference of opinion between the Treasurer and the Reserve Bank as to whether the monetary and banking policy of the Bank was 'directed to the greatest advantage of the people of Australia', as prescribed in its statute.*

Conclusion

It is clear from the foregoing survey that there has been a pronounced and persistent trend towards the extension of State ownership and control of central banks, and that it received its initial impetus during the thirties and forties, which can be attributed to the operation of various abnormal factors during that period, namely, the world-wide disruptive effects of the Great Depression of 1930–3; the universal abandonment of the gold standard and the consequent greater scope and need for monetary management which in one way or another involved Governments in taking direct or ultimate responsibility for the monetary policy to be followed by the central bank; the widespread adoption of a deliberate policy of cheap money as an anti-deflationary or reflationary measure during the thirties, and subsequently as a cheap and easy means of financing the war and post-war reconstruction; the obvious extension of general Government control and intervention during the war; and the marked trend of public opinion towards socialism and the 'welfare state' and, consequently, towards direct Government

* The specific objectives of monetary policy named in the Reserve Bank Act were: (*a*) the stability of the currency of Australia; (*b*) the maintenance of full employment in Australia; and (*c*) the economic prosperity and welfare of the people in Australia.

control of monetary policy as a means of ensuring full employment and social security under all circumstances.

This trend towards direct Government control of monetary policy continued to prevail, as shown previously, in varying forms and degrees in different countries. Thus, while in some countries it manifested itself, if at all, only in general terms in the statute of the central bank, other countries preferred, or found it necessary, not only to spell out the objectives of monetary policy but also to define the powers of the Government in the execution thereof and the relations between the central bank and the Government, in general. Admittedly, there are countries in the latter group where the Government has not actually had to exercise its legal powers to the extent of issuing specific directives to the central bank or vetoing its resolutions, but it might be claimed that the mere possession of such powers by the Government would usually serve to exert a sufficient persuasive effect on the central bank, in the same way as the possession by the central bank of adequate powers of credit control was claimed to have increased its capacity to exercise moral suasion in its dealings with commercial banks and other banking institutions concerned.

On the other hand, the absence of such specific legal powers on the part of the Government vis-à-vis the central bank, in some countries, must not be taken to mean that the central bank has always been free from Government pressure and able to adopt and carry out an independent monetary policy. As the Governor of the Bank of Norway[3] said recently about central banks in certain countries where 'the degree of autonomy in general is especially far-reaching': 'But the tendency also in these countries seems to be toward less freedom of action and more subordination to the goals of the Governments and the general economic policy.' Nevertheless, he also took the opportunity to point out an important fact which is relevant to many central banks, namely, that as compared with 'an official in the Ministry of Finance' who 'cannot appeal to the public to gain support for his points of view', it is 'a widely accepted part of the rules of the game . . . that the management of the (central) bank can turn to the public',[4] through such means as the annual address of the Governor or other publications of the central bank.

It must be acknowledged, however, that Governments generally have been compelled to take a more active part in the formulation of internal as well as international monetary policy, not only in view of the increasingly important role which they have come to play in financial and economic affairs, but also because of the more general recognition of the impact of monetary policy on both the internal economy and the balance of payments. Moreover, there is no doubt that every central bank, whether wholly or partly owned by the State or by private stockholders, has for years accepted the position that the broad monetary policy of the country should be laid down by the Government and/or the Legislature, and that, because of the great importance of its functions and operations to the material welfare of the nation, the central bank should be subject to some measure of State control. The important point is that the central bank, which has the machinery and the expertise to carry out the monetary policy, should constantly be consulted in the formulation thereof, and should also be placed in a position where it is able and free to give independent and objective advice to the Government.

This raises the fundamental question of the status of the central bank and the degree of independence which it should enjoy under its statute or through the appropriate attitude of the Government. While the central bank obviously has no right to claim 'independence of the Government', particularly in matters of monetary and exchange policy, it should be enabled to maintain a position of 'independence within the Government', as explained by the former Chairman of the Federal Reserve Board of the United States in evidence before a Congressional Committee. Experience has shown that such a position of semi-independence, in conjunction with regular and wholehearted co-operation and consultation between the central bank and the Government in the national economic interest, is of great importance for the effective performance of the central bank's special functions and duties, and in particular for the maintenance of confidence in the currency and credit of the country, externally as well as internally.

References

1 *See* Stokes, Milton L. *The Bank of Canada*. Macmillan, Toronto, 1939. p. 238.
2 Kim, B. K. *Central Banking Experiment in a Developing Economy*. Korean Research Centre, 1965. p. 24.
3 *Norges Bank Economic Bulletin*. December, 1972. p. 150.
4 *Ibid*. p. 155.

Index